I can think of no other time in my life when cultivating daily intimacy with the Lord mattered more than it does today. As the world around us undergoes unprecedented birth pangs—nation rising against nation, kingdom against kingdom—our souls long to abide in ever deepening union with the matchless, changeless, and unshakeable One. As you embark on the next 365-day journey in *Today God Is First for Women*, you will find your faith being strengthened, your hope being lifted, and your knowledge of God's Word being sharpened by the day. As marketplace leaders, we get the privilege of revealing the light of the world in meetings and boardrooms, on calls and in emails every day. Keep your lamp burning bright by soaking in the timeless truths and wisdom you will discover as you read each new day. May your spirit be captivated and empowered continuously as you encounter his presence in new, refreshing, and glorious ways!

—**Anna Kramer,** editor in chief, *World Changer Magazine*;
founder and chief creative officer, Pneuma33 Creative

Os Hillman has spent years listening closely to the heartbeat of the Father for his children and, specifically in this book, for his daughters. If you ever need a word of encouragement, inspiration from the lives of women who are walking this journey with you, or a fresh impartation of courage from those amazing daughters of the faith who have forged a path and gone ahead, you will most certainly find it here.

Filled with words of wisdom, strength, and support to equip and encourage you along life's way, this book will be a welcome companion each and every day.

—**Sharon Curtis-Gerlach,** president and CEO, Divine Exchange Inc.

I love the *TGIF* devotional. For me it is such a great companion in my quiet time as I journey through life. It is a signpost in some areas and a mile marker in other areas. It gives direction, it gives encouragement, and it gives strength. I just want to encourage you to enjoy *TGIF* every morning like I do.

—**Kathy Branzell,** national director, National Day of Prayer

This *Today God Is First for Women* devotional will help you praise when you are celebrating, will comfort you when you are struggling, will encourage you when you are doubting, and will be the balm of Gilead when you are hurting. Each day, Os points to the glory and goodness of God while God reveals himself to us in his Word. Whoever you are, there is rich treasure for you in this book of devotions for women.

—**Patti Plough,** founder and CEO, Excel Legacy Group LLC;
The ESOP Evangelist

Scripture is filled with messages from our heavenly Father to guide our daily lives. God continues to use Os Hillman to help Christ followers, and now specifically Christian working women, apply the Bible to their work. Through stories and Scripture, Os helps us see all that God intends when we read the Word through the lens of our work. Thank you, Os, for speaking directly to women in bite-sized nuggets of truth for us to consume daily.

—**Martha Brangenberg,** cohost, *iWork4Him Podcast*;
cohost, *sheWorks4Him Podcast*

I found the new devotional *Today God Is First for Women* to be thought-provoking as well as inspirational. Each morning I looked forward to the nugget I was going to receive for the day. Os is masterful in how he tells a story or educates with a historical fact; he makes a point practical to my life and my personal walk with God. Each day I took away a thought that caused me to ponder and reflect. Although each devotional is short, only about four minutes to read through, the impact it made was lasting. In one of my early readings, Os told a story about a little girl who was blind, yet she was able to see what those around her could not. I meditated on that for days, asking God to show me things that were not visible to the natural eye. Almost immediately, I was drawn to details of my day that I would have missed if my spiritual eyes had not been opened. I believe women who read this devotional will be blessed beyond measure and that their walk with the Father will be deepened.

—**Alicia Johnson, MS,** pastor;
licensed chemical dependency counselor (LCDC)

A powerful daily resource to help readers stay rooted in the truth that it is Christ through whom we live, work, and have our very being. Os, thank you for your continued commitment to helping men and women live their faith and fulfill their God-given callings through their work.

—**Shae Bynes,** founder, Kingdom Driven Entrepreneur; author, *Grace over Grind: How Grace Will Take Your Business Where Grinding Can't*

If you are a woman who wants daily encouragement to live fully authentic as your best self and empowered by God's love, this devotional is for you. Os Hillman joins with the Lord's heart in affirming and acknowledging the giftedness and the beloved nature of women at work in God's beautiful world.

—**Beth Bennett,** Atlanta-area director, Mission Increase

As the author of *Jesus, CEO*; *The Path*; *Jesus in Blue Jeans*; and others, I have to tell you, Os, how much I am enjoying your book *TGIF: Today God Is First*. What a visionary writer you are! I'm sure that your advertising background helped you develop such clear and concise messaging. *TGIF* is my new favorite devotional book, and I felt compelled to write to you and say, "Well done!"

—**Laurie Beth Jones,** founder, The Jones Group

TGIF

FOR
Women

365 DAILY DEVOTIONS
FOR THE WORKPLACE

OS HILLMAN

BroadStreet Publishing® Group, LLC
Savage, Minnesota, USA
BroadStreetPublishing.com

TGIF for Women: 365 Daily Devotions for the Workplace

9781424565238 (faux leather)
9781424565245 (ebook)

Printed in China

23 24 25 26 27 5 4 3 2 1

Dedication

To Pamela and Charis, the two most important women in my life.
Thank you for all you bring to my life.

Foreword

As a young Christian woman, I felt an undeniable tension between my career in the marketplace and the longing in my heart for full-time ministry. This was something I was unable to reconcile until I was introduced to Os Hillman's work in 2006. As I read his *TGIF: Today God Is First* devotional, I was reignited in my faith and received great clarity in my calling. I had the privilege of meeting Os in person at a Change Agent Weekend he facilitated in North Myrtle Beach in 2014. I was inspired by the authenticity of his leadership and genuine encouragement to me and the other women who were present. He challenged us to step out of the traditional "church" box and into our God-given identity as Spirit-led women who were called to become kingdom leaders in the marketplace. Os and I eventually became collaborators in marketplace ministry as we found ways to serve together from our respective organizations.

It was during these times that I have been able to watch Os herald the amazing accomplishments of his daughter and wife as their biggest cheerleader. I have witnessed these women overcome great adversity to now lead powerful ministries as God increases their influence and platforms for his glory.

Since Os's first *TGIF* devotional became a catalyst for my own calling, I am deeply honored to be one of the many contributors to his latest work *TGIF for Women: 365 Daily Devotions for the Workplace*. I pray you, too, will meditate on this life-changing devotional and discover clarity for your own calling in the marketplace. May you be affirmed in your God-given identity, and together we can link arms with our brothers and sisters around the world "for such a time as this"!

For the kingdom,
Nadya Dickson
National and international director, The Master's Program for Women

Preface

I first met Os in 2015 at a movie preview for *Captive*, a movie about a female drug addict who was abducted in her apartment by a man who had killed two other people that night in downtown Atlanta. She read *The Purpose Driven Life* to her captor and believed this saved her life.

When I met Os at the movie that night, I was introduced by my good friend Polly Harper, who had business dealings with Os years prior. She said, "This is Pamela Winderweedle. She has a prison and reentry ministry, and since you know the producer here, Os, maybe you could assist Pamela with the contract she has on a movie deal for her life story."

He responded, "What in the world would merit a movie about your life?"

I said, "It is very complicated and a very long story."

He handed me his card, and I gave him mine as he stated, "I am very interested in hearing more."

I had no idea who Os Hillman was nor how our lives would forever be connected after that night.

It just so happened that I worked at an engineering company two exits from where Os lived on Georgia State Route 400 in Cumming, Georgia. We had lunch almost every day, and during every meeting, Os handed me another one of his books or CD sets or magazines. The first was his *TGIF: Today God is First* devotional, which I loved and constantly commented to him about how he was reading my mail! I thought he was trying to impress me, and I told him quickly that I was moving from a thirty-acre property with a seven-bedroom house, three rentals, a large warehouse, three large kilns, and so much office equipment and ministry supplies. I had been there for a year but now had to move. I was trying to acquire property for my ministry and did not have time to read or listen to all his publications, but I promised I would at some point.

Os traveled nationally and internationally all the time, and we read devotions and prayed together no matter what state or country he was in.

One time while he was in Hawaii speaking at a conference, he mentioned his Change Agent Network, and I said, "Oh, that sounds like a great program."

He chuckled and said, "Have you even been to my website to see all that I do?"

I said, "No, I am sorry. I haven't. You know that I have been really busy all these months, trying to get packed and moved and with work also. No, I am so sorry I haven't. I promise I will do it when we get off this call though." I did, and I was *so* shocked! *Who is this man I have been dating all these months?* I thought. He was so humble and never really talked about all the things he had accomplished and done all over the world as a Christian leader. This really impressed me. I felt like I was so connected with him in so many ways. And we really were…for such a time as this. Within eight months, we were married. "For such a time as this" was our wedding theme.

Os will often share with me a testimony from a reader of *TGIF*, which truly blesses me. God has used a major adversity that Os went through in the midnineties to turn his Valley of Achor ("trouble" as described in Hosea 2) into a door of hope for many.

I am so grateful to God that I am married to Os. We have a wonderful life together, and God is using us in both of our ministries. I have a prison and reentry ministry called LifeChangers Legacy (LifeChangersLegacy.org). I, too, am a writer and developer of curriculum, including the "I See ME Free" Incentive Mentorship Program for those within the prisons desiring change. It is so beautiful how God brings his children together.

I pray this new *TGIF for Women* will be a blessing to you as much as it is to me.

May God richly bless you as you discover new insights about God and his dealings with his children—us.

Pamela Hillman

Introduction

The story behind *TGIF: Today God Is First* began in 1994 after I went through a major crisis. I lost over $500,000 from a "Bernie Madoff" type of scam. My financial advisor called me one day and said the investments he was handling for me had been taken by a scammer who fled the country. I would not recover one penny. I was also experiencing a marriage crisis at the time that would lead to a divorce. My largest client in my ad agency refused to pay a $140,000 bill. Life went from one place to a whole other place in the space of three months. This would take me into a seven-year crisis.

It was during this time I sought God for answers. I met a man in 1996 who told me I had a "Joseph Calling" on my life. He said it was a marketplace calling to be a spiritual and physical provider to others. But the key was I would have to press into Jesus with all my heart. He became my mentor that day. Everything he said has come true. I began writing *TGIF* as therapy for myself. I just happened to share some of the messages with friends. One friend owned a website. He asked if I would put the messages on his website. The rest is history. I began to get emails from people around the world. The common messages were, "You read my mind today" and "You spoke right into my situation. Thank you!" *TGIF* is now read in 105 countries, and hundreds of thousands of readers subscribed to receive its messages daily. I pray this devotional book will be a blessing and encouragement to you.

God turned my Valley of Achor ("trouble"; see Hosea 2:15) into a door of hope for many through my crisis. He restored my finances after seven years (just like Joseph), I married Pamela many years later, and I have traveled to twenty-six countries and have written twenty-four books as a result of the process God took me through.

He can do the same for you!
Os Hillman

Failing Forward

Suddenly Jesus appeared among them and said,
"Peace to you!"
JOHN 20:19 TPT

The first thing Jesus said to the disciples when he appeared before them after his resurrection was, "Peace to you!" He could have chastised them for their failure to be true to him. He could have expressed his disappointment in their lack of faithfulness. But he didn't.

Fear of failure can often keep you from success. However, failing forward brings us one step closer to success. God doesn't test us to find out something he already knows; he tests us to let us know ourselves so we can grow into maturity. If you hope to succeed, learn everything you can from your failures. God sees failure as preparation for success. Some things we can only discover by our failures.

Sara Blakely is the founder of Spanx, a women's garment company with sales of more than $400 million annually. She said her father taught her the greatest lesson in life: "Growing up, my dad used to encourage my brother and me to fail, and he would ask us at the dinner table what we had failed at that week. If we didn't have something to tell him, he would actually be disappointed. I didn't realize it at the time, but he was just redefining failure for me. Failure became about not trying, not the outcome…That was a real gift he had given me."[1]

Question

Do you ever not pursue something for fear of failure?

Ask God to give you the courage to pursue something you have in your heart and embrace the process, even if it means risk of failure.

One Tough Woman

She said, "I will surely go with you;
nevertheless there will be no glory for you in the journey you are taking,
for the LORD will sell Sisera into the hand of a woman."
JUDGES 4:9 NKJV

Deborah was one of the few women judges in the land of Israel. She had just won a major battle against the enemies of Israel and a general named Sisera. His army had been soundly defeated by Israel. At first, when she tried to recruit a warrior named Barak, he did not accept Deborah's invitation to the fight. As a result, she prophesied that a woman would be used to deliver the general into the hands of Israel. He later relented and joined her in battle.

A gentile couple named Heber and Jael were not known to have an alliance to either Israel or their enemy but had some form of relationship with the general, Sisera, who was now a fugitive. He thought he had loyalty from the couple. Unfortunately for him, Jael was sympathetic to the people of Israel, who had lost twenty thousand lives at Sisera's hand. When Sisera came to her tent and asked to hide, she invited him in and hid him under a rug. She gave him something to drink, and he fell asleep. She then proceeded to take a tent peg and drive it through his temple; he immediately died.

In her song of triumph, Deborah honored Jael for acting on behalf of Israel. It's one of the few places in Scripture where a woman is the subject of a prophecy related to battle.

Question

What spiritual battles are you facing today that you need to engage on behalf of the kingdom of God?

Father, give me the courage to fight the battles that come my way.

Your Positioning

Let another praise you, and not your own mouth;
someone else, and not your own lips.
PROVERBS 27:2 NET

What is your "position" among your peers?

I told my wife one time, "God obviously plays favorites. He gave you a level of beauty unlike any woman I have ever known! You are gorgeous!" (She liked that.)

During our lifetime, we develop a personal "brand." Just like Cadillac is a luxury car brand and Walmart is known for low prices, you and I are known for certain characteristics among friends, family, and associates.

Perhaps you, too, are known for your physical beauty. Or perhaps there are other qualities that represent you, like generosity or being a faithful friend. Or you could have a not-so-good brand as a person who is moody, controlling, or critical of others.

King David had a brand. He committed adultery and murder, and he failed many times in his family life. Yet, God later described David as a "man after my own heart" (Acts 13:22 NIV). Although David did make many mistakes, his heart became soft toward God, and God honored that despite any perfections David might have had.

Question

What is your "position" today among your peers? What do you think others say when your name is mentioned?

Father, make me a woman of integrity, love, and faithfulness. Bless me with the heart of a servant to others.

Ten Flights of Stairs

Beloved friends, what should be our proper response to God's marvelous mercies? To surrender yourselves to God to be his sacred, living sacrifices.
ROMANS 12:1 TPT

One Sunday in Copenhagen, Corrie ten Boom, who was eighty at the time, had spoken from Romans 12:1–2, urging listeners to present their bodies as living sacrifices to Christ. Two young nurses invited Corrie to their apartment for lunch, not thinking that they were inviting an eighty-year-old woman to scale ten flights of stairs because there was no elevator. (Perhaps they should have thought twice about putting that kind of burden on Corrie!) That seemed to be a monumental task at her age.

When Corrie discovered this was the situation, she complained to the Lord. Then the Lord whispered to Corrie that a special blessing awaited her on the tenth floor, so she bravely tackled ten flights of stairs, having to stop and rest along the way. The parents of one of the girls were in attendance, and neither were Christians, but they were eager to hear about the gospel. After hearing Corrie's testimony, they both invited Jesus into their lives. Returning down the steps, Corrie said to the Lord, "Thank you, Lord, for making me walk up all the steps. And next time, Lord, help me listen to my own sermon about being willing to go anywhere you tell me to go—even up ten flights of stairs."[2]

Question

Have you ever had to go the extra mile for God?

Father, help me be available at all times to share your love with others.

The Purpose of the Desert

"Therefore I am now going to allure her;
I will lead her into the wilderness and speak tenderly to her."
HOSEA 2:14 NIV

If you have an important message to convey to someone, what is the best means of getting the message through? Have you ever tried to talk with someone who was so busy you could not get them to hear you? God has his way of taking us aside to get our undivided attention. For Paul, it was Arabia for three years; for Moses, it was forty years in the desert; for Joseph, it was thirteen years in Egypt; for David, it was many years of fleeing from King Saul.

Sometimes God must take us into the desert wilderness in order to speak to us. Fear not the desert, for it is where you will hear God's voice like never before. It is where you become his bride. It is where you will have the idols of your life removed. Someone once said, "God uses enlarged trials to produce enlarged saints so he can put them in enlarged places!"

"He brought me out into a spacious place; he rescued me because he delighted in me" (2 Samuel 22:20).

Question

Are you too busy to spend time with God? Begin to change that today.

Father, help me spend time with you every day to know you better.

Receiving Only from God

To this John replied, "A person can receive
only what is given them from heaven."
JOHN 3:27 NIV

Good never gave you that property," said my friend, who had entered my life at a time of great turmoil. These were hard words at the time. My business, my personal finances, my marriage all seemed to be drying up at the same time. My friend had made an observation about some land we had purchased years before. His point was that I had acquired something that God had never given me. It was not a by-product of God's blessing; it was a source of sweat and toil born out of the wrong motives of the heart.

When John's disciples came to him and asked if he was the Messiah, he responded that he was not and that one could only receive what God had given him. He was a forerunner to the Messiah, and he was fulfilling a call God had given him. When we seek to acquire anything that God has not given us, he will remove that which we are not supposed to have.

David understood this principle when he said, "Everything comes from you, and we have given you only what comes from your hand" (1 Chronicles 29:14).

Question

Have you ever sought something God never intended you to have?

Father, help me to receive only what you have for me out of obedience and abiding in you.

Saved from Death's Door

"If you embrace the truth, it will release true freedom into your lives."
JOHN 8:32 TPT

My wife, Pamela, and I met in 2015. I learned that she was sexually abused growing up, which led to drug use for years, which led her to prison for eighteen months in 2010 and 2011. God changed her there, and today she has an international ministry for men and women in prison.

Lori Ann is a woman Pamela met in prison in 2010. Due to many years of drug use, her organs failed, and she was on life support for one and a half months in April 2021. She believed her fate was to die. With fingers amputated and no feeling in her foot, Lori Ann reached out to Pamela for help. Pamela poured herself into Lori Ann's life immediately. Lori Ann got on a disciplined plan that Pamela gave her, which included a health and wellness regimen of walking, hyperbaric oxygen therapy, nutrition shakes, and vitamins she had been so deficient in due to the extreme drug usage. Pamela used her "I See ME Free" workbook program to mentor Lori Ann.

Lori Ann could feel her mind and body improving in ways she never experienced before. She started getting feeling back in her foot and other parts of her body. Lori Ann began investing all her time in daily Bible studies and the "I See ME Free" workbook. She began seeing herself free. After follow-up doctor's visits, her vital signs were now normal, nearly perfect.

Today, Lori Ann is a transformed woman through Christ with renewed hope, and she wants to live her identity in Christ. She spends her time sharing her story and is working with LifeChangers Legacy, helping and mentoring others within the prison system to get the same freedom she found in Christ.

Question

Are you available to save someone from death's door?

Father, thank you that the truth makes us free!

God's Economy

"To console those who mourn in Zion, to give them beauty for ashes, the oil of joy for mourning, the garment of praise for the spirit of heaviness; that they may be called trees of righteousness, the planting of the Lord, that He may be glorified."

ISAIAH 61:3 NKJV

The world has its own economy that includes buying and selling, methods for getting ahead, and ways to advance a cause. It often includes distorting truth and manipulating people to get the desired outcome.

God has an economy in which we are called to operate that is very different from the world's economy. He says go low to get high, serve others instead of being served, give to receive, praise when you have heaviness, die to live, and forgive instead of getting even.

Living in God's economy is not always easy. However, when you live under this economy, your life will be blessed. You will experience supernatural living. You will receive from God things you never thought you'd receive or deserved to receive. We find a key truth of God's economy found in Joshua 24:13: "I have given you a land for which you did not labor, and cities which you did not build, and you dwell in them; you eat of the vineyards and olive groves which you did not plant."

What does this verse mean? It means sometimes, through your obedience, you might get less than what you think you should get, but other times, you may get more. Obedience is the key to opening the windows of heaven in your life. God will open doors based on your obedience versus your skill and abilities.

Question

Are you living in God's economy?
If not, what adjustments do you need to make?

Father, help me to live in your economy.

The Women in Jesus' Life

Many of the Samaritans of that city believed in Him because of the word of the woman who testified, "He told me all that I ever did."

JOHN 4:39 NKJV

Women were often second-class citizens in Bible times. But Jesus demonstrated respect and affirmed many of the women in his life and ministry. He often confronted the biases of the day.

The disciples questioned Jesus when he spoke to the Samaritan woman at the well. They could not understand how he would speak to a woman, not the least of which was a Samaritan woman, the worst of the worst in the eyes of the disciples. Custom taught that Jews had nothing to do with Samaritans. However, this encounter would lead to Jesus preaching to the residents of Samaria, with many embracing Jesus as their Savior. That would not have happened without the Samaritan woman.

Throughout his earthly ministry, Jesus involved women. We can see this in his words and actions. He saw their worth, unlike people of his time who regarded women as inferior.

When the disciples reproved the woman who poured perfume on Jesus' feet and the woman who touched his robe, Jesus acknowledged the faith and actions of the women.

When Jesus was crucified, women stood by the cross and prepared spices for his anointing. Jesus chose women as the messengers to bring the resurrection message to the fearful disciples after he rose from the dead.

Yes, Jesus built genuine relationships with women, defending them and depending on their influence.

Question

Is Jesus your best friend?

Father, thank you for sending Jesus to be my Savior and Lord.

Sarah Laughed

Therefore Sarah laughed within herself, saying, "After I have grown old, shall I have pleasure, my lord being old also?"
GENESIS 18:12 NKJV

Have you ever laughed at an instruction given to you from the Lord because it seemed so utterly preposterous? And not only that, but you denied that you laughed at the instruction? That's exactly what Sarah did when the angel of God paid Abraham a visit one day.

"But Sarah denied it, saying, 'I did not laugh,' for she was afraid. And He said, 'No, but you did laugh!'" (v. 15)

Abraham and Sarah thought God needed help in fulfilling his promise to give them a son by having Ishmael through Sarah's servant girl. Now they are confronted with their sin of not trusting God.

I once had a prophetic person say to me during a time of crisis in my life, "Os, whenever I look at you, I see the word *write* on your forehead. You are going to write many books!" I had never written one book. And I was a very poor student in school, making *D*s in English class. However, what she said that day actually came true. As of this title, I have written and had published twenty-three books!

Question

Have you ever laughed at the prospects of God doing something extraordinary in your life?

Father, I repent of my lack of faith and believe you can do anything in my life.

Obedience

"Ever since I went to Pharaoh to speak in your name,
he has brought trouble on this people,
and you have not rescued your people at all."

 EXODUS 5:23 NIV

Have you ever felt that the more obedient you are to following God, the more adversity there is? Moses had been instructed to go to Pharaoh and tell him to release the people of Israel. God had said he was going to deliver the people through Moses. The only problem was that God did not tell Moses at what point they actually would be released. When Moses complained to God, the Lord told Moses that he had to harden Pharaoh's heart in order to perform greater miracles. God was behind the hardening of Pharaoh's heart. Sometimes we forget that even the king's heart is in God's hand.

God has a reason for everything he does. These delays were designed to bring greater glory to God and were to be a lasting legacy of God's miracle-working power for generations to come.

Question

Are there delays that tempt you to attribute negative feelings toward God's character?

Father, help me to reconcile what I cannot control and trust you to move on my behalf when I cannot understand.

Wrestling with God

The sun rose above him as he passed Peniel,
and he was limping because of his hip.
GENESIS 32:31 NIV

Jacob was a man who was a controller. He connived and manipulated his way to get what he wanted. It was a generational stronghold passed down through his mother, who encouraged her son to play a trick on his father, Isaac, by pretending to be his brother, Esau. As a result, that trick caused Isaac to give the family blessing to Jacob. Jacob also learned control from his uncle Laban, who caused Jacob to work for fourteen years to take Rachel as his lifelong mate.

Control is a problem for men and women. People try to control others by keeping score of others' mistakes, blaming others, or constantly criticizing. Control is at the core of that which is opposite of the life Christ calls us to in serving others.

What delivers us from this fleshly nature of control? It often requires a crisis. Jacob's crisis came when he faced the prospect of meeting his brother, Esau, who had said he would kill him the next time he saw him after Jacob stole the birthright from him. An angel came to Jacob the night before he was to meet Esau, and he wrestled the angel, who dislodged his hip socket. Afterward, Jacob would walk with a limp. Jacob had to yield to God's will for his life related to his brother Esau. In essence, he could no longer control the outcome of his life.

Question

Do you struggle with control in your life?

Father, deliver me from controlling people and circumstances in my life.
I choose to trust you for my spouse and children today.

Sudden Ghosts in Life

When the disciples saw him walking on the lake, they were terrified.
"It's a ghost," they said, and cried out in fear.
MATTHEW 14:26 NIV

Have you ever had some unexpected event in your life that caused great fear? Sudden calamities can result in great fear unless we know who is behind the event. Such was the case for the disciples when they were out in their boat one night. Suddenly, they saw a figure walking on the water, and they assumed it was a ghost. They feared for their very lives. But as the figure got closer and closer, they could see that it was Jesus. Their fear turned to joy because now they knew whom they were confronting. This seemingly life-threatening event turned into one of the great miracles of the Bible. Peter was invited to walk on the water—and he did just that.

Are there some "ghosts" in your midst? Look beyond the appearance and let God turn your ghosts into a miracle.

Question

Has there been an event in your life that cause you to fear?

Father, thank you that you have not given me a spirit of fear but love, power, and a sound mind (2 Timothy 1:7).

Move On

"Why are you crying out to me?
Tell the Israelites to move on."
EXODUS 14:15 NIV

Moses had brought the whole nation of Israel, approximately six hundred thousand, to a dead end in the desert. The only thing between Israel and Pharaoh's pursuing army was the Red Sea. God did a strange thing. He directed Moses to take a route that led to the Red Sea instead of the northern route around the Red Sea. God explained that he didn't want them to fight the enemies they would have encountered on the northern route. But still, there was the issue of the Red Sea.

They finally arrived at the Red Sea, and the people were wondering where they would go from there. News hit the camp: Pharaoh had changed his mind. He was coming after them with his army. They had no place to go. Panic set in. They blamed Moses for their predicament.

God sometimes brings each of us to a "Red Sea" in our life. It may be a work problem that can't be solved. It may be a marriage that seems to be failing. It may be a debilitating disease. Whatever your Red Sea, God tells us one thing: "Keep moving!"

Question

Do you have a "Red Sea" in your life today?

Father, I trust you to part my "Red Sea" today.

Dealing with Barrenness

Don't be pulled in different directions or worried about a thing. Be saturated in prayer throughout each day, offering your faith-filled requests before God with overflowing gratitude.

PHILIPPIANS 4:6 TPT

Hannah was married to a man named Elkanah, who was financially secure enough to support two wives. He loved Hannah more than the other wife.

However, Hannah could not have children. The other wife had several children, and that was a cause for jealousy between the two women. She even jeered and insulted Hannah for not having children. This became a deep wound in Hannah's life. She cried out to the Lord, "If you will only look on your servant's misery and remember me, and not forget your servant" (1 Samuel 1:11 NIV). She told the Lord that if she could have a child, she would give him fully to the Lord for his service. God answered her prayer, and when young Samuel was weaned, she took him to Eli, the priest, to serve in his house. Every year she would make a robe for Samuel and take it to him.

Years earlier, Abraham, too, faced giving up his beloved child, a foreshadowing of what God himself did in sending us Jesus. Hannah was a committed believer, who sought God passionately and sacrificially in her life. She was a prayer warrior. God answered Hannah's prayer after she spent years seeking him.

Interestingly, God honored Hannah's faith and perseverance. She would later have three sons and two daughters.

Question

Is there anything in your life that you're desiring deeply?

Lord, I turn this desire over to you and ask to receive whatever it is you want me to receive.

The Value of Hard Places

So, then, death is at work in us but it releases life in you.
2 CORINTHIANS 4:12 TPT

Being forced into hard places gives us a whole new perspective on life. Things we once valued no longer hold the same value. Small things become big things, and what we once thought big no longer seems important.

These hard places allow us to identify with the sufferings of others. It keeps us from having a shallow view of the hardships of others and allows us to truly identify with them. Those who speak of such trials from no experience often judge others who have had such hardship.

Those who have walked in hard places immediately have a kinship with others who have walked there also. They do not need to explain; they merely look at one another with mutual respect and admiration for their common experience. They know that death has worked a special thing in them. This death leads to life in others because of the hard places God has taken them through.

It is impossible to appreciate any valley experience while you are in it. However, once you have reached the top of the mountain, you are able to appreciate what terrain you have passed through. You can appreciate the beauty of the experience and lay aside the sorrow and pain it may have produced.

Death works in you for a greater purpose. If you are there today, be assured that God is producing something of much greater value than you will ever know.

Question

Do you need special grace for the season in which you find yourself?

Father, thank you that your grace is sufficient for every trial I may encounter.

The Driving Counselor

We are convinced that every detail of our lives is continually woven together for good, for we are his lovers who have been called to fulfill his designed purpose.

ROMANS 8:28 TPT

Turn left here, honey. Slow down! You're driving too fast."

With each instruction, her husband exploded in anger, "Stop telling me how to drive!" was often his response. But it didn't matter. She felt compelled to instruct her husband.

After years of this behavior, Bill decided to pray. *Lord, I do not know why my wife feels compelled to tell me how to drive. But I am going to believe there is some reason this is taking place. I choose to give thanks for this behavior instead of responding in anger.*

"Turn right here, honey," said his wife the next time they were going somewhere.

"Thank you, dear, I appreciate your help," was his polite response.

A few weeks passed, and one day his wife walked in while he was reading his Bible. "Bill, I just got a revelation about something I have been doing. I realize now why I nag you when we are in the car together. It's because I was the oldest of five kids, and I was responsible for them when our parents died young. I was their parent and always had to instruct my siblings. Will you forgive me?" Bill nearly fell off his chair.

For Bill, driving with his wife is now pleasant since he gave it to the Lord. And he now better understands his wife and what might be a need behind certain behavior that he could meet.

Question

Are there behaviors in your life that might have a root cause?

Father, reveal any hidden wounds from my childhood that might be contributing to negative behaviors in me.

Kings and Priests

*[Jesus Christ] has made us kings and priests to His God and Father,
to Him be glory and dominion forever and ever.*
REVELATION 1:6 NKJV

After leaving Bible college, Nadya bought a small restaurant. She enjoyed business ownership, but she often felt like she was leaving her "ministry" to run a "secular business." She eventually sold the business to accept a pastoral role. After several pastoral roles, her love for entrepreneurship led her again to work with business start-ups. She became the vice president of a consulting firm that served investors and professional athletes. It was exciting, but she still feared she was missing her calling. One day she received a devotional I had written called *TGIF: Today God Is First*. For the first time, she felt affirmed with God's blessing on her work. She felt the Spirit of God and began to weep. She sensed God saying to her, *Nadya, I am going to use you to connect the kings and the priests*. Seven years later came the epiphany.

She became the managing partner of an organization that held events, connecting marketplace leaders to Christian nonprofit leaders who were looking for business counsel. One morning, when standing at the podium to pray for the meeting, God reminded her of the words he had spoken to her. He said, *Look! Look around. You are connecting the kings and the priests!* She caught her breath and began to pray with fire in her belly. Since then, she has been connecting and coaching marketplace leaders to discover their purpose and thrive in their calling.

Question

Have you ever fallen for Satan's lie that if you're in the workplace versus in vocational ministry, you have less of a commitment to God?

*Father, thank you that whatever we do, we do it unto the Lord
(see Colossians 3:23).*

The Purpose of Crucibles

The crucible for silver and the furnace for gold,
but the LORD tests the heart.
PROVERBS 17:3 NIV

W e don't often think of the Lord testing the heart. However, in this proverb, God reveals his way of refining us is by bringing crucibles into our lives. When we examine the lives of those God uses significantly, we can usually find a crucible they had to endure that helped prepare their lives for use in the kingdom. Those seasons of fire became the catalyst to take them to a deeper level of relationship with their heavenly Father. Often, the greater the use in the kingdom, the greater the fire of preparation that leads to greater revelation of himself and his ways. "Some of God's greatest crucibles are found where we live every day"—the workplace: the employee who betrays our trust, the client who refuses to pay, the vendor who falls short of our expectations. Each of these is a test from God to find out how we will respond.[3]

Question

What tests is God bringing your way today? He also provides his grace so you might pass the tests that he brings before you.

Father, I ask you for the grace to walk with you in whatever tests you have placed before me this day. Thank you that you are able to accomplish what you want for me.

The Prayer Handkerchief

For the "foolish" things of God have proven to be wiser than human wisdom.
1 CORINTHIANS 1:25 TPT

Frank is a businessman who was flying overseas and had settled into his seat for a quiet return trip when the man next to him started up a conversation. Frank politely conversed with the man, hoping it would be a brief conversation so he could rest. However, as time went on, the man began to ask more and more questions. Finally, the conversation turned to family, and the subject of babies came up. Frank confided in the man that his daughter and her husband had been hoping to become pregnant for years without success.

"That's it!" said the man. "I knew, for some reason, the Lord wanted me to talk with you, but until you said that, I was searching and searching." Frank did not even realize the man was a believer until that moment. The man continued, "This may sound strange to you, but God has given me a kind of gift to help women who struggle with infertility conceive. Whenever I pray for women, they get pregnant. May I ask you to do something rather unusual? I would like us to pray over this handkerchief. When you get back to your daughter, I would like you to lay this handkerchief on your daughter's belly and pray over it."

Frank returned to the States, and a short time later, he arranged a time for his daughter and her husband to come by the house. Frank felt very awkward because he knew his son-in-law would think this was foolishness. Nevertheless, Frank proceeded to explain what had happened on the plane, and his daughter agreed to his plan. He laid the handkerchief on his daughter's belly and prayed.

A few weeks passed, and Frank received a phone call from his daughter. "Dad, you will never guess what has happened. I am pregnant!" she exclaimed.

Question

Has God ever asked you to do something that seemed strange, even foolish?

Father, help me to always be open to your instructions.

The Skillful Worker

If you are uniquely gifted in your work, you will rise and be promoted.
You won't be held back—you'll stand before kings!
PROVERBS 22:29 TPT

The Lord has called each of us to be excellent in what we do. Those whom God uses in the kingdom as workplace ministers are skilled and exemplify excellence in their field. Not only were these men and women skilled, but they also are filled with God's Spirit.

When speaking to Moses, the Lord said,

See, I have chosen Bezalel son of Uri, the son of Hur, of the tribe of Judah, and I have filled him with the Spirit of God, with wisdom, with understanding, with knowledge and with all kinds of skills—to make artistic designs for work in gold, silver and bronze, to cut and set stones, to work in wood, and to engage in all kinds of crafts. (Exodus 31:1–5 NIV)

Consider Joseph, whose skill as an administrator was known throughout Egypt and the world. Consider Daniel, who served his king with great skill and integrity. Consider Priscilla and her husband, Aquila, who appear to have been successful business owners. They had recently emigrated from Italy to Corinth because Emperor Claudius had expelled all the Jews from Rome. They seem to have been a couple of means.

May we strive for excellence in all that we do for the Master of the universe.

Question

Are you committed to excellence in all you do?

Father, help me be a woman of excellence in all I do.

My God, My Provider

I know the thoughts that I think toward you, says the LORD,
thoughts of peace and not of evil, to give you a future and a hope.
Then you will call upon Me and go and pray to Me, and I will listen to you.
JEREMIAH 29:11–12 NKJV

When Ann was twelve years old, she was at a camp when God told her that he had something special planned for her. He gave her a special feeling in her heart that has stayed with her for sixty years now. In her senior year of college, God made it clear to her that he wanted her to go to seminary. So, she packed her car and headed to a seminary in Louisville, Kentucky.

God said she needed to get a master's degree in social work. The university had an agreement with the seminary to accept the social work students into the advanced nine-month program. Ann applied and was accepted into the program.

She immediately applied for a scholarship because it was very expensive with the out-of-state tuition. She was told that the only scholarship available was one that required a two-year commitment to work with people in Appalachia. School was to start in three weeks. She submitted this into God's hands, knowing that if he wanted her in this school, he would make a way. Two days later she received a letter that stated she had received a full scholarship plus one hundred dollars per month with no work commitment.

That began an exciting journey of one miracle after another for God to direct Ann to where he wanted her to serve.

Question

Do you trust God to lead you into your life calling?

Father, thank you that I can trust you in every area of my life to provide what I need.

Standing in the Gap

"I looked for someone among them who would build up the wall and stand before me in the gap on behalf of the land so I would not have to destroy it, but I found no one."

EZEKIEL 22:30 NIV

The people of Israel fell into sin when they worshiped the golden calf. It would not be the last time God's people would fall into idol worship. They had forgotten the great things God had done for them. This angered God so much that he was going to destroy the whole nation. Only one thing changed God's mind in the matter—Moses. Psalm 106:23 says God would have destroyed them "had not Moses, his chosen one, stood in the breach before him to keep his wrath from destroying them." Moses was willing to stand in the gap, sacrificially, for those who were not deserving of such sacrifice.

This sacrificial love by Moses is called for among his people today. Just as Christ did, we are to be those who will stand in the gap on behalf of others who are not aware of their own vulnerable condition. It is a proactive sacrificial position.

Question

Whom has God called you to stand in the gap for? Perhaps your husband, children, or work associates? Perhaps it is a wayward child who is fighting an addiction?

Father, I commit to stand in the gap for those you call me to stand for.

Mother Teresa

"When you saw me hungry, you gave me no food,
and when you saw me thirsty, you gave me no drink.
I had no place to stay, and you refused to take me in as your guest."

MATTHEW 25:42–43 TPT

Mother Teresa gave her life of service to the needs of the poor in Calcutta, India. She reveals in the following anecdote what she believes every believer in Jesus is called to do:

> It is not enough…for us to say, "I love God," but I also have to love my neighbor. St. John said that you are a liar if you say you love God and you don't love your neighbor. How can you love God, whom you do not see, if you do not love your neighbor whom you see, whom you touch, with whom you live? And so it is very important for us to realize that love, to be true, has to hurt. I must be willing to give whatever it takes not to harm other people and, in fact, to do good to them. This requires that I be willing to give until it hurts. Otherwise, there is not true love in me, and I bring injustice, not peace, to those around me.[4]

Question

How might Mother Teresa's words encourage you to do things differently?

Father, help me to be sensitive to how I might love the unloved.

Horizontal versus Vertical

Looking this way and that and seeing no one,
he killed the Egyptian and hid him in the sand.
EXODUS 2:12 NIV

Moses saw the pain of his people. He saw the bondage and the injustice. His heart was enraged, and he decided he would do something. He would take matters into his own hands. The result was murder. The motive was right, but the action was wrong. He went horizontal instead of vertical with God. Moses fled to the desert, where God prepared him to be the man who would ultimately deliver a nation. But it took forty years of preparation before God determined Moses was ready. It was during Moses' mundane activity of being a sheepherder that God called on him to be a deliverer.

Moses' identification with the plight of his people was not harnessed by the power of the Holy Spirit. But God was patient, just as he is patient with each of us. Sometimes he must put us in the desert for a time in order to season us so that Christ is allowed to reign supreme in the process.

Question

Have you ever acted out of your flesh for a righteous cause but instead experienced the consequences of doing it the wrong way?

Father, help me to be your vessel to fix those things that are important to you and lead me by the Holy Spirit.

Her First Car

Now Samuel did not yet know the LORD:
The word of the LORD had not yet been revealed to him.

1 SAMUEL 3:7 NIV

Charis, my daughter, was sixteen years old at the time—driving age. She had saved her hard-earned money to match her father's contribution to buy her first car. I told her that we needed to pray for God to lead us to that perfect car.

We prayed we would find the right car, even in the silver color and model that she wanted. Finally, after several weeks, she got discouraged and began to tear up as she said, "We will never find a car for this price." I told her the car was out there, but it was not God's time yet. This didn't go over well with a teenager.

Finally, one day I came upon a car on the internet that seemed like it fit our criteria. I called the owner. The parents of the boy who owned it answered the call and gave me more information. I liked the parents right away. They had a nice "spirit" about them.

We drove over to the house, and there in the front yard was a silver sports car—the model she had been looking for, complete with a fantastic stereo and speaker system. We noticed a small fish symbol on the back bumper. "These people may be believers!" I said.

The price was a little higher than our budget. We asked if they could meet our price. They did. My daughter had her new car with a personal imprint from God to show my daughter that he was the source of the new car.

One of the most important roles you and I have as parents is to transfer our faith to our children.

Question

Do your children live their faith in daily life?

Father, help me to live my faith so my children will live it too.

Seeing the Works of God

Some went out on the sea in ships;
they were merchants on the mighty waters.
They saw the works of the LORD.
PSALM 107:23–24 NIV

When you were a child, perhaps you went to the ocean with your family for a vacation. I recall wading out until the waves began crashing on my knees. As long as I could stand firm, the waves were of no concern to me. However, as I moved farther and farther into the ocean, I had less control over my ability to stand. Sometimes the current was so strong, it moved me down the beach, and I even lost my bearings at times. But I have never gone so far into the ocean that I was not able to control the situation.

Sometimes God takes us into the deep waters of life for an extended time. Joseph was taken into deep waters of adversity for thirteen years (see Genesis 37–50). The deep water was preparation for a task that was so great he never could have imagined it.

If God chooses to take you into deep waters, it is for a reason. The greater the calling, the deeper the water. Trust God that your deep waters are preparation to see the works of God in your life.

Question

Can you think of a time when God took you into "deep water"?

Father, I trust you today to guide me through deep waters in my life.

Microsoft Mary

*Trust in the LORD with all your heart, and lean not on your own understanding;
in all your ways acknowledge Him, and He shall direct your paths.*

PROVERBS 3:5–6 NKJV

One of the greatest modern-day technology inventions I've appreciated most is the GPS for cars. I remember a time when it especially came in handy when I was in Germany and Switzerland. We were able to program the GPS in English. We began our drive to our destination when a pleasant voice came on: "Turn left in two hundred yards." We called our invisible road counselor "Microsoft Mary."

Jesus gave us the Holy Spirit to help you and me navigate through life. "But when he, the Spirit of truth, comes, he will guide you into all the truth. He will not speak on his own; he will speak only what he hears, and he will tell you what is yet to come" (John 16:13 NIV).

A story was told years ago about the Chinese underground church having to rely on the Holy Spirit to tell them when and where they were to meet. It was too dangerous to announce public meetings. So, each member had to ask the Holy Spirit the time and place. They would all arrive at the same place at the same time.

Question

Is the Holy Spirit active in your work life? Are you asking for his direction to succeed in your work?

Father, I invite the Holy Spirit to direct me in all my daily affairs.

Tough as Nails

*"The Spirit of the Lord is upon me, and he has anointed me
to be hope for the poor, healing for the brokenhearted,
and new eyes for the blind, and to preach to prisoners."*

LUKE 4:18–19 TPT

In the 1600s, George Fox realized that women are often tougher than nails when it comes to working for Christ. He embraced women preachers in the Quaker movement. One of his first converts was a well-to-do woman from Nottingham, England, named Elizabeth Hooten. She was the Quaker's first woman preacher. She was persecuted for her faith and even put in jail in England.

Upon getting out at age sixty, she traveled to Boston, but authorities refused her entry. She sailed to Virginia instead and literally walked to New England. When Governor John Endicott asked her why she was coming to America, she replied, "To do the will of him that sent me." This landed her in jail again, and she was often beaten in spite of her age. In 1671, she left New England for the West Indies to do missionary work and to escape persecution. Shortly after, she fell ill and died on January 8 and was buried on the Jamaican beach just like a soldier who died in the line of duty.[5]

Question

What impresses you most about the life of Elizabeth Hooten?

Father, help me to have the same passion for sharing the gospel as Elizabeth.

A Call to Worship

They did not heed Moses,
because of anguish of spirit and cruel bondage.
EXODUS 6:9 NKJV

It is very difficult to lead when those you are leading believe they have been mistreated and have lost all hope. Such was the case when God called Moses to bring the people of Israel out of Egypt. They had lived under many years of oppression and slavery. Yet God heard their cry. He sent someone to bring them out of slavery so that they might worship God (see Exodus 8:1). God was bringing the people of Israel out of four hundred years of slavery. They were being transformed from slaves to sons and daughters of God. Little would they realize how difficult this transition would be over the next forty years. God was bringing them into a new identity.

In Proverbs, the writer tells us "Hope deferred makes the heart sick" (13:12 NIV). There can be times when life becomes so discouraging and desperate that we lose all hope, and it can actually make us sick. I have been at this place; it is a scary condition. It brings you to the edge of despair.

Question

What are you in bondage to today? What keeps you from entering true worship?

Father, show me the areas of bondage that I am living in so that I may worship you.

Sacrificing at What Cost

"I will not sacrifice to the LORD my God
burnt offerings that cost me nothing."
2 SAMUEL 24:24 NIV

One day I was having lunch with woman who had a certain amount of success and celebrity status in her life. After a time of getting to know each other, she said, "How can I help you?" Those words surprised me coming from a woman who obviously already had many requirements on her time. My first thought was that I was impressed with her humility. My next thought was to wonder whether it was a genuine offer or just an effort to impress me with her humility and Christian piety. I have since discovered she was sincere.

This encounter reminded me that each of us must be willing to give to others without a motive to get anything in return. It is simply an act of serving others. Jesus said that we must consider others more important than ourselves. Jesus said that if you want to be great, you must be the servant of all (Mark 10:43–44).

Question

When was the last time you sacrificed for another with no expectation of getting anything in return?

Father, help me to be a servant to others without regard for how my actions will benefit me.

Forgiving Ourselves

*If we freely admit our sins when his light uncovers them, he will be faithful
to forgive us every time. God is just to forgive us our sins because of Christ,
and he will continue to cleanse us from all unrighteousness.*

1 JOHN 1:9 TPT

The murderer was condemned to life in prison. Then one day something amazing happened. The guard came and opened the jail cell. "You are free to go. Someone else is taking your place," said the guard.

"How can this be? I am still guilty!" said the prisoner.

"Your debt has been paid. You are free to leave," said the guard once more.

The prisoner decided not to leave. "I cannot allow another to pay my debt," said the prisoner. Because of his pride he chose to remain in bondage.

Sometimes, the hardest person to forgive is ourselves. It is especially hard for high achievers to forgive themselves. We think we are above such failure. However, the Bible says we all sin, and it is impossible to remedy that sin by ourselves.

The question is not whether we will sin; the question is what we will do when we do sin. When you come to Jesus with your failures, there is nothing more you can do besides confessing and renouncing your sin. Sometimes it may require restitution with others. However, once you confess your sin and ask forgiveness, it is no longer on the ledger of debts.

Question

Is there any sin from which you need forgiveness?

Father, I give this sin to you and choose to walk free. The cell has been opened for me.

A Talking Donkey

The donkey said to Balaam, "Am I not your own donkey,
which you have always ridden, to this day?"
NUMBERS 22:30 NIV

Have you ever tried to force things to happen in life? Such was the case of Balaam. God was not pleased with the prophet Balaam's decision to respond to a pagan king's request that he curse Israel. As Balaam rode his donkey to keep his appointment with the king, God sent the angel of the Lord to stand in the way and oppose Balaam. Although Balaam did not see the angel, his donkey did. Three times the donkey turned from the path, and three times Balaam beat the animal in anger. Finally, the donkey turned around and, to Balaam's shock and amazement, began to speak to him, admonishing his master for beating him. He warned Balaam of the angel of death, who was standing in the road with a sword drawn, ready to kill Balaam if he continued.

Imagine a donkey talking to you! God may be doing one of four things when you encounter obstacles:

1. He's blocking it to protect you.
2. His timing to complete this stage is not the same as yours.
3. He may want other players to get in place, and the circumstances are not yet ready for them to enter.
4. He may be using the process to develop patience in you.

Question

Which of these might apply to your situation?

Father, help me rely on the Holy Spirit to know which one applies to my situation as I walk with you.

"I Can Hear!"

*Then he touched the right side of the injured man's head
and the ear grew back—he was healed!*
LUKE 22:51 TPT

Young twelve-year-old Jenny was born with a defect that prevented her from hearing out of her right ear. There was a church in her area that was experiencing miraculous healings when people were baptized. Jenny had heard that a man with stage four cancer had gotten in the waters and was healed of cancer.

Her parents agreed to take her to the Sunday evening services, during which they baptized anyone who wanted to be baptized. When she got into the water, the pastor said, "What brings you here tonight?"

She responded, "I heard about the man who had stage four cancer getting healed after being baptized. If Jesus can do that for him, he can heal my right ear."

At that moment, even before she was baptized, everyone saw the expression on her face change, (I was an eyewitness to this that night) as she proclaimed, "I can hear! I can hear!" That night God honored the young girl's faith and healed her of an ear problem that had plagued her since birth.

"Whoever continually humbles himself to become like this little child is the greatest one in heaven's kingdom realm" (Matthew 18:4).

Question

Do you have the faith of a child?

Father, help me to trust you just like this child trusted you for her healing.

Empty Mangers

The only clean stable is an empty stable. So if you want the work of an ox and to enjoy an abundant harvest, you'll have a mess or two to clean up!
PROVERBS 14:4 TPT

When Jesus came into this world, he chose to be born in a most unusual place—a manger. It was no more than a livery stable with goats, oxen, and other livestock. There is a distinctive characteristic about a place like this. It is filled with odors and dung from the animals. God seems to work best among the unpleasantness of circumstances. In fact, "Where there are no oxen, the manger is empty" (Proverbs 14:4 NIV). What is this really saying?

I believe it is saying that in order for Jesus to be present, we must not be afraid of those things that bring with them "messes to clean up." God works among the messy things in our lives. And from these messes comes an abundant harvest. This is what he did with all his servants in the Bible. God is filled with paradoxes. Sometimes God likes to show himself in the midst of the messes of life. So often, the bigger the mess, the bigger the harvest.

Question

Do you find that life is messy right now? It may be that God is allowing the mess to do a greater work in and through you.

Father, help me to allow messes to take place for your greater glory in and through me.

Obedience with a Cost

*"Ever since I went to Pharaoh to speak in your name,
he has brought trouble on this people,
and you have not rescued your people at all."*

EXODUS 5:23 NIV

Have you ever felt like you have been obedient to the Lord for something he called you to do and all you got were more roadblocks? This is the way Moses felt. When Moses went to tell Pharaoh to release the people because God said so, Pharaoh simply got angry and forced the people to make bricks without straw. The people blamed Moses for this. Moses was just learning what obedience really means in God's kingdom. Moses had not even begun to release plagues upon Egypt. He hadn't even gotten started in his calling, and he was already complaining to God about his circumstances. In the future, there would be many more plagues released with no deliverance in sight. Why would God tell Moses that he was going to deliver the Israelites and not do it?

It was all in timing.

God had a good reason for his delays. God not only wanted the people of Israel but also the Egyptians to know him. It would be the greatest show of God's power on earth. Often in our lives, God causes delays that we cannot understand in order to bring greater glory though our humility and trust.

Question

Does it seem like God is thwarting your plans at times?

Father, give me the patience to accept your timetable.

Understanding Your Gift

Now concerning spiritual gifts, brothers,
I do not want you to be ignorant.
1 CORINTHIANS 12:1 MEV

In 1 Corinthians 12 and Romans 12, the apostle Paul teaches us about the role of spiritual gifts. He correlates these gifts to a human body, with each person's gift helping the whole body of the church. This is an important principle for us to learn. A mentor once admonished me regarding my own gift.

"God will never speak as strongly to you as to someone else," said my mentor to me one day.

The statement shocked me. "What in the world do you mean by that?" I argued with him.

"Your spiritual gift of administration and leading is one of the most dangerous gifts in the whole body of Christ. The reason is that you can see the big picture better than anyone else. And you're so task-oriented that you will run people into the ground getting your project completed because you think you see it so clearly. That is why the best friend you could ever have is someone with a prophetic gift to discern whether the big picture you see is actually the picture God is directing."

When we discover the spiritual gifts God has placed in those around us, we are better able to see the body function as a real body, totally dependent on one another.

Question

What is your spiritual gift? How are you serving others through your gift?

Father, help me serve others in the body of Christ through my gifts.

Brainwashed

"How enriched you are when persecuted for doing what is right!
For then you experience the realm of heaven's kingdom."
MATTHEW 5:10 TPT

In his book *How to Be Born Again*, Billy Graham tells a story of a Japanese woman who had been imprisoned in China. There was a huge consequence to owning even a few verses from the Bible. She was given a portion of Scripture from the book of John and began to memorize it. She would do this at night, pulling her coat over her head and reading the verses and memorizing them. Over a period of time, she was able to memorize portions of the book of John and then destroyed the paper by flushing it down the drain to avoid being caught. She said, "That is the way that John and I departed company." She was interviewed by a *Time* reporter just before she was released.

When she was freed, she appeared full of joy while many of the other prisoners slowly walked from their captivity to freedom. One reporter said, "I wonder if they managed to brainwash her?"

The *Time* reporter who had previously interviewed the woman overheard the remark and answered, "God washed her brain!"[6]

Question

How might you have responded to the same situation as the missionary?

Father, give me the courage to live for you no matter the conditions.

The Black Hole

*"My grace is always more than enough for you,
and my power finds its full expression through your weakness."*

2 CORINTHIANS 12:9 TPT

In 1962, I remember watching on TV the early spacecraft launch with John Glenn. One of the tensest moments of his return to earth was his reentry to the earth's atmosphere. I remember NASA explaining the heat shield on the capsule that had to withstand incredible temperatures to avoid complete destruction. There was a blackout period for several minutes with no radio contact. He was in the "black hole." It was a tense time. Either he would make it through, or the spacecraft would burn up in the atmosphere. There were several minutes of silence during the television broadcast that seemed like an eternity. Then, mission control shouted with joy when they reestablished contact with the spacecraft. It was a time of rejoicing.

Have you ever had a time when you were in a spiritual black hole in your life? I have. The pressure was unbearable. I had no sense of God's presence. Just silence. I think every Christian who is called to make a significant difference in this world experiences times like these.

The apostle Paul asked God to remove the heat from his own life one time. God's answer was not what he wanted to hear

"But he said to me, 'My grace is enough for you'" (2 Corinthians 12:9 NET).

Question

How's your heat shield today? Can it withstand the heat that would want to burn up everything in your life that is not based in God?

I pray for your grace that is sufficient to be my heat shield today.

Decision-Making

*Trust in the Lord completely, and do not rely on your own opinions. With all your
heart rely on him to guide you, and he will lead you in every decision you make.
Become intimate with him in whatever you do, and he will lead you wherever you go.*

PROVERBS 3:5–6 TPT

This is one of the most quoted verses in the Bible related to gaining wisdom
and direction from God. Yet I have never heard one teaching on this passage
that teaches what I believe the writer is really saying. The first part is pretty
easy: we are to trust God with all our heart. Next, we are not to lean on our
own understanding. If we are not to lean on our own understanding, on whose
understanding are we to lean? God's!

God admonishes us to seek him in all our decisions so that he might
truly make our decisions. In the Old Testament, the priest made decisions
based on which way the Urim and Thummim fell inside his breastplate. Casting
of lots was another means of making a decision. Proverbs says, "The lot is cast
into the lap, but its every decision is from the LORD" (Proverbs 16:33 NIV). Still
another means of making a decision is through a multitude of counselors.

Question

How do you make decisions? Do you follow one of these examples?

*Father, help me make decisions by walking in obedience to your commands
and abiding in you.*

Never Leave You

"I promise that I will never leave you helpless or abandon you as orphans—
I will come back to you!"

JOHN 14:18 TPT

Jackie spent decades working to achieve power. She told herself that it was for a good cause. She was lying to herself.

She was born and grew up in South Africa, lived and worked in many countries, climbed the corporate ladder quickly, and earned promotions, titles (including partnership at a large accounting firm), money, and the perception of security. She was also a dedicated scholar, studying the practices of manifesting nirvana from renowned global leaders. Self-reliance became her carefully mastered skill. By the world's standards, she had it all, until she didn't.

She lost her career after twenty-two years. The people who promised they would never leave and that they loved her all left. She was faced with the questions: *Who am I? What am I here for? Where are you, God?* She hadn't needed God before while she was trusting herself. And then God answered. Jackie was sitting in a Starbucks in Canada when her life changed forever. She met a devotion writer with a doctorate in theology, who guided Jackie to God through weekly Bible studies.

This was several years ago. Jackie has since learned that self-rejection and self-reliance only serve to divide her from God, but when she surrendered, the gifts of peace, provision, healing, and forgiveness flowed to her. She also learned that faith does not mean ease, and that trials and tribulations do not mean God has abandoned her. The biggest gift? She knows that it is by God's grace, his indescribable love, and through the sacrifice of Jesus that she is saved.

Question

Have you ever felt like God abandoned you?

Father, thank you that you never abandon your daughters.

Confronting Those in Error

*At a lodging place on the way, the L*ORD *met Moses and was about to kill him. But Zipporah took a flint knife, cut off her son's foreskin and touched Moses' feet with it.*
EXODUS 4:24–25 NIV

Moses was called to deliver a people from slavery. Zipporah was the wife of Moses. No doubt, the calling on Moses' life impacted her life and the life of her son greatly. Somewhere in the journey, Zipporah learned that Moses had failed to circumcise their son, a very important instruction God gave to Moses. The instruction was for all the males in his family be circumcised.

God was going to kill Moses for his failure to circumcise his son. This oversight on Moses' part almost cost him his life. Imagine that—God prepared a man forty years, and yet, he was almost disqualified for disobeying one command. Zipporah confronted Moses and warned him of his error.

Zipporah was not very happy about Moses' failure to follow through, and she took it upon herself to fulfill God's instruction to Moses: "But Zipporah took a flint knife, cut off her son's foreskin and touched Moses' feet with it. 'Surely you are a bridegroom of blood to me,' she said" (v. 25).

Question

Do you need to speak boldly to your spouse or someone who is going down a wrong path?

Father, give me courage to speak truth to those who need to hear it.

Becoming a Fool

The fear of the LORD is the beginning of knowledge,
but fools despise wisdom and instruction.
PROVERBS 1:7 NIV

In biblical wisdom literature, the pupils of the sages and mentors are the unwise, often termed "fools" or "simple ones." The various Hebrew words for *fool* occur more than a hundred times in the book of Proverbs.

The reference to someone being a fool was not necessarily a negative term. A simple fool, or *peti*, was a person who made mistakes but quickly righted them and was restored to fellowship with God. King David was a simple fool, one who made mistakes but kept a repentant heart toward God, who did not turn away from David for his many sins.

The hardened fool, *kesil* and *ewil*, makes mistakes but never learns from them and will not listen to others. King Saul was a hardened fool.

The third level of fool mentioned in Proverbs is the mocking fool, or *letz*. The mocking fool mocks the things of God. Cynical people who disregard the things of God are "mocking fools."

The fourth level of fool is the God-denying fool, or *nabal*. These are morally wicked people who ignore the disgrace they bring on their family and who despise holiness. This person says, "There is no God" (Psalm 14:1).[7]

Question

What type of "fool" are you?

Father, help me be a simple fool, who learns from my mistakes to gain wisdom.

Going against Public Opinion

On the eighth day they came to circumcise the child, and they were going to name him after his father Zechariah, but his mother spoke up and said, "No! He is to be called John." They said to her, "There is no one among your relatives who has that name."

LUKE 1:59–61 NIV

Have you ever had to go against family tradition? Elizabeth had given birth to John the Baptist. It was time to name the child. Tradition said the name would be in honor of a family member. The family members were insistent. When Elizabeth didn't agree with them, they appealed to Zechariah, who supported Elizabeth.

Zechariah and Elizabeth were told by the angel Gabriel that the child's name was to be "John." They were being obedient to the Lord's command, which went against tradition and public opinion.

We live in a day when leaders are often driven more by public opinion than by what is right. We are each called to live a life making decisions based on obedience, not public opinion. Living a life of obedience will often go against the tide of public opinion. Jesus lived a life based on a purity of purpose and mission. The Pharisees wanted him to conform to the rules of religious tradition. The result was that he died because he lived to obey an audience of One, not public opinion.

Question

Are you challenged to live a life of conviction versus trying to please others?

Father, help me to do what you call me to do no matter the cost.

The Lord Sings over You

*"The L*ORD *your God in your midst, The Mighty One, will save; He will rejoice over you with gladness, He will quiet you with His love, He will rejoice over you with singing."*

ZEPHANIAH 3:17 NKJV

W hen I first read today's Scripture passage, I found it difficult to believe. *The* LORD *sings over me?* I wondered. *But Lord, don't you know how much I fail? Don't you know how weak my faith is? Don't you know how much I fall short?*

His response was, *No, I sing over you. My love for you is not based on your performance but simply being my child.*

We've all had different experiences with our earthly fathers. Some have had good experiences, while others have had very bad experiences that can impact our view of our heavenly Father. Know that your heavenly Father cares deeply about you and has only thoughts of love toward you as his daughter.

This is Valentine's Day in America. It's a time to do something special for the special person in our life. Today, allow God to send his love letter to you. Because today he is singing over you!

Question

Do you struggle to allow God and others to love you unconditionally?

Father, help me to receive your unconditional love for me today.

Called to Politics

So Timothy, my son, I am entrusting you with this responsibility,
in keeping with the very first prophecies that were spoken over your life,
and are now in the process of fulfillment in this great work of ministry,
in keeping with the prophecies spoken over you.

1 TIMOTHY 1:18–19 TPT

The Bible tells us that we can all hear God speak. Paul said, "I wish you all spoke with tongues, but even more that you prophesied" (1 Corinthians 14:5 NKJV).

I have a one-on-one coaching program for Christian CEOs. One of our clients was a Christian woman who is a CEO over a large company. God has done an amazing work in her life. She had a time in her life where she struggled with her own sexuality. God helped her reconcile the conflicts she was having, and this led to starting a ministry to help other people dealing with similar issues.

We have a peer-to-peer time to allow CEOs to present issues to the other CEOs in the group and get their feedback. She was sensing that God may be calling her into politics, something she had never done before. But she was looking for confirmation from God.

I gathered five other godly leaders who were prayer warriors to meet on a video conference call. They were not told anything about the CEO. We began our prayer time, and about ten minutes into our prayer, one of our prayer leaders said to the woman, "You're called to politics!"

He had no idea the significance of his statement, again, not knowing anything about her. The rest of the prayer time confirmed many things in the CEO's heart.

Question

Do you believe God knows the number of hairs on your head
(see Matthew 10:30)?

Ask God to confirm any decision you may be wrestling with.

Time to Hear

*"Whoever passionately loves me will be passionately loved by my Father.
And I will passionately love him in return and will reveal myself to him."*
JOHN 14:21 TPT

Have you ever wondered how you can guarantee a greater revelation of Jesus in your life? Jesus tells us how this can be done. It is all tied to seeking him.

The key can be found in the last four words of today's Scripture verse. He will show himself to us when we love him by seeking him in our life. The more we seek him, the more revelation of his presence we will experience in our life. Through Jeremiah, God tells us, "Call to me and I will answer you and tell you great and unsearchable things you do not know" (Jeremiah 33:3 NIV).

At a certain point in my life, I realized if I was going to hear God's voice, I had to make time to seek him and hear him. I had to spend focused time alone, reading, studying, and seeking his face only. Jesus set the model for this when he often left the crowds to be alone and seek his heavenly Father. I also had to tune my "radio" to his frequency. Static comes into that frequency when I am disobedient. My level of seeking determines the power of my "radio" to reach him. The more I seek him, the more I hear him.

Question

Are you intentional about seeking God in your life?

Father, I desire to know you and the power of your resurrection in my life.

Fulfilling Your Purpose

Lord, you know everything there is to know about me. You perceive every movement of my heart and soul, and you understand my every thought before it even enters my mind.

PSALM 139:1–2 TPT

Your purpose in life is chosen by God. It is like calling water "wet"—there is no changing that fact, and there's no changing God's purpose for your life. While you may not *fulfill* the purpose for which you were made, you still *have a purpose* that God intends for you to fulfill. This is your blueprint from God. In the same way that he had a specific purpose for Jesus, he has a specific purpose in mind for your life.

This doesn't mean, however, that there is one highly specific work for you to do and that if you miss it, too bad. It is my belief that you can achieve your purpose in many different and creative ways. This should take the pressure off. You won't throw your entire life off course by choosing the wrong college, job, or mate. God is much bigger than any miscalculation or disobedience on our part. "The LORD will fulfill his purpose for me" (Psalm 138:8 CSB). Isn't that comforting to know?

Defining your purpose will help you to determine the activities that you should be involved in.

Remember, Jesus did only what he saw the Father doing—and he was able to see what his Father was doing because of his intimate relationship with him.

Question

Can you cite your purpose in one sentence?

Father, help me discover my purpose so I fulfill that purpose.

Deliverance from Abuse

Love never brings fear, for fear is always related to punishment.
But love's perfection drives the fear of punishment far from our hearts.

1 JOHN 4:18 TPT

Life was very tough for Knadia. She was living in an abusive relationship. One day in a fit of violence, her husband ran to get his gun. She left the relationship for her and her children's sake, but she still experienced many sleepless nights of fear after escaping from her house. She had expected an instant sense of relief once she got out of that relationship. Instead, she experienced something completely different. She often felt depressed and anxious. Instead of joy, she felt guilt. At times, she felt nothing at all. She was numb. On top of all that, she had financial struggles.

Today Knadia no longer is just surviving but thriving! What happened? Jesus transformed her life. His love allowed her to heal in those hidden and broken places. She learned to forgive and fully submit to God and allow him to rewrite the story of her life. God used her heartaches and hardships to bring freedom to others. She realized she had a Joseph calling. Joseph overcame his hardship to fulfill a larger story of his life. So, she was doing the same.

Knadia learned how to use the pain from her trauma to discover her God-given purpose and is now walking in that purpose, living free of emotional and financial shackles, spending quality time with her kids. She is helping thousands daily with a message of hope for those who have experienced domestic violence—a hope that comes only from a relationship with Jesus. Today she is a nurse practitioner, an entrepreneur, a speaker, and an author.

Question

Are you caught in a destructive relationship? Take steps to get deliverance.

God, give me the courage to make the decisions I must make for me and my family.

Finding the Will of God

*"I delight to do Your will, O my God,
and Your law is within my heart."*
PSALM 40:8 NKJV

How would you describe the process by which you, as a woman of God, find and do God's will in your life? For some, finding God's will is like playing bumper cars. We keep going in one direction until we bump into an obstacle, and then we turn and go in another direction. It is a constant process of elimination, failure, or success. Is this the way God would have us find his will? No. There is much more relationship between hearing God's voice and living within the mystery of his omnipotence in our lives.

Occasionally, we come to a sharp turn in the contours of our life. For those times, God allows us to stretch our normal response to change. We cannot go with God and stay where we are. Finding and doing God's will always require change and seeking him in our lives. "Call to Me, and I will answer you, and show you great and mighty things, which you do not know" (Jeremiah 33:3).

Question

What changes are necessary in your life to join God in what he is already doing?

Father, I commit myself to seeking you more in my life by spending more time with you.

Understanding Your Role

They said, "Has the LORD indeed spoken only through Moses?
Has He not spoken through us also?" And the LORD heard it.
NUMBERS 12:2 NKJV

Miriam was the older brother of Moses. Moses' mother, Jochebed, decided to wrap baby Moses up in a blanket and place him in a basket that could float down the Nile River in hopes it would catch the attention of the Egyptian pharaoh's daughter. The plan worked. It was Moses' older sister, a child herself, who monitored the situation and even talked with Pharaoh's daughter and suggested she get someone to nurse the child for her. That person was Moses' own mother. Jochebed cared for baby Moses for three years and got paid for it. You've got to love the irony!

Aaron and Miriam were brother and sister to Moses. In the desert, the daily management of affairs fell on Aaron and Miriam. Miriam had some prophetic gifts in her and was referred to as "Miriam the prophetess" (Exodus 15:20). She often led worship and dancing among the people (vv. 20–21).

But there came a time when Miriam decided her role should be more, believing God could speak to her just as much as he did to Moses. She conspired with Aaron to challenge Moses' leadership. God was not pleased.

We can assume Miriam was the instigator because God struck her with leprosy, but he did not punish Aaron. God told Moses to put her out of the camp for seven days. Moses interceded for her, and she was restored.

Pride can affect all of us. We want affirmation and to be recognized. But this becomes a dangerous place when we seek to fill a role God never intended us to fulfill.

Question

Are you fulfilling the role God has called you to serve?

God, help me to stay in the lane where you have called me to be.

A Josephine Calling

He sent a man before them—
Joseph, sold as a slave.
PSALM 105:17 NIV

God is doing a unique work around the world today. He is raising up Josephs and Josephines throughout the world. Some are still in the "pit" stage of their pilgrimage, while others are heading toward fruitfulness. What does it take for a woman to become a true Josephine? It takes years of preparation and testing.

A true Josephine is one who is a provider, both spiritually and materially, for those in the body of Christ. She is a person who understands that she is simply a manager of all that God has entrusted to her. She is a person who has humility and a broken and contrite heart before God. But how does God prepare modern-day Josephines?

Modern-day Josephines are prepared through their own versions of feet bruised with shackles and necks put in irons (v. 18). It is often through the adversity of failed finances, failed marriages, failed relationships, and broken dreams. These are the things that try us the most. These are the things God uses to allow the Josephines of our day to be proven by the Word of the Lord. Once these women are proven, God brings them out of their prisons and uses them mightily for his purposes. Joseph went through his own trials not because of any failure of his but because of an incredible calling: to save and provide for an entire nation.

Question

Are you willing to allow God to do whatever it takes for you to become a true Josephine?

Father, do whatever is necessary to fully use my gifts and talents for your eternal purpose.

The Proper Foundation

Unless the LORD builds the house,
the builders labor in vain.

PSALM 127:1 NIV

Imagine spending years building an expensive home with the finest materials and the highest quality craftsmanship. It is a work of art, and the project is almost complete. As the day arrives to move in, a building inspector arrives and hands you a notice that condemns your beautiful home because it doesn't meet code.

Many Christian workplace believers who invest years in their businesses will one day stand before the Lord and realize they, not the Lord, were building the house. God is very picky about motives behind the actions. Before we act, we must ask why? Why are we doing what we are doing? Has God called us to this task? Or is the real motive purely financial? Or control. Or prestige.

"If anyone builds on this foundation with gold, silver, precious stones, wood, hay, straw, each one's work will become clear; for the Day will declare it, because it will be revealed by fire; and the fire will test each one's work, of what sort it is" (1 Corinthians 3:12–13 NKJV).

Question

What is your motive behind the activities you do?

Father, help me to examine my heart to ensure I have a godly motive behind what I do.

Spiritual Strongholds

The weapons we fight with are not the weapons of the world.
On the contrary, they have divine power to demolish strongholds.
2 CORINTHIANS 10:4 NIV

One of the great discoveries I made in later years in my walk with God has to do with living in victory over generational spiritual strongholds.

A stronghold is a fortress of thoughts that control and influence our attitudes. They color how we view certain situations, circumstances, or people. When these thoughts and activities become habitual, we allow a spiritual fortress to be built around us. We become so used to responding to the "voice" of that spirit that its abode in us is secure. All of this happens on a subconscious level.

The Bible speaks of punishing the children for the sins of the fathers to the third and fourth generations (see Exodus 20:5). The only way out from living under the curses of generational strongholds is to acknowledge them before the Father and repent of their reign in our lives. This breaks the curse's future effects.

Question

What are the true motivations of your heart? Have you ever looked deeply at these motivations? You might find that these subconscious motivations may be preventing you from experiencing the fullness of Christ in your life.

Father, reveal any strongholds that keep me from experiencing your deep love for me.

Seeing Greater Purpose in Adversity

Paul shouted, "Don't harm yourself!
We are all here!"
ACTS 16:28 NIV

Paul and Silas had just been thrown into prison. An earthquake occurred, and the jail cell was opened. It was Paul and Silas' opportunity for escape. "Deliverance! Praise God!" might be the appropriate response. But this is not what Paul and Silas did. In fact, rather than leave, they sat quietly in their cell area. The guard, in fear for his life, knew that it would be an automatic death sentence if prisoners escaped. Paul and Silas did not leave because they saw a higher purpose for which they were in prison. The story goes on to explain how Paul and Silas went home with the guard and his family. Not only did the guard get saved but his entire household as well.

How often we are so busy looking for deliverance from our circumstance that we miss God completely. God wants to do miracles in our circumstances if we will only look for them.

When God says that "all things work together for good for those who love God, who are called according to his purpose" (Romans 8:28 NET), he means *all* things. It is up to us to find the "work together for good" part by being faithful to the process.

Question

Is there a circumstance in your life for which you need to understand a higher purpose?

Father, help me to see your hand in every daily circumstance I encounter.

Placing Trust in Our Strength

The LORD sent a plague on Israel,
and seventy thousand men of Israel fell dead.
1 CHRONICLES 21:14 NIV

When was the last time your overconfidence cost the lives of seventy thousand men? That is exactly what happened to David. David made what might appear to be an innocent request of his general, Joab, to count the troops. But the minute Joab heard the request he cringed. You see, to number the troops was a great sin in Israel because it was against the law. Why? Because it demonstrated that you were placing more trust in numbers than in the living God. David's pride cost the lives of seventy thousand fighting men. God gave him three choices of punishment for his sin. A plague was the one he chose, and it resulted in the loss of seventy thousand.

The minute you and I place more trust in our abilities than in God, we are guilty of numbering the troops. How does he punish us? Sometimes it's through letting a deal go sour. Sometimes it's through problems with a client or vendor. Sometimes it results in a conflict with our spouse.

Question

Have you ever depended on your own abilities alone to accomplish a task and suffered the consequences?

Father, forgive me for trying to make things happen out of my own strength instead of trusting you to solve my problem.

God's Image in Ebony

Whatever your hand finds to do, do it with your might; for there is no work or device or knowledge or wisdom in the grave where you are going.
ECCLESIASTES 9:10 NKJV

Amanda grew up in a time of slavery in America. She was a hard worker, a trait she learned from her father. To earn money for his children's freedom, her father worked jobs making brooms and farming that did not earn a lot of money. Still he provided for his family even though he was often in the fields until one or two in the morning. He only slept a few hours then began the same drill every day. Amazingly, he purchased freedom for his entire family.

Amanda accepted Christ into her life and her mother and grandmother had amazing faith. She grew during the Methodist revivals, which deeply affected her life.

She worked in the kitchen and became known for her Maryland biscuits and fried chicken. And she was known as the best scrubwoman in the area.

She was passionate about sharing Christ with others and gained notice as an evangelist. She began speaking in revivals and churches. Her fame spread as far as England, then India, then Africa. She organized many ministries to help women and children grow in their relationships with Christ while also adopting homeless kids and establishing an orphanage near Chicago. People referred to her as "God's image carved in ebony."

Consider the obstacles this young black woman overcame to be one of God's ambassadors around the world. How about you? Are you God's ambassador for Christ?[8]

Question

How can you use your gifts to be Christ's ambassador like Amanda?

Father, help me be a faithful and overcoming woman like Amanda.

Unexplainable Power

"Very truly I tell you, we speak of what we know,
and we testify to what we have seen,
but still you people do not accept our testimony."
JOHN 3:11 NIV

When is the last time something happened in your work life that can only be explained as God? Was it yesterday? Was it just last week? A month ago? A year ago? The answer to this question may mean several things. If it has been some time since you saw God's activity in such a way that you know it was his hand, you may not be trusting to a level that requires faith.

The converts in the early church changed the world they lived in because of what they saw and heard. It was the power of the gospel that changed lives, not what they learned from mere teaching.

God wants to show himself in ways you and I cannot imagine. Let God demonstrate his power in your work and life today. Then, you will see God "draw all peoples to Myself" (John 12:32 NKJV). Many of us live a wholesome, moral life, but those we associate with do not see this activity as anything they cannot achieve on their own. That is why many are not drawn to our lives. God's power is not evident.

Question

Is faith with power the kind of faith you are experiencing in your life?

Father, help me to experience the power of God in my daily life so that others will see and experience your love through me.

Saved from Such People

By your hand save me from such people, LORD,
from those of this world whose reward is in this life.

PSALM 17:14 NIV

How do you view your lifetime compared to eternity? Your life is a speck on the timeline of history of thousands of years.

Yet, every day, millions of people will go to work seeking to gain that elusive thing called success. The rewards of this life continue to provide the incentive for sixty-hour weeks or the extra weekend away from the family. Sometimes we get entrenched in the message of the world. This message is an appealing, seductive call to sell out eternity for the temporal. What are the priorities in your life? One of the ways we can determine where our priorities are is to evaluate our checkbooks. What are we spending our money on? Are we investing in kingdom initiatives and projects that have a redeeming value?

As a Christian businesswoman, perhaps today's message is a wake-up call. Real life is only in what is built on eternity through our work on earth.

Question

How does this verse line up with where you are today? Are you building a world whose reward is in this lifetime or an eternal one? Do those with whom you associate live in such a way that they demonstrate how their reward does not concern this life?

Father, Jesus said to seek first his kingdom and all these things will be added.
Help me to see my work with an overriding spiritual purpose to it.

Filled with the Holy Spirit

Ananias went to the house and entered it. Placing his hands on Saul, he said, "Brother Saul, the Lord—Jesus, who appeared to you on the road as you were coming here—has sent me so that you may see again and be filled with the Holy Spirit."

ACTS 9:17 NIV

Billy Graham, the great evangelist, shared a personal story about the role of the Holy Spirit in his lifelong ministry and how he came to see the importance of being filled with the Holy Spirit.

> In my own life there have been times when I have also had the sense of being filled with the Spirit, knowing that some special strength was added for some task I was being called to perform.
>
> We sailed for England in 1954 for a crusade that was to last for three months. While on the ship, I experienced a definite sense of oppression. Satan [attacked me] by a sense of depression, accomplished by a frightening feeling of inadequacy for the task that lay ahead. Almost night and day I prayed…Then one day in a prayer meeting with my wife and colleagues, a break came…I was filled with deep assurance that power belonged to God and he was faithful. I had been baptized by the Spirit into the body of Christ when I was saved, but I believe God gave me a special anointing on the way to England. From that moment on I was confident that God the Holy Spirit was in control for the task…That proved true.[9]

Question

Have you ever invited the Holy Spirit to fill you and baptize you for his assignment for you?

Father, I invite the Holy Spirit to fill me and baptize me so that I might live out the calling you have for me.

Exceeding Expectations

She said to the king, "The report I heard in my own country about your achievements and your wisdom is true. But I did not believe these things until I came and saw with my own eyes. Indeed, not even half was told me; in wisdom and wealth you have far exceeded the report I heard."

1 KINGS 10:6–7 NIV

I'm shocked," said the woman on the phone. "I've just seen your picture. I was expecting a grey-haired, old man. You are too young to have the wisdom that I read in your messages."

When people meet you or experience your work-life skills, would they say that you far exceeded their expectations? Do you undersell and overproduce or oversell and underproduce? Solomon's wisdom far exceeded any man's wisdom, and it was evident to others.

"If you are uniquely gifted in your work, you will rise and be promoted. You won't be held back—you'll stand before kings!" (Proverbs 22:29 TPT). If there were a kingdom assignment to be done, would God recommend you for the job? God calls you and me to live our lives and do our work with excellence.

Question

When people come in contact with you, do they come away with a greater appreciation of you?

Father, help me to do my work with excellence so that I might represent you well to others.

Appearing to the Little Child

*At that time Jesus said, "I praise you, Father, Lord of heaven and earth,
because you have hidden these things from the wise and learned,
and revealed them to little children."*
MATTHEW 11:25 NIV

Twelve-year-old Jordan was deaf. One typical Sunday morning church service, she took her regular first-row seat. She liked to sit with her friend in the front row even though she could not understand the message without a sign language interpreter. On this day, there was no interpreter for the service. However, her friend and her friend's mother sat next to her, and they both knew sign language.

The visiting preacher asked people to come forward to be prayed for.

Jordan used sign language to ask her friend if she saw what Jordan was seeing. Jordan's friend asked, "See what?"

Jordan replied, "The angels and Jesus!"

The friend signed, "Where?"

Jordan again pointed to the platform. "There!" she signed. "By the guitar!"

It was then that Jordan's mother, Pattie, saw the girls talking. Pattie knew her daughter was seeing something because of her face and her reactions. Jordan never took her eyes off the platform. Jordan began describing what she was seeing to her friend's mother through sign language, who then began telling Jordan's mother, who was sitting next to her, what she was seeing. Jordan was seeing Jesus on the platform and a host of angels surrounding him. As Jordan looked on the stage at Jesus, who was standing behind the preacher, Jesus looked back at her and signed to her, "I love you."

Question

Are you open to seeing Jesus in ways you have never seen him?

Father, open my eyes to see you when others cannot see.

Our Counselor

"When the Father sends the Spirit of Holiness, the One like me who sets you free, he will teach you all things in my name. And he will inspire you to remember every word that I've told you."

JOHN 14:26 TPT

I was driving down the interstate feeling discouraged from an appointment I had just had. A former employee's company was seeking to displace me and my company for our services. It had been one of many difficult events during those months. As I was driving, some words popped into my mind, "No weapon formed against you shall prosper." I did not know where those words came from other than I knew the Holy Spirit was speaking them to me; I knew they were in the Bible. I knew they were in the Old Testament.

When I returned to my office that day, I searched for the key words in my concordance and found the verse. "No weapon forged against you will prevail, and you will refute every tongue that accuses you" (Isaiah 54:17 NIV).

Jesus said that the Holy Spirit would remind us of the things he desires us to know. There are times in our lives when the Holy Spirit speaks into our spirit words designed to encourage us or give us what we need at the moment. That is just one of the roles of the Holy Spirit in the life of the believer.

Question

Do you spend time in God's Word each day?

Father, help me be a student of your Word so the Holy Spirit can help me recall his Word when I need it.

Loose Your Donkey

"Go to the village ahead of you, and at once you will find a donkey tied there, with her colt by her. Untie them and bring them to me. If anyone says anything to you, say that the Lord needs them."

MATTHEW 21:2–3 NIV

A donkey was an animal of commerce in Jesus' day. It was used to carry great burdens of goods from place to place, and it was known as the "beast of the burden." The donkey in Matthew 21 was surely owned by a village workplace believer. But Jesus told his disciples to fetch the donkey and her colt, for "the Lord needs them." This donkey played an important part in Jesus' triumphal entry into Jerusalem. It was a day that was the culmination of three years of ministry. Jesus chose to use a vehicle of commerce to bring him into his most important public display.

God is saying to workplace believers, "Loose your donkey for my purposes. I have need of it." He is preparing his remnant who are like a tribe within the church, to be a major force in the great harvest.

Is your donkey tied to the living Vine, the choicest branch of Jesus himself? When we are tied to the living Vine, designed for his use, we will be useful in God's kingdom.

Question

Is your donkey available for his use?

Today, ask Jesus to allow the Vine to flow through you in every area of your life.

Aging Well

As he was about to enter Egypt, he said to his wife Sarai, "I know what a beautiful woman you are. When the Egyptians see you, they will say, 'This is his wife.' Then they will kill me but will let you live. Say you are my sister, so that I will be treated well for your sake and my life will be spared because of you."

GENESIS 12:11–13 NIV

At sixty-five years old, Sarai was still beautiful. Men noticed her wherever she and Abram went. "When Abram came to Egypt, the Egyptians saw that Sarai was a very beautiful woman. And when Pharaoh's officials saw her, they praised her to Pharaoh, and she was taken into his palace. He treated Abram well for her sake" (vv. 14–16).

Abram knew his wife was beautiful, even at age sixty-five. Twice he told a lie to a ruler to protect himself because he knew kings of that day might kill him to take his wife. But there was an unwritten law even among pharaohs that you don't take another man's wife. So, when Pharaoh discovered Abram lied to him, he was angry that Abram almost made him sin.

Many a woman has felt used in her relationship with her husband. The biblical account of Sarai is a story of God's faithful protection.

Question

In what ways have you seen God's protection in your life?

Pray for faith to believe God will protect you even in difficult times.

Taking Control

Sarai said to Abram, "See now, the Lord has restrained me from bearing children. Please, go in to my maid; perhaps I shall obtain children by her."
GENESIS 16:2 NKJV

*C*ontrol. It is a concept that many people struggle with. Husbands and wives both encounter times when they feel their spouse exerts too much control over them.

Let's face it, when we find ourselves in a vulnerable place, our natural tendency is to try to control the situation to avoid being hurt or used or to get a desired outcome.

When we don't see God moving in our situation, we are tempted to take control to ensure a desired outcome. The root of control is fear, fear that if we don't take control, our lives will be impacted negatively. We remove God from the equation.

That was the case for Sarai. She believed her husband Abram was called to be father of many nations, and there was a son promised to him. But he must not have gotten things right. He needed an heir, but she was now ninety years old.

Sarai decides to have Abram sleep with Hagar to conceive a son that would be hers. Bad idea! That decision would result in two nations that would be at war against one another to this very day.

Question

Are you tempted to take control of a situation because you cannot see how you will reach your desired outcome unless you take control?

Father, give me the faith to trust you for my situation and prevent me from trying to control the outcome.

Finding Jewels in the Desert

"Therefore I am now going to allure her;
I will lead her into the wilderness and speak tenderly to her."
HOSEA 2:14 NIV

An ancient Arabian fable tells of three merchants who crossed the desert, riding their camels in the cool of the night. At one point, the merchants crossed a dry riverbed full of pebbles.

"Halt!" said a voice from the darkness.

All three men jumped down from their camels and huddled in fear.

"Don't be afraid," said the voice in the dark. "I won't harm you if you do as I say. See those pebbles at your feet? Each of you, put one in your pocket."

The three merchants obeyed. Each took a pebble from the riverbed.

"Now leave this place," the voice said, "and don't stop until daybreak. In the morning, you will be happy—and sad. Now, go!"

When morning came, the merchants stopped. Each man pulled the single pebble from his own pocket and saw that it sparkled in the morning sunlight. The "pebbles" were precious gems.

"Jewels!" one merchant said, his face shining with joy.

"Oh, no!" wailed the second. "There were *thousands* of jewels all over the riverbed. Each of us took only one. Why didn't we grab handfuls?"

"Look!" shouted the third, pointing behind them. A desert wind had whipped up, erasing their tracks. "We can never find our way back!"

The voice in the desert had spoken truly. The merchants were happy and sad. They had found wealth in the desert—but they could have taken more![10]

Question

Have you ever been led to the desert to find true treasure?

Father, help me to embrace times in the desert to find true treasure.

Paneled Houses

"Is it a time for you yourselves to be living in your paneled houses,
while this house remains a ruin?"
Haggai 1:4 NIV

A crisis of grand proportions is in the spiritual house of God today. The moral fiber of our world has eroded. Greed, idolatry, and pleasure are the gods of our day. And it is no different in the body of Christ.

The prophet Haggai wrote about a people who had lost concern for the need to build God's house in lieu of worldly pleasure. When our world begins to focus around increasing our pleasure, building bigger and better homes, and failing to make what is important to God important in our own lives, this should be a warning to us.

Jesus entered the temple area and drove out all who were buying and selling there. He overturned the tables of the moneychangers and the benches of those selling doves. "'It is written,' he said to them, '"My house will be called a house of prayer," but you are making it a "den of robbers"'" (Matthew 21:13).

Jesus got angry because they had stepped into a place of complacency that was not acceptable to the Lord. When we begin to blend in with the moral condition of an ungodly world, we begin losing God's perspective on life.

Question

Do you have a proper balance in your lifestyle?

Father, help me to give attention to those things that are important to you.

Spiritual Mentors

"Where you go, I will go; where you lodge, I will lodge; your people shall be my people and your God my God. Where you die, I will die, and there will I be buried."
RUTH 1:16–17 NRSVUE

Whom has God placed in your life for you to learn from? A mentor is one who takes responsibility for the spiritual and, sometimes, physical care of another. It requires a commitment from the teacher and the student.

The book of Ruth tells the story of Ruth and Orpah, two women of Moab, who married two sons of Elimelech and Naomi, Judeans who had settled in Moab to escape a famine in Judah. The husbands of all three women die; Naomi plans to return to her native Bethlehem and urges her daughters-in-law to return to their families. Orpah does so, but Ruth refuses to leave Naomi, declaring, "Where you go, I will go; where you lodge, I will lodge; your people shall be my people and your God my God. Where you die, I will die, and there will I be buried." Ruth follows Naomi to Bethlehem and later marries Boaz, a distant relative of her late father-in-law. He becomes her kinsman-redeemer. Ruth is a symbol of abiding loyalty and devotion. Generations later, King David and Jesus would come from their family lineage.

Question

Who are the people of God he has placed in your life? Are you learning from them?

Father, show me the women in my life from whom you desire me to learn.

Godly Rewards

"You have said, 'It is futile to serve God. What do we gain by carrying out his requirements and going about like mourners before the LORD Almighty?'"

MALACHI 3:14 NIV

Have you ever felt that serving God had little reward and that the ungodly seemed to be more blessed than you? This is what the people of God felt in the days of the prophet Malachi. God heard their cry and responded through Malachi to explain God's view on this matter.

A scroll of remembrance was written in his presence concerning those who feared the Lord and honored his name.

"On the day when I act," says the LORD Almighty, "they will be my treasured possession. I will spare them, just as a father has compassion and spares his son who serves him. And you will again see the distinction between the righteous and the wicked, between those who serve God and those who do not." (vv. 17–18 NIV)

Notice that after the people complained about this, they began to talk to each other, and the Lord listened and heard. God had been taking note of those who were serving him and honoring him. We will see that there is a distinction between the righteous and the wicked on that day when "the Sun of Righteousness shall arise with healing in His wings; and you shall go out and grow fat like stall-fed calves" (4:2 NKJV). What a beautiful picture of what we will feel like on that day!

Question

Do you ever feel like God has overlooked you?

Father, thank you that you know every circumstance I am walking through and that you are with me.

Fruitful Suffering

"It is because God has made me fruitful
in the land of my suffering."

GENESIS 41:52 NIV

Joseph named his second son Ephraim. Ephraim was given to him after Joseph had been delivered from his suffering of thirteen years. Joseph said that he named him this because God had made him fruitful in the land of his suffering. *Ephraim* means "twice fruitful."

Joseph was fruitful in two instances. He was fruitful during his time of adversity and in his prosperity. When God brings us into a time of suffering, it can be a fruitful time. It's rare for us to see the fruit during the suffering period. But know that the roots are going deep into the spiritual soil of our soul because of our pressing into God during our time of suffering. This is producing a work in our character that cannot be seen until it finishes the process. Such was the case for Joseph.

It was not until several years after such a time of suffering that I began to see the fruit of the trials that the Lord allowed me to experience. How grateful I am to understand some of the reasons that have led to a new life in him that I would never have had without this period.

Question

Do you find yourself in a time of suffering? Now is the time to press in to God.

Father, let your roots grow deeper in me through my suffering and create a deep-rooted faith that creates lasting spiritual fruit in my life.

Spiritual Warfare

For our struggle is not against flesh and blood.
EPHESIANS 6:12 NIV

Have you ever heard someone say, "I will never do business with another Christian"? Several years ago, I heard this quite often in my dealings with Christian workplace believers. This comment represents the battle that rages against us by the enemy of our souls to destroy the witness and effectiveness of Christian workplace believers.

Satan's ploy in the life of Christian workplace believers is to do several things to make them ineffective. First, he wants to discredit them by allowing them to fail in some way. This often manifests itself when workers fail to perform what they commit to do or perform the work in an unsatisfactory way. Sometimes, this is a result of the believer simply not striving for excellence. In other cases, it may be a misunderstanding that causes strife.

There are times when each of us is thrust into situations out of our control. Sometimes this results in our inability to pay a bill on time or to deliver a service. Defeating Satan in these battles requires extra communication with those with whom we are dealing. If the motive of your heart is to do right, then God will give you favor in order to work through these difficult spots. Realize we wage a spiritual war that is not flesh and blood. We must fight this war with spiritual weapons applied to practical daily living.

Question

Have you ever been let down by a fellow believer who caused conflict in your relationship?

Father, show me where the enemy is seeking to make me ineffective. Help me stay on the high ground to defeat the enemy's scheme.

Knowing versus Doing

*I continually long to know the wonders of Jesus
and to experience the overflowing power of his resurrection.*
PHILIPPIANS 3:10 TPT

If I asked you the purpose for which God made you, what might you say? You might give a lot of answers that involve some action on your part. However, the simplest answer to that question relates to one primary thing: fellowship. The most important thing God desires from us today is to have a deep and intimate fellowship with us personally.

The apostle Paul said he wanted to know Christ, and by knowing Christ, he could experience the power of his resurrection. I find this to be the hardest thing for many of us to do. So often it is much easier to be busy with the urgent or even with Christian activities rather than spending quiet moments before the Lord. Before we realize it, days have passed since our last quiet time with Jesus.

Jesus understood the importance of quiet moments with the Father. "After he had dismissed them, he went up on a mountainside by himself to pray. Later that night, he was there alone" (Matthew 14:23 NIV). The more mature we become in our relationship with the Lord, the more precious this time becomes to us. An interesting thing happens when we make prayer a priority: urgent things seem to wane as we focus on him. He makes all these other things fall into place.

Question

Are you taking the time to get to know the Lord today?

Father, help me to make time with you a priority each day.

Coming out of Babylon

*"'Come out of her, my people,' so that you will not share in her sins,
so that you will not receive any of her plagues; for her sins are piled up to heaven,
and God has remembered her crimes."*

REVELATION 18:4–5 NIV

There is a day when God is going to judge the system of Babylon around the world. What is Babylon? Babylon is a system of doing business. The stronghold of the workplace is mammon and pride. Dependence on money and misplaced trust are at the core of a Babylonian philosophy of life.

Revelation 18 describes a time when God will judge this Babylonian system. It is the one place that we see a system destroyed in one day, even one hour. I do not believe Babylon is a particular city but a world system.

Christian women in the workplace are called to understand the signs of the times. When the Soviet Union fell, many knew it was going to happen because they could recognize the signs of the times. God has a way of shaking things up. These shakings force us to determine in whom and in what we will place our trust.

Question

Are you still doing business as if you were living in Babylon? If so, expect to share in the sins of Babylon when God decides to judge her.

Father, show me where I might be operating in a "Babylonian" system of work and allow me to come out of it so I might worship you in all my actions.

Developing Our Heart for God

I will arouse your sons, O Zion, against your sons, O Greece,
and wield you like a warrior's sword.

ZECHARIAH 9:13 NRSVUE

In the third and fourth centuries, followers of Socratic teaching and other Greek scholars began to influence the church in ways that were different from the Hebraic roots of the early church. The Greek influence appeals more to the intellect, whereas the Hebraic model of the early church appeals to the heart. The Greek influence resulted in more emphasis on oratory skills and cognitive knowledge of God. Over the many centuries, this influence has shown itself in a more programmatic approach to the gospel rather than a process of living out our faith. So why is it important for us to understand this?

Knowledge without power to express the life within is of little value. The more programmatic the focus, the less emphasis we place on building deep and caring relationships that result in changed lives. Our early church fathers knew there was a cost to living out the Word of God, not simply giving mental assent to it.

Question

Are you walking with God today in an intimate fellowship? Or has your involvement in programs and activities designed to do good things replaced your relationship with the Lord? Reflect on Proverbs 23:12: "Apply your heart to instruction and your ears to words of knowledge" (NIV).

Father, help me respond with my heart to increase my intimacy with you.

Tapping into Our Secret Weapon

His prayers are filled with requests to God that you would grow and mature,
standing complete and perfect in the beauty of God's plan for your lives.
COLOSSIANS 4:12–13 TPT

Good morning. Before we begin our staff business meeting, I wish to ask John to give us the intercessors' report regarding the direction of our new business development program."

"Our intercessors have been prayerfully reviewing the action plan I gave them. We believe the Lord is directing us in this way. However, our intercessors believe we may need to adjust our direction on this."

Does this sound like a far-fetched illustration of a modern-day company? If we are truly going to remove the separation of what we perceive as holy versus unholy, then we must make some paradigm shifts in our thinking.

The Lord has called you and me to be ministers of the gospel in and through the workplace. This means we must fight our battles, grow our companies, and minister to our employees and vendors through the power of the Holy Spirit. Intercessory prayer is the secret weapon of Spirit-led activity. Imagine having intercessors who are part of your team, committed to helping you make decisions in your business life "that you may stand firm in all the will of God, mature and fully assured" (v. 12 NIV).

Question

Do you have trusted people who pray for you in your work-life calling?

Father, please lead me to those who can partner with me in prayer for my life and work.

Comforting Others

All praises belong to the God and Father of our Lord Jesus Christ. For he is the Father of tender mercy and the God of endless comfort. He always comes alongside us to comfort us in every suffering so that we can come alongside those who are in any painful trial. We can bring them this same comfort that God has poured out upon us.

2 Corinthians 1:3–4 tpt

I was fourteen years old in September 1966. I was home watching *I Dream of Jeannie* on television when the program was interrupted by a news bulletin: "Three prominent local businessmen have died in a plane crash in the mountains of Tennessee." That's how I learned of the death of my father.

It was difficult and painful growing up without a father. I loved and needed my dad. I couldn't understand why God would take him away from me so suddenly. I certainly didn't see the death of my father as a "blessing" in any sense of the word.

Because of my own loss, I had an instant connection with others who suffered similar losses. We shared an experience that other people couldn't fully understand.

Although adversity may never be a blessing, God in his grace can bring blessing out of our adversity and can bring the needed healing to our lives. Why not give your circumstance to the Lord today and let him use it in the lives of others? This will be the first step toward healing.

Question

Has God allowed you to experience difficult losses in your life? If so, allow his grace to use those losses for his purposes.

Father, give me the grace to accept the things I cannot change to allow you to use them for your purposes.

I Just Wanted a Puppy

Therefore, if anyone is in Christ, he is a new creation;
old things have passed away; behold, all things have become new.
2 CORINTHIANS 5:17 NKJV

On a wet snowy day, the five-year-old little girl is enraptured with the puppy she found. As she ties it up, she looks up and begs her dad, who is standing at the door, "Can I have it, Daddy, please…can I have it?"

With alcohol reeking from his breath, her dad says, "Come upstairs with me, and I'll let you have the puppy."

What took place next was something no child should experience. Her mother made him leave immediately upon discovering what he had done. The sexual abuse happened again through other men when she got a bit older. She discovered drugs would deaden the pain temporarily, which led her into an addiction to drugs, a dependence on alcohol, and prostitution with wealthy men.

Her Christian grandmother was the positive influence in her life. A preacher once laid his hand on her head and said, "This one is special. God is going to use this one." She never forgot those words, even in the drug world.

She continually cried out to God in her pain. She was sent to prison to serve an eighteen-month sentence, which became her ticket to true freedom. She poured herself into the Scriptures every day. She began helping other women reach spiritual freedom also. When released in 2010, she started Chebar Ministries Inc. LifeChangers Legacy Prison and Reentry Programs. We married in 2016. Pamela's ministry helps men and women in prison across the nation and the world.[11]

Question

Would you like to help those, like Pamela, who have been or are in prison?

Father, I pray for those in prison. Lead me become a mentor to someone who needs Jesus through a local prison ministry.

Knowledge + Action = Faith

For we have heard the good news of deliverance just as they did,
yet they didn't join their faith with the Word.
Instead, what they heard didn't affect them deeply, for they doubted.
HEBREWS 4:2 TPT

The people of Israel were called out of the bondage of Egyptian slavery. God said they would be brought out of four hundred years of slavery so that they might worship him. God desired to bring them into a place of milk and honey—the promised land. Yet that generation never entered into the promised land. Why? They never took what they knew in their heads and transferred it to their hearts. It never resulted in actions that were based on what they believed.

When I was a new Christian, I heard an illustration of what belief and faith looked like when combined. If you were a trapeze artist and were skilled at walking across tightropes over high places, you might even be willing to walk across Niagara Falls. In fact, I might have confidence that you could because I had seen your abilities as a trapeze artist. However, if you asked me if you could push me in a wheelbarrow across Niagara Falls, you would be challenging me to put my beliefs into action. This requires faith, participation, and risk, which, until now, was based only on mental assent.

Question

Has God spoken to you about an area in your life that requires a step of faith?

Father, I will move in faith, believing you will provide what I need today.

Striving versus Abiding

Unless the Lord builds the house, the builders labor in vain…In vain you rise early and stay up late, toiling for food to eat—for he grants sleep to those he loves.
PSALM 127:1–2 NIV

What does it mean for the Lord to build the house? It almost seems a contradiction when we consider that we might be the builders in this passage. God wants us to allow him to build the house.

God is telling us there is a way of working without striving. There is a way to conduct business without sweating and toiling for outcome. His warning to each of us is to avoid thinking that outcome is based on our sweat and toil instead of our obedience. Outcome is sometimes more than we deserve and sometimes less than we hoped for. His desire for each of us is to see him working in our daily work life. He wants us to avoid looking to our own effort to gain an outcome.

One day Jesus called out to Peter from the shore of the lake and suggested he throw his net on the other side of the boat. It was this simple act of obedience that yielded a tremendous catch that Peter would not have received unless he obeyed.

We are called to work; he will bring forth the fruit. He is the Vine. We are the branches. Fruit comes forth naturally from a healthy tree.

Question

Is there any area of life in which you are striving?

Heavenly Father, please show me the difference between loving trust and obedience and striving for outcome.

Speak to Your Circumstance

"You will also declare a thing, and it will be established for you;
so light will shine on your ways."

JOB 22:28 NKJV

God gives us spiritual authority to gain breakthroughs if we are listening to the Holy Spirit.

When I was dating my wife, there was a period when she had to move from her current home to another home before we got married. It was hard finding a rental home that would allow her five dogs, so when we found one, we placed an offer. We were going to meet at the house for a second look when the agent called back and said, "Os, you will need to hunt for another property. This one has been contracted by an executive from Apple. His credit is good, and that is normally what will disqualify someone."

I called my Pamela and told her the bad news. "I guess we don't need to go to the house now," I said.

"No! That is my house!" she insisted. "We need to go to the house and walk around it and claim it."

"Are you sure, honey?" I asked.

"Yes, that is our house!" We went to the house and, just like Joshua walked around the city, we walked around the house and claimed it for Pamela. We *canceled* the contract in prayer.

A few hours later, I got a phone call from the owner of the business. He said, "Os, I have no idea what happened to this contract; the client has changed his mind. The house is yours if you still want it."

I had to repent for my lack of faith.

Question

Have you ever made a decree over a problem?

Father, give me the boldness to speak over problems where I need a breakthrough.

Called to Be a Josephine

God's promise to Joseph purged his character
until it was time for his dreams to come true.
PSALM 105:19 TPT

Denise D. Campbell was a successful advertising executive from Chicago with two master's degrees. Life was good in 2007. She gave her life to the Lord in November of that same year. She had a six-figure income and was heading up the ladder of success as a media sales executive. But that all changed in July of 2008 when the recession hit.

She was laid off from her job, which ushered her into a seven-year season of adversity. She would be thrust into the greatest time of hardship of her life. Denise lost all tangible evidence of the success she had experienced in her career. Her life had been emptied of all that was "Egypt!"

Denise called me one day, and I began to help her navigate her season of adversity. God gave Denise tremendous experiences that allowed her to learn to trust and to be led by the Holy Spirit. He was teaching her about his economy of provision in a desert season. She was, like Joseph in prison, manifesting supernatural gifts of healing and discernment for others. The Bible says God prospered Joseph while he was in prison. God was prospering Denise in her "prison."

Denise is no longer the person she was in 2008. She has been transformed and equipped by this process to do the work of the kingdom. She has come to a place of trusting God daily and looking forward to the next stage of her Joseph journey.

Question

Do you find yourself in a season of major adversity?

Father, you say your grace is sufficient for all things. Give me the grace
I need today.

Changing Our Paradigm

As Peter was in deep thought, trying to interpret the vision, the Spirit said to him,
"Go downstairs now, for three men are looking for you.
Don't hesitate to go with them, because I have sent them."

Acts 10:19–20 TPT

Peter had never preached to the gentiles. In fact, he believed it was against Jewish law to associate with the gentiles. God needed to change Peter's attitude about this, so during the night, God gave Peter a vision that showed him it was permissible to preach to the gentiles. The Spirit came to Peter and informed him that some men were about to come visit him, and he was to go with them. As God instructed, Peter went with the men, and the Lord did great miracles in the lives of gentiles through Peter.

Sometimes we are so bent on our particular belief that the Holy Spirit must do something miraculous to change our paradigm.

I was once asked to attend a conference overseas. At the time, finances were such that the very idea of spending money on an international trip was ridiculous to me. The very next day, a man I had met only once before informed me of this event and asked if I would come if my expenses were covered. I was dumbfounded! The Lord had sent a messenger to change my paradigm because he knew I didn't have the faith to think of the possibility. He knew I needed help.

Question

Do you need a paradigm shift in some area of belief?

Father, show me any area in my life that I need to change my belief or assumptions.

Your Calling's Depth and Width

If troubles weigh us down, that just means that we will receive even more comfort to pass on to you for your deliverance! For the comfort pouring into us empowers us to bring comfort to you.

2 CORINTHIANS 1:6 TPT

God must love you a lot! He doesn't allow someone to go through the kinds of adversity you have experienced unless he has a special calling on your life." Those were the words said to me by two different mentors at two different times within a three-year period.

Later I would learn another related truth from a respected man of God whom God uses throughout the globe. "The depth and width of your faith experiences are directly proportional to your calling." What were these men of God saying?

They were describing a process of preparation that God takes each of his leaders through when he plans to use them in significant ways. A "faith experience" is an event or "spiritual marker" in your life about which you can say, "That is where I saw God personally moving in my life." It is an unmistakable event in which God shows himself personally to you. It was the burning bush for Moses, the crossing of the Red Sea or the Jordan River for the nation of Israel, Jacob's encounter with the angel. It was the feeding of the five thousand for the disciples. It was the time when you saw God face-to-face in your life.

Question

Do you need a personal faith experience right now in your life?

God, reveal yourself to me in a personal and powerful way today.

Living for a Greater Cause

I can do everything through Christ,
who gives me strength.
PHILIPPIANS 4:13 NLT

In the thirteenth century, a man named William Wallace became the instrument of freedom from England's tyranny over Scotland. A very wicked king ruled England, and the king killed William's wife. This tragedy in the life of William Wallace launched him into living for a cause. Initially his cause was revenge, but soon his cause turned to something bigger than himself—freedom for a nation.

When he challenged the commoners to fight for this freedom, they responded that the enemy was too great and that they might die on the battlefield. They also refused to fight for the nobles, the knights and leaders who had a vested interest in gaining more land for themselves instead of fighting for a pure cause of freedom. Wallace's response in the movie *Braveheart* is "Yes, we might die. We will all die sooner or later. But we will die for a cause worth dying for. So that our children and their children might live in freedom."[12]

Today we find many Christian workplace believers living a status quo relationship with God that is more characterized as "business as usual" than a life demonstrating God's power.

God has called each of us to live for a cause greater than ourselves—a life that is dependent on his grace and power to achieve things we never thought possible through our lives. This is his plan for your life.

Question

Are you living for a cause greater than yourself?

Dear Lord, show me what you want me to achieve through my life today.

Bitterness versus Grace

Watch over each other to make sure that no one misses the revelation of God's grace. And make sure no one lives with a root of bitterness sprouting within them which will only cause trouble and poison the hearts of many.
HEBREWS 12:15 TPT

In business and life, the opportunity is great for harboring bitterness over a wrong suffered. We are given plenty of opportunities to grow bitter from relationships that bring hurt and pain. The above verse cautions us against bitterness because the author of Hebrews knows that a bitter root grows and grows until it eventually defiles many others through a wake of bitterness. If bitterness is allowed to take root, we become imprisoned to it. God's grace will no longer have as great an effect in our lives. We become ineffective, insensitive, and spiritually dead. We can even become physically ill from it. God does not live in bitterness. He lives in grace. He has provided grace for every person to walk in.

One day I was challenged to deal with an individual who hurt me terribly. I was faced with a decision. Would I choose bitterness, or would I choose grace? Oh, how my natural tendency was to choose bitterness! But God provided the courage for me to choose grace. With that grace came freedom—a freedom to love and even accept the person who was the source of such pain.

Question

Are you in need of grace today to forgive someone?

Father, give me the courage and grace to forgive those who have wronged me.

A Job versus a Calling

"But this is not your calling. You will lead by a completely different model. The greatest one among you will live as the one who is called to serve others, because the greatest honor and authority is reserved for the one with the heart of a servant. For even the Son of Man did not come expecting to be served but to serve and give his life in exchange for the salvation of many."

MATTHEW 20:26–28 TPT

Before my mom died, she was living in an elderly care nursing facility for Alzheimer's and dementia patients. It was easy to distinguish those nurses who saw their work as a job versus those who saw it as a calling.

There was one woman there we all loved. Her name was Carolyn. We knew that if Carolyn was on duty, our mom would be well cared for. Carolyn exemplified one who was doing her job because she actually loved her work. Carolyn's job involved caring for difficult patients who often had little appreciation for what she did for them. When asked about her view of her job, Carolyn's response was quite remarkable: "I enjoy it."

Carolyn was recognized by her organization as caregiver of the year. She didn't do her job because she wanted that recognition. Instead, it was the fruit of living out her calling to be a caregiver.

Carolyn's view of life was in sharp contrast to others who worked at the same facility. It was often difficult to get them to meet the basic necessities of care for my mother. The attitude with which many on the staff did their job was that their tasks were compulsory instead of an opportunity to serve.

This attitude can be seen in almost any vocational area.

Question

Which person are you in this story?

Father, help me to see my job as a calling and an avenue to express the life of Jesus through my work life.

Seeing through God's Eyes

They mourned and wept and fasted till evening for Saul and his son Jonathan, and for the army of the LORD and for the nation of Israel, because they had fallen by the sword.

2 SAMUEL 1:12 NIV

How would you respond if you heard something bad happened to someone who had been trying to cut off your head for several years? King Saul had been seeking to kill David for many years before Saul was thrust into battle against the Amalekites. In this final battle, a sword killed Saul. When the news reached David, instead of rejoicing that his enemy was no longer a problem for him, he responded in a totally unexpected manner. He mourned. Imagine that; he mourned for the one who had sought to kill him.

This is a sign of one who can look past an individual who is the source of pain and consider how God views him. When we begin to see people as God does, we'll no longer look at them as enemies but as souls in need of grace. This is how Jesus could give up his life for us. He saw our great need, not what we did to him.

Question

When someone wrongs you, do you seek to retaliate, or do you pray to understand the need behind the offender's actions?

Father, help me to see past the behavior of those who betray me and give me the grace to pray for them and forgive them.

When God Restores What Locusts Eat

"I will repay you for the years the locusts have eaten—
the great locust and the young locust, the other locusts and the locust swarm—
my great army that I sent among you."

JOEL 2:25 NIV

There are seasons in our lives that involve times of famine and times of restoration. Solomon tells us that God has made everything beautiful in its time and that there is a time for everything and a season for every activity under heaven (see Ecclesiastes 3:1, 11).

God brings about both the good and the bad. The seasons of famine have a divine purpose in our lives. They accomplish things that only these hard places can accomplish. But there is a time when those hard places have accomplished their purpose and God begins to restore. God did this with the nation of Israel after a season of famine and devastation.

God wants each of us to know that there is a time when he will restore in order to demonstrate his gracious hand in our lives. He is a loving father who tenderly guides his children through the difficult places.

Question

Has God taken you through a time of famine?

Father, may I know you as the restorer of that which the locusts have eaten. I will wait patiently for you to bring about my restoration.

Suffering for Another's Salvation

"How blessed you are when people insult and persecute you and speak all kinds of cruel lies about you because of your love for me!"
MATTHEW 5:11 TPT

Recently, a friend told a true story about one of his closest friends who experienced great suffering for the soul of his persecutor. This man worked on a cargo ship. His boss was the captain. This friend was a committed Christian who shared his faith with others and was a good worker. He even led the sea captain's girlfriend to Christ. The sea captain already hated and ridiculed the Christian worker because of his faith in Christ. When his girlfriend came to Christ, she stopped sleeping with the captain because she knew it was a sin. This took a great deal of courage and faith to change her habits and lifestyle. The captain blamed the Christian man for the change in his girlfriend.

One day he entered the restaurant where the Christian man was having lunch. The captain walked over to his table and began hurling obscenities, and then he began beating the man. The Christian man simply tried to protect himself but did not fight back. The captain kept beating him until eventually the man lay on the floor bleeding.

Two men who saw what happened took the captain outside and began beating him. The Christian worker left the restaurant and began helping the injured captain. The sea captain was so moved that this man could do this after he had literally beaten him bloody that he began to weep, not understanding what could move a man to have such love in the face of such violent hatred. The sea captain accepted Jesus at that moment.

Question

Have you ever been persecuted for your faith?

Father, give me the courage to stand in the gap for someone who needs salvation, no matter the cost.

Understanding the Source of Anger

A fool gives full vent to his anger,
but a wise man quietly holds it back.
PROVERBS 29:11 RSV

The workplace can be a pressure-packed world. The demands that are often put on us can bring out things that we never knew were inside us. Sometimes we begin to think that the source of that pressure is to blame for our response to the pressure. It could be an event, a spouse, a boss, a client, a child, or even a driver who cuts us off in traffic.

Have you ever said, "If you had not done that, I would never have responded that way!" We all choose to get angry. No one else is to blame for our anger.

Dr. Sam Peeples wrote, "The circumstances in my life, the people in my life, and the events of my life do not make me the way I am…but reveal the way I am!"[13] This simple quote has had a profound impact on how I view my anger now. Anger only reveals what is inside of me. I can't blame anyone but me for my response to a situation. I have learned that anger is only the symptom of something else that is going on inside of me.

It has been said that anger is like the warning light on the dash of your car. It is the light that tells us something is going on under the hood, and we need to find out what is the source of the problem.

Question

Do you struggle with anger?

Father, reveal to me the source of my anger. Heal me of any fears that may be the root of my anger.

Beware of Unusual Circumstances

Each believer is given continuous revelation by the Holy Spirit
to benefit not just himself but all.

1 CORINTHIANS 12:7 TPT

Whenever something unusual happens in daily life, these are often signs that God is up to something. We must have a heightened sense of awareness of what God may want to do in these situations.

My mentor once shared how he was upgraded on an airline unexpectedly. In his new seat on the plane, a woman who was very troubled sat next to him. He began to quietly pray for the woman, and God gave him supernatural insights that her problem related to the fact that she had not forgiven her mother in a family-related issue. He decided to politely share his insight. The woman was shocked. My mentor began to minister to her on the airplane and ultimately led her to Christ.

God is raising the spiritual bar for Christians who want to impact the world for Christ today. He wants to break through into people's lives supernaturally by giving them insights into the needs of other people in order to bring them to Christ.

Jesus often spoke supernaturally into the lives of others based on the circumstance of the moment. He often spoke of their current condition in life and invited them to make a change.

Question

Are you available to hear God speak to you about someone who needs encouragement?

Father, help me to be sensitive to the leading of the Holy Spirit in my life.

Deliverance from a False Identity

"If you want to test my teachings and discover where I received them, first be passionate to do God's will, and then you will be able to discern if my teachings are from the heart of God or from my own opinions."

JOHN 7:17 TPT

Dee struggled with her sexuality early in her life. She was raised as a Christian. Yet the way she lived did not line up with what the Word of God said. She acknowledged that she believed in Jesus, yet she was not convicted that her life of sexual promiscuity was wrong.

One day, a friend, who was struggling just as she was, acknowledged that her lifestyle was wrong but was simply not motivated to change. She told Dee that the Bible speaks about their issue in Romans.

She decided to read for herself. She was able to read with her heart and mind open to what God was saying through his Word. She did not read it with any preconceived idea of what she wanted the Scriptures to say. She was not instantly delivered that day of sexual sin, but she began to seek to know God and soon after fully surrendered her life to Jesus.

John 7:17 tells us that if our will is truly to do the will of our Father in heaven, we will know what the Scriptures are truly saying. We will know the truth. And no man's commentary will have to tell us.

Today it has been over thirty years since Dee had those struggles. She came to know her heavenly Father through Jesus Christ who helped her understand how she was created in his image.

Question

Do you know someone who is struggling with sexual promiscuity?

Lord, please help me be a friend to others in my life. Give me courage to be a source of truth to allow others to gain true freedom.

The First Requirement of Ministry

The priests are in mourning,
*those who minister before the L*ORD.*

JOEL 1:9 NIV

The first requirement for being used by God in the life of others is to mourn on their behalf. We must identify with their pain and suffering. Each of us must be broken for others first.

In order to be fully used by God in the workplace, we need to understand what breaks God's heart. When we understand what breaks God's heart, we are able to mourn on behalf of a grieving person or a nation we are called to serve. What breaks God's heart? When we begin to answer this question, we begin the first step to becoming instruments of change for those things that are important to God. Perhaps it is an overemphasis in our own talent and abilities or a lack of complete trust in Jesus. Perhaps it is the lack of respect for human life that leads to the killing of innocent babies. Perhaps it is the deceit and pride that often rule the workplace of commerce. When we begin to mourn over our own sins in these areas, God starts to use us as instruments of righteousness to affect these things. It is only when God lets me see my own sins and how they break his heart that I can be an instrument for his purposes.

Question

Is your heart broken over the things that break God's heart?

Father, how might you want me to be the instrument to affect these things for you? The first step is identification with what breaks your heart. Help me to know this.

Understanding Our Own Calling

"If I want him to remain alive until I return, what is that to you?
You must follow me."

JOHN 21:22 NIV

Jesus was talking to Peter after he had just had a very important encounter with him. It was one of the last meetings the two would have. This was the third time Jesus had shown himself to the disciples after his resurrection. It is the famous dialogue between Jesus and Peter in which Jesus asked three times if Peter loved him. Jesus followed by telling Peter, "Feed my sheep" (v. 17 NET). Jesus went on to foretell of Peter's death. Peter asked Jesus about John and whether he would die also. Jesus reacted sharply to Peter's comment, telling him not to worry about what John's role or purpose was in life. All Peter had to do was to concern himself only with his own purpose.

Even as Christians, we are often confronted with the temptation to believe that someone is blessed if they have achieved prominence. In his discussion with Peter, Jesus was getting at the very heart of the matter of a person's calling. Peter was to concern himself only with one thing: his own calling before God.

Question

Are you tempted to compare yourself with where others are in their lives? Are you dissatisfied with where God has you right now?

Father, today I choose to be of good cheer and to be "confident of this, that he who began a good work" in me "will carry it on to completion until the day of Christ Jesus" (Philippians 1:6 NIV).

Following Only the Father's Commands

So Jesus said,…"I only do the works that I see the Father doing,
for the Son does the same works as his Father."
JOHN 5:19 TPT

Have you ever thought about a typical day in Jesus' life? Perhaps he might have had questions like these, "Whom am I going to heal today? Whom will I visit today? Which person will I deliver from demons this day?" and so on. The demands on Jesus' time were great. Yet we see that Jesus allocated his time very deliberately. We don't get the idea that Jesus was flustered or stressed from the activity he was involved in. He often sought times of prayer and reflection away from the disciples. His life appeared to have a balance of quiet moments and active ministry to the lives with which he came in contact.

How do we determine what we will be involved in each day of our lives? What keeps us in sync with the will of our heavenly Father for the daily tasks he calls us to? Jesus tells us that he was only involved in those things the Father was involved in. Nothing more, nothing less. So often we determine our participation in an activity based on whether we have the time to do it or whether we desire to participate. The real question we should ask is, "Does the Father want me to participate in this activity?"

Question

How do you determine which things you will be involved in?

Father, show me how to spend quality time with you each day.

Sitting at His Feet

Ruth gleaned in the field until evening. Then she threshed the barley she had gathered, and it amounted to about an ephah.

RUTH 2:17 NIV

The story of Ruth provides an excellent illustration of the connection between spending time in the presence of God and receiving physical provision. Naomi was married to Elimelech. They had two married sons. Elimelech died, and ten years later, both of the sons also died. Ruth was married to one of the sons.

The other daughter-in-law moved back to her family, but Ruth, in spite of Naomi's encouragement for Ruth to return to her own family, insisted on staying with Naomi. The only way for the family line to continue would have been for Ruth to marry another son or direct relative. Now, through a custom known as the kinsman-redeemer, Ruth could be married to a relative in the family line. Naomi had a relative named Boaz, who was a prominent landowner and farmer. She sent Ruth to glean in the fields of Boaz all day. She yielded one ephah of grain (about thirty-five liters or a little less than six gallons).

Naomi realized the only way Ruth was going to have any kind of future was if a kinsman-redeemer came to her rescue. She instructed Ruth to go to the threshing floor and quietly sit at the feet of Boaz all night. Her hope was that Boaz would exercise his right to be her kinsmen-redeemer.

Boaz sent Ruth home and took the necessary steps to become her redeemer. But before he sent her home, he gave her six ephahs of barley—six times what she got working all day. Her sitting at the feet of her kinsman-redeemer turned out to be more productive than toiling all day in the fields.

Question

Have you come to a place of hopelessness in a situation in life?

Father, help me to sit at your feet daily.

Death and Birth of a Vision

"Let me make this clear: A single grain of wheat will never be more than a single grain of wheat unless it drops into the ground and dies. Because then it sprouts and produces a great harvest of wheat—all because one grain died."
JOHN 12:24 TPT

Almost every significant thing God births he allows to die before the vision is fulfilled in his own way.

- Abraham had a vision of being the father of a great nation (birth). Sarah was barren and became too old to have children (death). God gave Abraham and Sarah a son in their old age. He became the father of a great nation (fulfillment).
- Moses had a vision of leading his people out of the bondage of Egypt (birth). Pharaoh drove Moses out of Egypt after Moses' first attempt to relieve their bondage (death). God gave Moses signs and wonders to convince Pharaoh to free the people and bring them out of Egypt and into the promised land (fulfillment).
- A grain of wheat has a "vision" of reproducing itself and many more grains of wheat (birth). The grain dies in the ground (death). A harvest springs up out of the very process of "death" in the ground (fulfillment).

Question

Has God given you a vision that is yet unfulfilled?

Father, I willingly lay down my desire so that you may fulfill it in your way and your time.

A Refiner's Fire

For he will be like a refiner's fire or a launderer's soap.
MALACHI 3:2 NIV

The Lord has a specific manner of preparing his people for useful service. God desires to turn his children from rough, hard-edged stones into gems of gold and silver.

The refiner's fire can only accomplish its purposes when the heat is turned up to extraordinary temperatures. It breaks down the metal in order for it to become moldable and shapeable. Only when the temperatures reach this level can the work be fully accomplished. So it is in our lives.

Until the Lord completes his refining process, the offerings we make are not made in righteousness and cannot be acceptable. Thank God that Jesus is our righteousness and that there is no righteousness apart from him. Still, the Lord continues to purge out of our lives all that is not of his righteousness. This comes through trials that bring each of us to the end of ourselves so that he may only reflect that which is himself. Be encouraged because it is his overriding commitment to turn you from a rough, hard-edged stone to a precious metal.

Question

Is God taking you through a refiner's fire?

Father, thank you for making me more like you through your refining fire.

Night Visions

"God may speak in one way, or in another, yet man does not perceive it. In a dream, in a vision of the night, when deep sleep falls upon men, while slumbering on their beds."

JOB 33:14–15 NKJV

Cheryl has always been a dreamer. She recalls that, as a young child, she had many dreams of Jesus coming to her window and calling her. So much so that her mother had thoughts that Cheryl might die soon because it seemed that Jesus could be calling her home to heaven. While in high school, Cheryl would go to school each day and tell her friends what she dreamed the night before. However, she never really considered that God was speaking to her through her dreams.

During her adult years, Cheryl would occasionally receive a dream where she knew it was God speaking to her about a particular situation, and that dream would guide her to a solution.

However, in 2018, Cheryl's dream life exploded when she began having had a recurring dream that really grabbed her attention. Recognizing that God was indeed speaking to her through that dream, Cheryl then began regularly writing down her dreams, as ridiculous as some may have seemed, and started responding to what God was saying to her through them.

Since that eye-opening encounter, Cheryl's dreams have been a constant source of encouragement, guidance, and connection with God. Others have sought her out to help them interpret their dreams.

Question

Could God be trying to get your attention through your dreams?

Father, open up my heart to be sensitive to your voice, in whatever form it may come.

I Want It My Way

Then the LORD opened the mouth of the donkey, and she said to Balaam,
"What have I done to you, that you have struck me these three times?"
NUMBERS 22:28 NKJV

Have you ever wanted something so badly that you were willing to do anything to see that it happened? Such was the case the prophet Balaam, who was going to prophesy against Israel to satisfy a king who was going to pay him.

God used an unusual circumstance to bring correction to Balaam. It seems an angel of the Lord was standing in the road in front of Balaam's donkey, and the donkey could see him, but Balaam could not. When Balaam's donkey refused to move, it veered off the road to avoid the angel. Then, when Balaam could not get her to cooperate, he beat the donkey with a stick. Then the donkey spoke to him, and the Lord opened Balaam's eyes, and he saw the angel of the Lord standing in the way with his drawn sword in his hand; he bowed his head and fell flat on his face.

The old saying "two wrongs never make a right" certainly applies here. Balaam was wanting to prophesy for money. And he was seeing his donkey standing in the way of his scheme. It took an angel of the Lord and a talking donkey to change his plans.

Question

Have you ever forced a situation you did not believe was God's will?

Father, help me to be led by your Spirit, not by my emotions or fears.

Full-Time Christian Work

Put your heart and soul into every activity you do, as though you are doing it for the Lord himself and not merely for others. For we know that we will receive a reward, an inheritance from the Lord, as we serve the Lord Yahweh, the Anointed One!

COLOSSIANS 3:23–24 TPT

I didn't know you were in full-time Christian work," said my close friend.

I responded, "Every person who has followed the will of God in their life is in full-time Christian work." God calls some to the mission field, others to be accountants, advertising executives, and construction workers. God never made a distinction between sacred and secular. In fact, the Hebrew word *avodah* is the root word having the same meaning of both "work" and "worship." God wants us to see all work as worship.

We have incorrectly elevated the role of those Christians who work exclusively in ministry to be holier and more committed than the person who is serving in a more secular environment. Yet the call to the secular workplace is as important as any other calling. God has to have his people in every sphere of life. Otherwise, if all Christians were separated from society, many in the world would never come to know Jesus.

We are all on missions. Some are called to foreign lands. Some are called to the workplace. Wherever you are called, serve the Lord in that place.

Question

Have you ever thought those in vocational ministry were more spiritual than you?

Father, thank you that we are all in "full-time Christian work" because there are no part-time Christians.

The Anguish of Faith

Let the morning bring me word of your unfailing love,
for I have put my trust in you.
PSALM 143:8 NIV

Of all the biblical characters, David gives us a glimpse of a person who walked with God with great emotion—in victory and in defeat. David never lost a battle throughout his many years of serving as king of Israel. In many of the Psalms, David often lamented about the difficult places where God had placed him. He talked of his enemies and the need for God to deliver him. He talked of God's everlasting love for him. How do you suppose David realized this after years of being sought by King Saul, who wanted to take his life? His years of turmoil within his family gave him many reasons to lose all hope in a loving God.

David often began his psalms in a place of discouragement and loss of hope. But he never ended one psalm in defeat. He always came to a place of victory in God by the end of the psalm. David always placed his life in God's hands, knowing God would care for him.

It is okay to feel discouragement. It is part of the process of grieving and working through those times of pain. But God wants each of us to allow him to walk with us in these places. If you find yourself in one of these places, do what David did. Ask God to show you the way and let him bring the word of his unfailing love to you.

Question

Are you ever tempted to believe God does not love and care for you?

Father, help me to experience your deep love for me today.

Toe in the Water

"When the soles of the feet of the priests carrying the Chest of God, Master of all the earth, touch the Jordan's water, the flow of water will be stopped— the water coming from upstream will pile up in a heap."
JOSHUA 3:9–13 MSG

In sales, they say that the first sale you have to make is the one to sell yourself. It was 2007, and Deb was at a crossroads. She'd already experienced success as a sales coach and then as a sales leader in the software industry. It was time to choose between working for someone else or working for herself again. That's when she could no longer ignore the full measure of her doublemindedness. She loved sales and hated sales. Working for others was like wearing snowshoes on deep snow; the stress to hit quota could be spread out and shared with others, lessening the pressure. But there are no "snowshoes" for the solo entrepreneur.

Add to the fact that the Lord had been prompting her to restart her sales consultancy for a while. "Let's see…choose to stay in the golden handcuffs or obey to the Lord?" Everything changed the day she renounced her doublemindedness at a gathering of Christian business owners. She introduced herself, confessed, and repented of her love–hate relationship with sales. She declared, "God made me good at sales, so I embrace his call to restart my business and purpose to walk in it going forward."

Three months later, she restarted her business and has never looked back. God blessed her with favor that allowed her to triple her first-year earnings in year two and to triple year two earnings and again in year three. She learned that blessings awaited her when she followed God's plan for her life. He was waiting on her to take the first step to "put her toe in the water."

Question

Are you postponing something God may want you to do?

Father, give me the faith to put my toe in the water.

David's Source of Direction

Let the morning bring me word of your unfailing love, for I have put my trust in you.
Show me the way I should go, for to you I entrust my life.

PSALM 143:8 NIV

David is the only person in the Bible whom God describes as a man after his own heart (1 Samuel 13:14). Despite David's many setbacks he continually sought to know and do God's will in his life. Like many of us, his will got in the way.

In the morning hour, David sought to hear from God. I can imagine David sitting on the open deck of his palace looking over the hills of Jerusalem, listening to God. There, in his morning watch, he felt God's unfailing love. He reaffirmed his trust in God. He also understood that the key to knowing God's will lay in spending such moments alone to reflect on what God had done and was doing in his life.

Sometimes we fall prey to believing that God is not concerned and that he does not lead us in our work life. We are tempted to think that he leads us in other areas but not in our daily workplace. The truth is that God is in every aspect of life and desires to direct us.

Question

Do you need direction in your life today? If so, David provides the best example of gaining direction.

Father, help me to seek you in the morning each day so that you might teach me to walk with you.

For Such a Time as This

"For if you remain silent at this time, relief and deliverance for the Jews will arise from another place, but you and your father's family will perish. And who knows but that you have come to your royal position for such a time as this?"

ESTHER 4:14 NIV

Esther was a Jewish orphan living in the land of Persia after her people were taken into captivity from Jerusalem. Raised by her cousin Mordecai, she lived during the time of King Xerxes who reigned over Persia.

An edict was sent out to bring all the virgins to the king's palace from the surrounding regions to replace Queen Vashti, who found disfavor with the king and was deposed. Esther was one of the young women taken and was ultimately selected to be the next queen.

Mordecai had a high-ranking position in the government that allowed him to learn of a plot by Haman, an official of the king, to kill all of the Jews. Now, the only way to stop this edict from being carried out was if Esther asked for an audience with the king to request that the plot be abandoned on her behalf. However, if the king refused to meet her, the penalty for her was death.

"For if you remain silent at this time, relief and deliverance for the Jews will arise from another place, but you and your father's family will perish." Mordecai was giving her a choice.

She responded, "If I perish, I perish" (v. 16). Esther realized this could be the reason God created her—to save her people from destruction.

Question

Have you ever faced a decision that had the potential for severe consequences?

Father, give me the courage to make a right decision when faced with difficult choice.

No Confidence in the Flesh

*It's true that I once relied on all that I had become.
I had a reason to boast and impress people with my accomplishments—
more than others—for my pedigree was impeccable.*

PHILIPPIANS 3:4 TPT

The apostle Paul surely could relate to the experiences many business executives face. Paul reached the height of his profession only to have it completely stripped and torn from him. What he thought mattered in life became rubbish compared to what God did in his heart as God destroyed what seemed valuable at the time. It took a dramatic event to bring Paul into this revelation. It took a bright light, blindness, and the most fearful experience a human could have—having Jesus personally address him and question why Paul was persecuting Jesus' people.

Paul would later write, "Yet all of the accomplishments that I once took credit for, I've now forsaken them and I regard it all as nothing compared to the delight of experiencing Jesus Christ as my Lord!" (Philippians 3:7).

Sometimes God lets us experience great pain to learn the lessons of greatest importance. Knowing Christ intimately is the most important lesson we can learn.

Question

Where do you find your greatest pleasure?

Father, help me avoid placing my confidence in things that are but rubbish so that I might know you more intimately.

Peace: A Weapon against Satan

Even when your path takes me through the valley of deepest darkness,
fear will never conquer me, for you already have!

PSALM 23:4 TPT

Your peace is actually a weapon to fight spiritual battles. The workplace creates many opportunities to rob us of our peace. Your confidence in the God of peace declares that you are not falling for the lies of the devil. You see, the first step toward having spiritual authority over the adversary is having peace in spite of your circumstance. When Jesus confronted the devil, he did not confront Satan with his emotions or in fear. Knowing that the devil is a liar, Jesus simply refused to be influenced by any voice other than God's. His peace overwhelmed Satan; his authority then shattered the lie, which sent demons fleeing.

There is a place of walking with God where you simply fear no evil. David faced a lion, a bear, and a giant. In this psalm, he stood in the "shadow of death" itself, yet he "fear[ed] no evil." David's trust was in the Lord. He said, "for thou art with me" (RSV). Because God is with you, every adversity you face will unfold in victory as you maintain your faith in God! Only God's peace will quell your fleshly reactions in battle. The source of God's peace is God himself. If fear has been knocking at your door, begin to face that fear with God's peace. It is God's secret weapon to destroy fear.

Question

Are you experiencing peace even in the midst of your battles?

Father, thank you for giving me peace to fight my battles today.

God's Power in the Clothing Industry

*God intended that your faith not be established on man's wisdom
but by trusting in his almighty power.*

1 CORINTHIANS 2:5 TPT

Years ago, a mentor said he feared that my exceptional marketing skills would "outmarket" God. I learned a principle from him to withhold my natural gifting to ensure that God is in whatever I was doing. If God led me to knock on a door three times, then I was to knock three times, not five times. It was a way of seeing God's hand in my activity instead of forcing things to happen.

Crystal is a businesswoman involved in the manufacture of designer clothing. Her designs are known for their elaborate detail and accessories sewn into each article. One day a call came from a retailer requesting that Crystal send four designs to them for consideration for the next season's clothing line. It was going to be very difficult to meet the deadline due to other circumstances that were going on in her life.

Finally, the deadline came, and she had not added the elaborate detail and finish work for which she was known on two of the four pieces they had requested from her. The retailer told her to send all four.

Crystal is a perfectionist. The idea of sending unfinished designs made her very uncomfortable. Then, she recalled my teaching on this principle. She decided to send the two pieces of clothing to the retailer along with the other two "finished" pieces. To her shock and amazement, the retailer chose the two pieces of clothing that had not been "finished" and declined the other two.

Crystal realized that God was demonstrating his power through this principle of withholding her natural gifting.

Question

Are you placing too much emphasis on your own skill?

Father, help me to trust you even when I may think you are falling short.

Making Adjustments

*"Throw your net on the right side of the boat
and you will find some."*
JOHN 21:6 NIV

A former client of mine was the marketing director of a large grocery food brokerage company and told me a story about one of their client grocery stores located in the upper Midwest. It seems that the store could not understand why, at a certain time every winter, sales plummeted. They studied their product line and interviewed customers. They did everything possible to uncover the mystery. Finally, someone made a remarkable discovery that changed everything.

It seemed that whenever it was really cold outside, the manager raised the temperature in the store. When customers came into the store, it was too warm for them, so they removed their coats and placed them in their shopping carts. This meant there was less room in their carts for food, which resulted in reduced sales overall. The manager then lowered the temperature of the store, customers kept their coats on, and sales went up!

Jesus stood on the shoreline and watched Peter and his companions fish. Jesus called from the shoreline to ask if they had caught anything. They had not. He then suggested they cast their line on the other side of the boat. Without knowing the person who was addressing them, the fishermen took his advice. They began catching so many fish they could not bring them in.

Adjusting our lives to God is the first thing that has to happen in order to begin experiencing him in our daily lives.

Question

What adjustments do you need to make in your life in order for things to work better?

Father, help me to discern the adjustments I need to make in my life.

Living a Life of Conviction

*Our gospel came to you not merely in the form of words
but in mighty power infused with the Holy Spirit and deep conviction.*
1 THESSALONIANS 1:5 TPT

Everyone lives a life of conviction. Whatever we give the most time, our greatest energies, and our greatest resources to is a good indication of where our convictions lie. Some live a life of conviction about work. Some live a life of conviction around pleasure. Still others live a life of conviction about very little that matters at all.

Whenever God chooses to do a deep work in a life, a strong conviction is born of the Holy Spirit. Conversions in the early church resulted in changed lives that held to a deep, life-transforming conviction regarding what they believed and how they lived out that belief. Paul explains that the gospel they received came not just in words but also in power, with the Holy Spirit and with deep conviction.

In order to impact others for Jesus Christ, each of us must be reflecting a faith that is demonstrated through deeply held convictions. Paul was willing to suffer great persecution for his faith. God calls each of us to a life that is supernatural, not simply a good, moral life. The early church understood the role the Holy Spirit played in demonstrating this power of the gospel.

Question

Are you living a life of deep conviction that spurs you on to reflect the power of Christ in your life and the lives of others?

Father, fill me and baptize me with the Holy Spirit that I might live a life of power in you.

Remedy for Depression

To console those who mourn in Zion, to give them beauty for ashes,
the oil of joy for mourning, the garment of praise for the spirit of heaviness.
ISAIAH 61:3 NKJV

A 1988 article in *Psychology Today* reported on an experiment involving seventeen hundred women. The women participated in various projects that involved helping other people. Of those surveyed, 13 percent noticed a decrease in aches and pains, and many women reported that they had felt relief from symptoms that included "stress-related disorders such as headaches, voice loss and even pain accompanying lupus and multiple sclerosis."[14]

I suspect many people could save thousands of dollars on therapy and antidepressants if they would just take time to serve others. The best way to get *beyond* our pain is to get *outside* of it. I discovered this in my own journey through a particularly dark time. I decided to serve others even though I was in great emotional pain. This had a remarkably positive effect on my emotional state.

When we refocus our attention on the needs of others when we ourselves are in turmoil, it allows the burden of our circumstance to be removed from us. The more you focus on your own problems, the more likely you are to become depressed.

Question

Do you find yourself depressed because of a circumstance in your life? Take Isaiah's advice: begin to praise the Lord in spite of the circumstances you see.

Father, today I choose to praise you in spite of the circumstances in which I find myself. I will find ways to serve others.

Treasures in Darkness

"I will give you hidden treasures, riches stored in secret places, so that you may know that I am the Lord, the God of Israel, who summons you by name."
ISAIAH 45:3 NIV

I have never been in this place before. I am way out of my comfort zone. I am scared to death to trust him at this level." Those were the words I expressed to a friend when I was in a difficult place in my life. That day, God led me to the above passage of Scripture.

What we perceive as dark periods in our lives are designed to be treasures from God. They are actually riches stored in secret places. We cannot see those times in this light because of the often-accompanying pain or fear that prevents us from accepting these times as treasures. They have a particular purpose from God's viewpoint: "So that you may know that I am the Lord…who summons you by name."

Unless we are cast into times in which we are completely at God's mercy, we will never experience God's faithfulness in those areas. We will never know how personal he is or that he can be trusted to meet the deepest needs in our lives. God wants each of us to know that we are "summoned by name." Every hair of our head is numbered. He knows every activity in which we are involved. His love for you and me knows no bounds, and he will take every opportunity to demonstrate this to us.

Question

Has God brought you into a place of darkness?

Father, I choose to trust you today to reveal that hidden treasure that can be found in this darkness.

Resolving the Ownership Issue

Yahweh claims the world as his. Everything and everyone belong to him!
He's the one who pushed back oceans to let the dry ground appear,
planting firm foundations for the earth.

PSALM 24:1–2 TPT

As Christian workplace believers, God calls us to view him as the owner of everything. We are to be stewards of all that he entrusts to us. This is one of the hardest of all commandments to follow for the Christian workplace believer because, if we work hard at our jobs, we receive all the material benefits of that work. It appears as though all that we have achieved was through our hand. Yet God says that it is by his hand that we are able to make wealth (see Deuteronomy 8:17–18). He is the source of that ability. As soon as we become owners and not managers, we fall into trouble with God.

Joseph understood that he was a steward of all the resources of Egypt. God promoted him to affect an entire region of the world. Joseph had more power, prestige, and wealth than any thirty-year-old who ever lived before him. The temptation for him in this newfound role in life must have been great.

As a quote often attributed to Oswald Chambers says, "Not every man can carry a full cup. Sudden elevation frequently leads to pride and a fall. The most exacting test of all to survive is prosperity."

Question

Are you living as a steward or an owner? Ask the Lord today to help you put on his altar whatever skills and resources you possess.

Father, I lay all my abilities before you today and acknowledge your lordship over them.

Lydia, a Workplace Minister

A woman named Lydia, a dealer in purple cloth from the city of Thyatira, who worshiped God, was listening.

ACTS 16:14 HCSB

There was a businesswoman named Lydia, whom Paul encountered in Thyatira. She was an early church entrepreneur dealing in purple cloth, the most expensive type of cloth in the first century Middle East. Most accounts believe she was Paul's first convert. I find it interesting that his first convert was both a woman and an entrepreneur. Women were often subservient to men in biblical times, and few were business owners. Kudos to Paul, who did not let societal biases keep him from spiritually investing in Lydia.

"We sat down and began to speak to the women who had gathered there…The Lord opened her heart to respond to Paul's message. When she and the members of her household were baptized, she invited us to her home" (Acts 16:13–15 NIV).

This encounter with Lydia and her women associates ultimately opened the way for ministry in that region. God often worked in and through women in the early church. Lydia was an influential businesswoman, and the gospel was affecting all strata of society, just as it does today.

Evidence of her conversion was immediate. She told the men if they considered her a believer in the Lord, she would like for them to come and stay at her house. Evidently, she had plenty of room to accommodate the four of them; Silas, Timothy, and Luke were with Paul also. They accepted her invitation and stayed at her house.

Question

Are you one of God's "Lydias"?

Pray that you will be the instrument, like Paul, to bring the gospel to influential women entrepreneurs.

Embracing the Lean Times

"Blessed is the one who trusts in the LORD,
whose confidence is in him."
JEREMIAH 17:7 NIV

Have you ever considered at what point a test becomes so difficult that you decide you can no longer trust in God and must take over to solve the problem yourself? The prophet Jeremiah describes a situation in which the temptation to solve a financial problem can become so great that we trust in man's way to solve it.

This is what the Lord says: "But blessed is the one who trusts in the LORD, whose confidence is in him. They will be like a tree planted by the water that sends out its roots by the stream. It does not fear when heat comes; its leaves are always green. It has no worries in a year of drought and never fails to bear fruit" (Jeremiah 17:7–8).

Jeremiah drew a sharp comparison between the man who trusts in his own effort to solve his problem and the man who trusts in God when he cannot see the outcome. The man who trusts in God bears fruit despite the circumstances in his life. He does not shrivel when the heat comes; in fact, his roots go deeper into God's grace. He continues to bear fruit in spite of his circumstances.

Question

Do you find yourself in a difficult place financially?

Father, today I choose to see you as my resource and faithful provider of all I need.

An Eternal View of Circumstances

I want you to know, dear ones, what has happened to me has not hindered,
but helped my ministry of preaching the gospel, causing it to expand
and spread to many people.

PHILIPPIANS 1:12 TPT

Are your life circumstances advancing the gospel? Can you see the Lord's hand in your life in such a way that all of your life experiences, joys, sorrows, hardships, and training have resulted in advancing the gospel?

Paul was a tentmaker by trade. But he had an overall ministry objective in his business life. That objective left him imprisoned and persecuted at times. But Paul saw these events not as roadblocks to his mission. Rather, they were catalysts to advancing the cause of Christ. Paul's revelation of this kept him from despairing about his circumstances.

One day a little-known pastor who lived in the small African nation of Benin began to pray for his Marxist president. For two years he prayed. Then the Lord told the pastor to go to meet this president and share the gospel with him. The president rejected the gospel, but after another such visit, the president accepted the gospel and became a Christian. He was removed from power but was discipled by this pastor. Sometime later this same president was elected again.

Question

Are your work and life experiences serving to advance the gospel?

Father, help me see my life the way you see it and fulfill my purpose here on earth.

Opening Our Spiritual Eyes

Elisha prayed, "Open his eyes, Lord, so that he may see."
Then the Lord opened the servant's eyes, and he looked
and saw the hills full of horses and chariots of fire all around Elisha.

2 Kings 6:17 NIV

Elisha was counseling the nation of Israel against the impending attack of the king of Aram. The Lord revealed the king's plans to Elisha. Elisha warned Israel of each intended attack. The king could not understand why his plans were continually foiled. He was furious when he was told it was the God of Israel who was to blame for this inside information. The king decided the only way to resolve the situation was to get rid of the problem by killing Elisha.

The king's forces surrounded Elisha and his servant. Elisha's servant was upset. Elisha immediately prayed that his servant's eyes might be opened to see that there was no need to be afraid because the angels were protecting them.

Elisha prayed, "Open his eyes, Lord, so that he may see." Then the Lord opened the servant's eyes, and he looked and saw the hills full of horses and chariots of fire all around Elisha. As the enemy came down toward him, Elisha prayed to the Lord, "Strike this army with blindness." So he struck them with blindness, as Elisha had asked. (vv. 17–18)

Question

Who is the Elisha in your life? Do you have a mentor friend who can see the activity of God in your life when you cannot see it?

Father, open my eyes to see what I need to see in the spiritual realm of my life.

Spiritual Contracts

In the first year of his reign, I, Daniel, understood from the Scriptures,
according to the word of the LORD given to Jeremiah the prophet,
that the desolation of Jerusalem would last seventy years.

DANIEL 9:2 NIV

When you enter a legal contract, it binds the two parties to fulfill the terms of that contract. In heaven, there are legal contracts that, when fulfilled, allow the spiritual to impact the physical.

Israel had been in captivity to Babylon for seventy years. Daniel, when he investigated the history of his nation, found the prophecy of Jeremiah, which revealed there would be seventy years of captivity. He recognized that in order to release his nation from this captivity, there had to be a confession of sin on the part of the nation. Daniel took that responsibility. When Daniel acknowledged this sin before God, something took place in heaven. God responded by sending his angel Gabriel to Daniel's side.

Confronting spiritual forces that have dominion over a situation requires finding the source of the problem. Once you find the source of the problem, you must take the necessary steps in the spiritual realm to release God's power into that situation. For Daniel, it meant taking responsibility for the sin of the nation by confessing its sins and asking forgiveness on behalf of the entire nation. God began the process of releasing the nation.

Question

Are there destructive forces among you that need to be torn down?

Father, show me the source of problems that may exist in my city or my workplace or the people you want me to free to fulfill God's purposes in their lives.

The Slinky

We know that all things work together for good to those who love God,
to those who are the called according to His purpose.

ROMANS 8:28 NKJV

Richard James was an engineer who worked for Cramp Shipbuilding in Port Richard, Pennsylvania. One day a torsion spring fell off the table in front of him, and he noticed how the spring fell end over end. He thought this might be a good toy, so he and his wife, Betty, pursued perfecting the spring.

Betty came up with the name *Slinky* after thumbing through the dictionary. She thought the word described the motion of the spring. They made four hundred Slinkys, and during the 1945 Christmas season, they convinced the Gimbels department store in Philadelphia to carry the toy for Christmas for one dollar each. They displayed the toy on a ramp while Richard showed customers how it unfolded. The first models were sold within ninety minutes.[15]

Richard became eccentric, giving large sums of money to Christian causes while the company started losing money.[16] One day, out of the blue, Richard walked in and informed Betty he was leaving to become a missionary in Bolivia. He left his wife and their six children. He told her she could have the company and give it up to creditors if need be. However, Betty decided to try and rebuild the company on her own. She launched a TV ad campaign with a catchy jingle that caught on. Sales skyrocketed, and she would run the company successfully for over forty years.[17] More than 300 million Slinkys were sold in her lifetime.[18]

Question

Have you ever experienced a crisis where someone left you, placing you in a very vulnerable place?

Father, help me to see my crisis as an opportunity.

The Dangers of Overcontrol

"For rebellion is like the sin of divination, and arrogance like the evil of idolatry. Because you have rejected the word of the LORD, he has rejected you as king."
1 SAMUEL 15:23 NIV

A friend of mine who is a jet pilot once told me that whenever a jet goes out of control and begins to spin, the only thing to do is take your hands completely off the controls and the plane will right itself. This goes against our natural inclination to manage and manipulate in order to bring things back under our power. It is scary to be out of control. Or is it?

Saul was a man out of control. He was losing control of his kingdom to David. He was losing the favor of God and the people. It began as compromises. He was instructed to kill the Amalekites completely, but he failed to follow through. Saul obeyed partially but not fully. It was partial obedience that led to his removal as king of Israel and his calling from God. But why did Saul do such a thing? "I was afraid of the people and did what they demanded" (v. 24 NLT).

Question

How many of us are in danger of losing God's blessing due to partial obedience? How many of us have such a need to control people and circumstances that we fail to fully walk in obedience to God's voice in our lives?

Father, help me be fully obedient to what you call me to do this day and avoid being put on the shelf for disobedience.

The Reaper

"Don't keep hoarding for yourselves earthly treasures that can be stolen by thieves. Material wealth eventually rusts, decays, and loses its value. Instead, stockpile heavenly treasures for yourselves that cannot be stolen and will never rust, decay, or lose their value. For your heart will always pursue what you esteem as your treasure."
MATTHEW 6:19–21 TPT

Cyrus McCormick's father dreamed of inventing a machine to harvest crops. For years he experimented with various reaper machines. At age thirty-eight, Cyrus drove to Chicago and opened his first factory. His success made him a millionaire at forty. He met Nettie Fowler, who was from New York. Nettie was beautiful, tall, full of grace and had striking brown eyes. Her relationship with Christ emanated from her countenance and attracted Cyrus immediately after meeting her. They fell in love and married in 1859. She was twenty-six years younger than Cyrus. They had twenty-six years of marriage together before Cyrus died.

Nettie inherited millions her husband's death. She established McCormick Theological Seminary in Chicago for young Presbyterian ministers. She helped establish student missions through the John R. Mott Student Volunteer Movement and was a major financial supporter for evangelistic campaigns of D. L. Moody.

This was just the beginning. She gave to hundreds of organizations.

She never thought of herself as a great philanthropist. She always felt others did more, and she once said, "The greatest gift of all comes from the self-sacrifice and devotion of missionaries. You can tell where people's hearts are by looking at their check stubs."[19]

Question

What does your checkbook reveal about your giving?

Father, help me to be a generous giver to your kingdom purposes.

New Workplace Believers

"Is it a time for you yourselves to be living in your paneled houses, while this house remains a ruin?"

HAGGAI 1:4 NIV

Zerubbabel was the governor of Judah sixty years after the great temple built by Solomon had been destroyed. The temple lay in ruins, and the Lord spoke to the prophet Haggai. God was calling for a remnant of his people to come out of their comfort zones and restore the glory of God's house.

God is doing this same thing today among Christian workplace believers throughout the world. He is raising up a remnant of workplace believers who are being handpicked to use their resources, skills, and experience to affect nations that have not heard the message of Jesus Christ. The only way some people can hear the gospel is through Christian workplace believers bringing commerce into their nations because these regions are closed to normal missionary efforts.

The remnant of workplace believers God is calling today understands that they have to come out of Egypt from their past work life. Egypt signifies the way of the world. It represents sweat and toil. It is the flesh. This new way is exemplified by a pioneer spirit. God assures us that his Spirit is with anyone who seeks to live in the realm of supernatural faith.

Question

Are you part of these remnants God has handpicked in these days? Has he called you out of Egypt in order to do extraordinary things in your life for his kingdom?

Father, please show me how you want to use me in the workplace.

Going without Jesus

A full day after they began their journey home,
Joseph and Mary realized that Jesus was missing.

LUKE 2:43 TPT

Bob and Janice had five kids. When they went on any trip, ten-year-old Benjamin, the youngest, always slept under the seat in their minivan. In the rush of preparing for their visit to the grocery store and getting the other kids situated, they failed to pick up Benjamin, who was standing outside at the other end of the store. As they proceeded down the road, they assumed that Benjamin was quietly sleeping in his normal place under the seat in the back of the van.

Meanwhile, about an hour later, young Benjamin was wondering why his parents had not picked him up. He went back into the store and told the manager his plight. The manager called the police. The young boy was eventually picked up by a police officer and reunited with his family.

Mary and Joseph traveled to Jerusalem for the Feast of the Passover. Jesus was twelve years old. They were evidently very distracted by the excitement and business of the feast. They realized Jesus was nowhere to be found.

As a parent, I find this story truly amazing. Yet, this story illustrates how each of us can become so busy that we continue to operate not realizing Jesus is no longer with us.

We can walk away from Jesus. Do not let this happen to you.

Question

Ask yourself if Jesus is accompanying you in your daily activities. He desires to walk with you each and every day.

Father, may I abide in you all day today to experience your presence and power in my life.

Faith Experiences

These only reveal the sterling core of your faith, which is far more valuable than gold that perishes, for even gold is refined by fire. Your authentic faith will result in even more praise, glory, and honor when Jesus the Anointed One is revealed.

1 PETER 1:7 TPT

One of the great tragedies of the Christian life is that if we fail to enter into a relationship with God that is born of the Holy Spirit, we are left with a religion, not a relationship. Many a person today lives with an intellectual belief in God but without a relationship that is based on two-way communication. This is the greatest tragedy of all. Their faith is reduced to "dos and don'ts" versus an experiential relationship with God.

Faith experiences with God allow us to know firsthand the faithfulness of God, the love of God, and the personal nature of God. If you cannot recount several instances when God has met you personally, then chances are your faith has not been born of the Holy Spirit into a living relationship with God. It is easy to fall prey to a relationship to God that never experiences his real presence; rather, it is based on knowledge only. This is a tragic place to be.

Question

Is this where you have been in your Christian experience?

Father, show me your personal nature and love. I know you desire this for me: "He who loves me will be loved by my Father, and I will love him and manifest myself to him" (John 14:21 ESV).

Using a Pen to Reform a Nation

He has made My mouth like a sharp sword; in the shadow of His hand He has hidden Me, and made Me a polished shaft; in His quiver He has hidden Me.

ISAIAH 49:2 NKJV

Harriet Beecher Stowe was an overachiever. She was born in the early 1800s, and her father, Lyman Beecher, was a nationally known evangelist. Harriet was raised in a middle-class family and became a successful writer and abolitionist during a time when the Civil War and slavery threatened to split the United States. She was married to Calvin Stowe, a college professor and scholar, and would have five children.

Harriet was deeply troubled by slavery in America and began to be very vocal about its injustice. One day her brother, a leader of the Boston abolitionists, made a comment that stirred Harriet. "Hattie, if I could use a pen as you can, I would write something that would make the whole nation feel what an accursed thing slavery is." That statement triggered Harriet to write her now-famous book, *Uncle Tom's Cabin*, a story about people who were enslaved in America, their plight, and the injustice of slavery. In March of 1852, the first printing of five thousand copies were gone in two days. By May, an incredible fifty thousand copies had been sold. It would sell three hundred thousand copies in its first year of publication.

It was in 1851 in a church service that God gave her a vision of an elderly black man being flogged to death that deeply affected her and led her to finishing her book and making the connection to Christ's suffering.

In 1862 Harriet met Abraham Lincoln who said to her, "So, you're the little woman who wrote the book that made this big war."[20]

Question

Has God given you a burden to address an issue that needs reform?

Father, give me the faith and boldness to be used to fight injustice.

Twins

Behold, children are a heritage from the Lord,
the fruit of the womb is a reward.
PSALM 127:3 NKJV

I grew up in a family of five kids. I was number four among my four sisters. My two oldest sisters were identical twins. They looked so much alike that many friends had trouble telling them apart. They were and are very close in spite of living in different cities today, often talking several times a week on the phone.

When they were younger, my twin sisters lived near each other. They often shopped at the same grocery store. One day one of my sisters did her weekly grocery shopping in the morning, and on this particular afternoon, the other twin did her weekly grocery shopping at the same store. A bag boy was helping my sister take her groceries to the car when he said, "Ma'am, you must have a really big family. I helped you earlier in the day with just as many groceries!"

My sister laughed. "Oh, that was my twin sister. We both shop here."

As we get older, we appreciate our families more and more. At least that is the way it should be. Every Thanksgiving, our large family of forty plus people gets together for a Thanksgiving meal. I am saddened when I hear of families that are torn apart because of an incident that caused a breach in a family relationship. I have heard of siblings who have no relationship because of a breach that happened in the family.

Question

Is there someone in your family that you need to forgive?

Father, give me the grace to forgive those who need your forgiveness.

Pursuing Your Passion

*I can do all things through Christ
who strengthens me.*
PHILIPPIANS 4:13 NKJV

It was the 1950s, and there were very few novels being written in the Christian arena. Eugenia was living in Chicago and was making a name for herself as a young radio writer and producer. She was not a follower of Christ at the time. She had the best of everything; she lived in a beautiful apartment, ate out at great restaurants, traveled by limousine, and had very influential friends.

But something was missing. She had attended church as a child, but during college, she proclaimed herself an agnostic.

She decided to follow her father's footsteps and pursue a career as a dentist. She was the only woman student at Northwestern Dental School that year, but she quickly grew bored and dropped out. For the next ten years she became more disenchanted with life. However, in 1949 her childhood friend had become a Christian. It was the influence of her friend Ellen that led Eugenia to have an encounter with Christ that changed her life forever.

Eugenia broke into the Christian media market when a Catholic FM station invited her to host an hour-and-a-half show five days a week called "A Visit with Genie." This was the beginning of a new opportunity to write and produce. She would eventually begin writing books and in 1965 wrote her first book entitled *Beloved Invader*.

Eugenia Price would go on to write thirty-five books with more than fifteen million sales. Her books would be translated into seventeen languages. Her crisis had led her to a new calling and new purpose.[21]

Question

Is there a passion in your life you need to pursue?

Father, give me the faith and courage to pursue my passion.

Friendship in the Pit

A dear friend will love you no matter what,
and a family sticks together through all kinds of trouble.
PROVERBS 17:17 TPT

I am in there again," I told my friend. "The pit." There can be times when no one can cheer you up, and you wonder if there is or ever was a God. Have you ever had such times?

The writer of Proverbs phrased it well when he said, "Hope deferred makes the heart sick" (Proverbs 13:12 NIV). Sometimes we get so low that we despair to unbelief.

"I'm coming over," my friend said. "We're going to pray."

About thirty minutes later, my friend walked in the door. We sat in my living room, and my friend began to pray. I didn't feel like praying. I was too deep in the pit. All I could do was listen. After a while my friend was quiet. We both sat quietly for ten to fifteen minutes, praying quietly to ourselves. Suddenly my friend said, "First Thessalonians 5:24!"

"What verse is that?" I asked.

"I don't know," she said. "That is the verse he spoke to me."

I grabbed my Bible and looked up the verse. "The one who calls you is faithful, and he will do it" (NIV).

We laughed. Can he be so personal? Can he care that much? That night I grew more in my love of my two friends, the friend beside me and Jesus, not to mention being brought out of the pit.

Question

Do you have a friend who is there when you need somebody at any hour of the day? Are you there for your friend?

Father, show me how I can be a better friend to someone today.

When Life Is Overwhelming

*Jesus refused to listen to what they were told and said to the Jewish official,
"Don't yield to fear. All you need to do is to keep on believing."*

MARK 5:36 TPT

Sometimes life can be overwhelming. Ann was in such a season. Whenever she tried to pray, she couldn't even put her concerns into words. Every prayer just came out, "Help me, God…God, help me!" Nevertheless, she kept reading her Bible and singing songs of worship. After all, if God couldn't help her, who could?

Slowly, her rescue came as she read familiar verses like: "I will never leave you nor forsake you" (Hebrews 13:5 NKJV); "My sheep listen to my voice; I know them, and they follow me. I give them eternal life, and they will never perish. No one can snatch them away from me" (John 10:27–28 NLT); "Don't be afraid; just believe" (Mark 5:36 NIV). Just believe. Just believe. Just believe. It was time for her to believe. It was time to choose to believe that God loved her, and he always had her best interest at heart, his path was the best path, and she was not alone.

Now, she calls that season and the rescue that followed "boot camp." It wasn't fun. It was her personal discipleship training. Surrendering to his teaching and believing that he was her loving coach brought her to a place of much joy, peace, and trust.

You are a daughter of the King!

Question

Do you ever feel overwhelmed with life?

Father, help me to see and experience your love and grace you have for me.

The Strength of Brokenness

*"The bows of the warriors are broken,
but those who stumbled are armed with strength."*
1 SAMUEL 2:4 NIV

There is an oxymoron throughout the Bible. It says that brokenness is strength. How can this be? How can brokenness be strength? In order to use men and women to their fullest extent, the Lord has to break his servants so that they might have a new kind of strength that is not human in origin. It is strength in spirit that is born only through brokenness.

Paul was broken on the Damascus road. Peter was broken after Jesus was taken prisoner. Jacob was broken at Peniel. David was broken after his sin with Bathsheba. The list could go on of those the Lord had to break in different ways before they could be used in the kingdom.

When we are broken, we see the frailty of human strength and come to grips with the reality that we can do nothing in our own strength. Then, new strength emerges that God uses mightily. God resists the proud but gives grace to the humble. This brokenness will become your authority for your assignment.

Question

Do you fear brokenness? Don't, for it may be the missing ingredient to a life that emerges with a new kind of strength and experience you did not know before.

Father, help me have a broken and contrite heart that you can bless.

Barbie

Now to Him who is able to do exceedingly abundantly above all that we ask or think, according to the power that works in us, to Him be glory in the church by Christ Jesus to all generations, forever and ever. Amen.

EPHESIANS 3:20–21 NKJV

Ruth Handler had a daughter named Barbara. Barbara loved to play with paper dolls, pretending they were adults.

Ruth was married to Elliot. They, along with Harold "Matt" Matson, began a small company to manufacture picture frames, calling it "Mattel" by combining part of their names ("Matt" and "Elliot"). Ruth made dollhouse furniture from the leftover scraps. The furniture became more profitable than the picture frames, and they decided to concentrate on toy manufacturing.

While traveling overseas in Switzerland, Ruth passed by a toy shop window and noticed that her daughter was attracted to a doll that had an adult body that was very sleek and attractive. She and her team began designing a similar doll and fitted clothes. She called the doll Barbie, after her daughter Barbara.

However, she was not prepared for the onslaught of negative reaction. Toy stores and marketers totally rejected her idea on the premise that kids would not embrace this doll and parents wouldn't let their kids play with a doll that had an adult figure. Ruth proved them wrong!

Barbie debuted at the New York Toy Fair on March 9, 1959, but it was not an immediate success. When Disney introduced *The Mickey Mouse Club* children's television show, Mattel invested heavily in television advertising. The TV commercials for the Barbie doll paid off, and Barbie rocketed Mattel and the Handlers to fame and fortune.[22]

Question

Do you have an idea God has given you that you need to pursue?

Father, give me the faith and courage to pursue my dreams.

Trusting in Chariots

Woe to those who go down to Egypt for help, and rely on horses, who trust in chariots because they are many, and in horsemen because they are very strong, but who do not look to the Holy One of Israel, nor seek the LORD!

ISAIAH 31:1 NKJV

It is human nature to want to use whatever means available to us to succeed. However, a conflict arises when we place our total trust in ourselves instead of God. The idea of maintaining a proper balance between trust and obedience to God versus placing an over dependence upon our natural skill and resources has created problems since Genesis. We are prone to build strong defenses through our natural gifts to avoid failure and use all of our might to be successful in our endeavors. However, we often do this at the expense of the supernatural in our lives. When it comes to receiving from God, it is important we don't make the same mistake Moses made when God told him to speak to the rock in order to receive water for the people. Instead, Moses struck the rock, and this resulted in God barring him from entering the promised land. The people of Israel often fell back to trusting in their own abilities, and God had to send a reproof into their lives.

How do we avoid the trap and maintain a proper balance between the natural and the spiritual? The rule of thumb is to submit every activity to God and use your skill as God directs you. Be sensitive to God's leading in all your activities. Avoid trying to build resources for the sake of insulating yourself against calamity that is rooted in fear.

Finally, follow Solomon's advice: "Trust in the LORD with all your heart, and lean not on your own understanding; in all your ways acknowledge Him, and He shall direct your paths" (Proverbs 3:5–6).

Question

Are you trusting in God for your success?

Father, help me trust you to achieve success in my life and work.

Planning for Success

LORD, I know that people's lives are not their own;
it is not for them to direct their steps.
JEREMIAH 10:23 NIV

In business, I hear a lot about planning. Every January, I hear workplace believers making their plans for the year. Corporations establish plans that cover anywhere from one to five years. Individuals create personal life plans. There is only one problem that I see with most planning done by well-meaning believers. If God is not the originator and director of the plan, then that plan is doomed for failure. So often, Christian workplace believers set out to plan something that seems good in their own mind. The merits of what is being planned can look great, and it can even be a worthy endeavor. However, that is not the point. When Jesus said he came only to do the will of the Father, he could not consider doing anything that was not what the Father wanted, no matter how good or righteous it might appear to be.

"In their hearts humans plan their course, but the LORD establishes their steps" (Proverbs 16:9). God must give us the vision for what he calls us to do. After we have the vision, we must ask him if he wants us to take action on that vision and what the action steps entail. The Lord wants to direct each step of the planning process.

Question

Are you allowing God to direct your planning?

Father, lead me in the way I should go and establish my plans according to your will.

Seeing Hardships as Opportunities

Arise, my soul, and sing his praises! I will awaken the dawn with my worship, greeting the daybreak with my songs of light.

PSALM 108:2 TPT

Fanny could have become a victim to her circumstance in life. Born in 1820 in a small cottage in Southeast, New York, Fanny one day woke up with a cold in her eyes. A doctor prescribed mustard poultices, which resulted in permanent damage to her eyes. She was blind for life. But she had a persevering spirit as a child and refused to let her disability determine her life. At age eight she wrote, "O what a happy soul I am! Although I cannot see, I am resolved that in this world I contend I will be."

For many years, Fanny studied and worked at The New York Institute for the Blind. She began as a student, then advanced to be a teacher and writer in residence. She quickly became known for her poems, even sharing one before Congress, and she was known among the most influential in the nation.

In 1851, Fanny accepted Jesus as her Lord and Savior at a revival meeting. She recalled, "My very soul was flooded with celestial light" while singing the line, "Here, Lord, I give myself away," from the old hymn "Alas! And Did My Savior Bleed." God revealed himself to her in an unusual way.

Time passed, and she meet hymnist William Bradbury fourteen years later.

He told her, "Fanny, I thank God we have met, for I think you can write hymns." Bradbury suggested a song idea, and on February 5, 1864, inspired by his idea, she wrote her first hymn at age forty-four. She would write eight thousand more hymns before she would go to be with the Lord.[23]

Question

Have you ever had something bad happen at the hand of others?

Father, help me use even hardships for your purposes.

The Gospel of the Kingdom

We can be sure that we've truly come to live in intimacy with God, not just by saying, "I am intimate with God," but by walking in the footsteps of Jesus.
1 JOHN 2:5–6 TPT

When Christ came to earth, he came to bring mankind the gospel of the kingdom. Over the centuries, the church has tended to emphasize only a portion of the gospel. That portion is the gospel of salvation.

Many of us come to Christ out of a need for salvation. Our hearts have been touched by his call on our lives. We reason and analyze the claims of Christ and make a decision to follow him.

However, there is a second stage that is the crisis stage. A crisis takes place in our lives, and we are newly motivated to seek Christ with a whole heart. We are motivated by the desire to get out of the pain of living. This stage is best characterized as *Help me, Lord.*

The third stage is the gospel of the kingdom. It is the place where Jesus resided in his walk with his heavenly Father. We are motivated by a deep love for him. When you are in this stage, you will have an attitude characterized as, *Have me, Lord.* "Though He slay me, yet will I trust Him" (Job 13:15 NKJV).

Question

Where are you today? Have you accepted his salvation to simply float along? Or do you seek him with a whole heart only when a crisis occurs?

Father, fill me with your Holy Spirit and give me a hunger for more of you.

When Hope Is Deferred

Satan went out from the presence of the LORD, and struck Job with painful boils from the sole of his foot to the crown of his head. And he took for himself a potsherd with which to scrape himself while he sat in the midst of the ashes. Then his wife said to him, "Do you still hold fast to your integrity? Curse God and die!"

JOB 2:7–9 NKJV

I walked into our home group, and Jennifer burst out crying. "I'm so discouraged! I don't know what else to do. Will I ever get better?" After three years of fighting a medical condition, the doctor just told her no progress had been made in the last six months of treatments.

Great men of God with healing ministries had prayed for her. Thousands had prayed for Jennifer through her ministry. A string of doctors had failed to yield any positive results. When hope is deferred, the psalmist says, the heart becomes sick (see Proverbs 13:12). During these seasons, we can only do one thing. We must hang on to whatever faith we have to get through each day and rejoice in the Lord (see Habakkuk 3:17–18).

Later that day, Jennifer talked to a friend who once had the same issues but was now better. "Jennifer, God is going to reveal things to you through this season of adversity that you would never receive had you not gone through this. This is part of your calling even though Satan is the instrument. God is always bigger than Satan's afflictions."

Our greatest tests come when we cannot see positive results from our faith and obedience. In such cases we must die to our expectations and entrust them to our Lord.

Question

Are you fighting a battle that seems cruel and unjust?

Father, give me the faith to fight my battle with your grace.

Knowledge That Is Productive

Since these virtues are already planted deep within, and you possess them in abundant supply, they will keep you from being inactive or fruitless in your pursuit of knowing Jesus Christ more intimately.

2 PETER 1:8 TPT

Productivity is a term all workplace believers can relate to. It is the by-product of what we desire from our work. Without productivity, we do not make sales, we do not deliver goods, and we do not achieve our goals. There are things in our work lives that can creep in, making us unproductive. The same is true in our walk with God.

The apostle Peter tells us that we can become knowledgeable of Jesus but fail to be effective and productive in our relationship with him. The apostle Peter tells us there is a solution to this dilemma.

> Devote yourselves to lavishly supplementing your faith with goodness,
> and to goodness add understanding,
> and to understanding add the strength of self-control,
> and to self-control add patient endurance,
> and to patient endurance add godliness,
> and to godliness add mercy toward your brothers and sisters,
> and to mercy toward others add unending love.
> Since these virtues are already planted deep within, and you possess them in abundant supply, they will keep you from being inactive or fruitless in your pursuit of knowing Jesus Christ more intimately. (vv. 5–8)

Question

Is your Christian experience filled with knowledge but little power? Is there staleness in your walk with God? Is there unrest in your soul?

Father, I pray I can receive these qualities in my life so that I can be productive as a soldier of Jesus Christ.

Your Work

*"I have brought you glory on earth
by finishing the work you gave me to do."*
JOHN 17:4 NIV

The Lord has revealed to us that the number one thing we are to do is love the Lord our God with all our heart and to love our neighbor as ourselves (see Matthew 22:36–40). His desire is for us to know him and the power of his resurrection. The fruit of this relationship must then be our glorifying him by completing the work he has given each of us to do.

What is the work God has called you to do? Jesus never did anything the Father had not instructed him to do. He lived in such communion with the Father that he knew when to turn left and when to turn to the right. Is it possible to have such a relationship with our heavenly Father?

"Call to me and I will answer you and tell you great and unsearchable things you do not know" (Jeremiah 33:3). What has he called you to do? Perhaps you are called to be the best CPA in your city or the best advertising executive or the best office worker or entrepreneur. Whatever work he has called you to do, he will use you as his instrument to accomplish something that he has uniquely prepared you to do.

Question

Do you view your work as a place of worship?

Father, help me to worship you every day through my work life.

Using Satan for God's Purposes

Release this man over to Satan for the destruction of his rebellious flesh,
in hope that his spirit may be rescued and restored in the day of the Lord.
1 CORINTHIANS 5:5 TPT

Paul encountered a believer who was involved in an incestuous relationship in the Corinthian church. The man was unwilling to change his behavior, so Paul recommended to the church that tough actions be taken. He spiritually handed this man over to Satan for the destruction of his flesh for the benefit of his soul. We know this man was a Christian because only a Christian can be subjected to church discipline.

Have you ever known someone who was walking in disobedience, and no matter how much you prayed, he or she seemed oblivious to his or her sin? God's weapon is to let Satan have access to them fully so that their lives become so miserable they cry out to God for mercy. Probably few of us have ever had to pray this prayer. However, you should not be fearful of this prayer for any believer who is willingly walking in disobedience. This is tough love. There is a time and place for tough love. I have seen this principal work. God restores his children when his body takes a stand against sin. It is not comfortable for those who take this action.

Question

Do you know someone who needs tough love in his or her life right now?

Father, I pray "in hope that [my] spirit may be rescued and restored in the day of the Lord."

Fostering the Right Environment

A shepherd should pay close attention to the faces of his flock
and hold close to his heart the condition of those he cares for.
PROVERBS 27:23 TPT

Janice was a high-level executive who required excellence and exceptional performance from those under her leadership in the Fortune 500 financial services company where she worked. She was the general manager of a credit card unit when five of her two thousand employees were found to have deliberately hidden $24 million in losses that she was accountable for. Her "no failure" policy had brought great pressure upon her employees, and she failed to recognize how this leadership style affected others. Her subordinates were fearful of reporting any bad news, so they lied about it.

Perfectionism is often mistakenly seen in our society as desirable or even necessary for success. However, studies show that perfectionist attitudes interfere with success. The desire to be perfect can both rob you of a sense of personal satisfaction and cause you and others to fail to achieve as much as people who have more realistic strivings.

Janice lost her job over this situation but was later offered another chance to salvage one of the company's smaller businesses. She realized that she needed to be much more understanding of people around her. She learned from her experience and succeeded in her next assignment with the company. Today, she looks back on this failure as one of her great life lessons, which has now allowed her to become one of the best executives in the company. Failure can be the greatest stepping-stone for success if we learn from it.

Question

What would others say about your relationship style? Do you foster dialogue and encourage others to bring issues to your attention?

Father, help me have a leadership style that invites input from others.

God at Work

For God so loved the world that he gave his one and only Son,
that whoever believes in him shall not perish but have eternal life.
JOHN 3:16 NIV

I'd like you to help us develop our marketing program beginning in January," said the CEO of a sports product company. The consultant was delighted to have the opportunity. He had just come out of some very difficult business and personal circumstances in the last few years. One day the CEO asked the consultant to manage the entire marketing department, placing him over the current marketing staff. It appeared that God was blessing his efforts with several successful initiatives. The consultant began to build a relationship with a few of the executives. One day, the sales manager came into his office and asked for help on a personal crisis. One thing led to another, and the consultant found himself leading the sales manager in the sinner's prayer in the sales manager's office.

God is at work every workday in the lives of his people. The circumstances may be different, but the results are the same. God allows his representatives to be a provider physically and spiritually to others.

Do not fret at the difficult training ground you may be required to endure. He has a plan. If you'll allow him to carry out his plan, you'll be privileged to be used by the master's hand. I know because I am that consultant in the story.

Question

Is God preparing you to be a provider in the workplace?

Father, use me in the marketplace to be your representative to lead others to you.

Spouses and Making Decisions

A fool is in love with his own opinion,
but wisdom means being teachable.
PROVERBS 12:15 TPT

When John Benson decided to make some financial investments in a new business venture, he was very excited about the possibilities for a handsome financial return. His business and financial background had served him well. John felt strongly that his wife, Jenny, would not understand the complexity of his investment, so he casually mentioned it to her. When she asked a few simple questions, John became defensive and justified his plans for investing in the venture.

A year later, after investing a large sum of money, John received a phone call from the investment company. All the investors who had put money in the company were going to lose their investment with no ability to recoup it.

This story could be retold repeatedly across the world. God's principles for making decisions require input from both spouses, regardless of their level of expertise. I learned this lesson the hard way after making many independent decisions outside the counsel of my wife. Today, whenever I am faced with a major decision, I first consult the Lord, and then I consult my wife. She may disagree totally with something that seems very straightforward to me, but I have learned not to move forward if we are not in agreement.

If we seek to make decisions independently from our spouses, we benefit from only 50 percent of the intended resource God has placed within our grasp.

Question

Do you consult your spouse before making important decisions?

Father, help me see my spouse as a source of protection for me.

A Life God Blesses

This is what the Sovereign Lord says: "See, I lay a stone in Zion,
a tested stone, a precious cornerstone for a sure foundation;
the one who relies on it will never be stricken with panic."

ISAIAH 28:16 NIV

Whenever God calls us into a consecrated life, it is made up of four distinct stages. Christ often compared this process to building a house. First, we must prepare to build by laying a foundation. That foundation is none other than Jesus Christ himself. Any foundation other than Christ will not stand.

Second, as we enter a walk of faith with God, he allows each of us to experience trials, testing, miracles, and challenges in life that are designed to provide "faith experiences," tangible evidence of his work in our life: Moses' burning-bush experience, Peter's walk on the water, Joshua's parting of the Jordan River. These experiences built the faith of these people.

The third stage deals with motives. "All a person's ways seem pure to them, but motives are weighed by the Lord" (Proverbs 16:2). What is the motive behind my actions? Is it only financial accumulation? Is it to gain control? Is it to create independence?

Finally, we are prepared to take action. Here we must ask, *Do I have the skill, quality, and ability to enter into this activity?* So often, we have not trained ourselves adequately to be successful in our endeavor.

Question

What is the foundation this project is based on?

Father, help me weigh my motives in every endeavor.

The Graduate-Level Test: Self-Defense

*"Love your enemies
and continue to treat them well."*
LUKE 6:35 TPT

As a believer grows in trusting obedience and love, God often brings a test that seems uncharacteristically cruel: being wrongfully judged by those close to you. It is not for the reactionary. It cannot be passed over by simply gutting it out. Supernatural grace is the only means of passing this one. It is one of those tests the Savior had to experience himself when being tried by the court of public opinion, the religious community, and the government of his day. His response to the government was silence. His response to the religious establishment was silence at the final judgment. To the rest of his accusers, he remained quiet and left vindication to the Father.

When God brings a measured assault against one of his children, it is to find out if she truly believes in the cross. The cross is where each of us is given the opportunity to die to our pride, our reputations, and our ego. When he allows a measured assault upon us, it is to find out if the cross is sufficient. He wants to see if we will seek to rescue ourselves. Thank God for the opportunity to be crucified with Christ. Then your righteousness will shine like the noonday sun, and the justice of your cause will be in his hands.

Question

How do you react when you are accused or mistreated for no reason? Do you listen quietly, or do you justify each and every action?

Father, give me grace to love those who persecute me and trust you to protect me.

Higher Education

*To another, the same Spirit gives the gift of the
word of revelation knowledge.*
1 CORINTHIANS 12:8 TPT

I walked out of the church parking lot after participating in a training class on hearing the voice of God. As I was talking to a friend, I looked over at a woman who was talking to her friend. The words *higher education* popped into my mind.

We had just learned that whenever something pops into our minds that seems foreign to our normal thinking, it is often the Holy Spirit speaking to us. We must connect the thought to an action.

I decided to be bold, and I walked over to the woman. "Pardon me, can I ask you if you have had a good bit of education in your life?"

The woman responded immediately, "Why, yes. I have two MBAs."

I was encouraged to proceed. "I believe the Lord wants me to tell you that he has directed you in your education, and although you cannot see the results of that investment in time and money, he is going to use it for his purposes. He wants you to be encouraged to know this."

The woman was very motivated by the words I spoke to her.

Every believer has been wired to hear the Holy Spirit's promptings in our lives. One of the primary ways he encourages believers is through other believers.

Today, be especially sensitive to that still, small voice inside of you. It might be the Holy Spirit speaking to you.

Question

Do you believe God speaks to you? Be assured that he does!

Father, help me recognize your promptings so I can be a blessing of encouragement to others.

Defining Moments

Then Moses stretched out his hand over the sea, and all that night the LORD drove the sea back with a strong east wind and turned it into dry land. The waters were divided, and the Israelites went through the sea on dry ground, with a wall of water on their right and on their left.

EXODUS 14:21–22 NIV

History often remembers people because of a defining moment that took place in their life. There are good defining moments and bad defining moments. September 11, 2001, was a bad defining moment for the United States of America. Many people's lives were negatively impacted as a result of the simultaneous terrorist attacks across the country. Moses had a defining moment when he parted the Red Sea with his staff.

Mary's defining moment came when the angel told her she was pregnant with the Son of God. Sarah laughed at the comment by the angel that she could be pregnant in her old age. Esther chose to appeal to the king on behalf of her people to save them from destruction. Rosa Parks will be remembered for refusing to give up her seat on the bus. Mother Teresa was traveling on a train when she heard the Lord's words, "I thirst," which prompted her to give her life to serve the poor in Calcutta.

For most of us, we can still define our moments for the future. God may yet have a defining moment when you will discover something new or see the work of God in your life in a unique way. God wants you to have an experience with him that is memorable.

Question

How would you like to be remembered? Is there a defining moment in your life that others will associate with your name?

Father, allow me to have a defining moment that will impact others.

Competition among Sisters

Rachel said, "God has vindicated me;
he has listened to my plea and given me a son."
GENESIS 30:6 NIV

Jacob had fled his family home because of the conflict with Esau when he stole the birthright from him. He had fled to his uncle Laban hundreds of miles from his home. When Jacob saw Rachel for the first time, he was smitten with her beauty. Rachel had a sister named Leah. She was the daughter of his uncle Laban and did not have the beauty of Rachel. Jacob offered to work for his uncle Laban for seven years to have the right to marry Rachel. Unfortunately, Laban set up Jacob after the seven years by tricking him into sleeping with Leah on his wedding night. (I have no idea how this could have happened, but that is what the story says.)

Laban required Jacob to marry Leah and work for him seven more years to be able to marry Rachel. The situation created competition between Leah and Rachel because Leah was very fertile and gave birth to many children while Rachel was barren.

This caused great pain in Rachel because a woman's value in those days was based on her ability to bear sons. Leah was grappling with God and her own sister. She thought God had abandoned her, but he had not. Rachel gave birth to Joseph and Benjamin. Sadly, she would die giving birth to Benjamin.

Have you ever felt God was not listening to your prayers? It may simply be a timing issue. Stand firm and wait on the Lord.

Question

Are you trusting God for a breakthrough in some area of your life?

Father, give me the patience and grace to accept your timing for my breakthrough.

Wanted: Dead or Alive

*Your hand-to-hand combat is not with human beings, but with the highest
principalities and authorities operating in rebellion under the heavenly realms.
For they are a powerful class of demon-gods and evil spirits that hold this dark
world in bondage.*

EPHESIANS 6:12 TPT

In the Old West, it was common to see a poster on the wall of the town jail or
post office with a someone's picture below the words *Wanted: Dead or Alive!*
These depicted the most notorious criminals who posed the greatest danger to
society.

Let me ask you some difficult questions. Is there a "Wanted: Dead or
Alive" poster in hell with your name on it? Are you a real danger to hell? Do you
cause problems for Satan's legion of demons? Are you pushing back Satan's
agenda on planet earth?

Millions of believers sit on the sidelines every day, having no impact on
the kingdom of darkness. Their names will never appear on a wanted poster in
hell because Satan sees that they are no threat. However, God wants you to be
a threat to Satan's kingdom.

What are some things you can do that will pose a threat to Satan's agenda?
Perhaps you can begin praying for one of Satan's most vocal personalities that
use their celebrity status to promote unrighteousness. He or she might be the
next Paul. There are many ways you can earn a reputation in hell.

Question

Are you willing to be a force that Satan's legions will have to reckon with?

Father, make me a threat to the kingdom of darkness.

The Spirit of Competition

"I in them and you in me—so that they may be brought to complete unity. Then the world will know that you sent me and have loved them even as you have loved me."
JOHN 17:23 NIV

A story is told about F. B. Meyer, the great Bible teacher and pastor who lived a century ago. He was pastoring a church and began to notice that attendance was suffering. This continued until he finally asked some members of his congregation one Sunday morning why they thought attendance was down.

I imagine one member saying, "It is because of this new church down the road. The young preacher has everyone talking, and many are going to hear him speak." His name was Charles Spurgeon.

Meyer, rather than seeking to discourage this, exhorted the entire congregation to join him and go participate in seeing this movement of God.[24]

In his humility, Meyer displayed the attitude that if this was happening, then God must be at work. He once said, "I find in my own ministry that supposing I pray for my own little flock, 'God bless me, God fill my pews, God send me a revival,' I miss the blessing; but as I pray for my big brother, Mr. Spurgeon, on the right-hand side of my church, 'God bless him'…I am sure to get a blessing without praying for it, for the overflow of their cups fills my little bucket."[25]

Can you imagine this story taking place in our competitive world today? Competition has penetrated the church so much that many churches and Christian organizations approach ministry like a sports event. They view their mission as a business that seeks to gain market share among Christians— donors, members, influence—all in the name of serving God.

Question

Are you contributing to unity in the body of Christ? Or are you contributing to a spirit of competition?

Father, help me be one of your instruments of unity in your body.

A Place of Strength

*Abram went to live near the great trees of Mamre at Hebron,
where he pitched his tents. There he built an altar to the LORD.*
GENESIS 13:18 NIV

Abraham took a totally different approach to solving the problem of fighting
over land. He told Lot to choose which land he wanted. Imagine, Abraham
could have been dooming himself and his family if he were unable to find
adequate land and water for them. He gave up his rights in the matter, and Lot
took full advantage. Lot left and took up residence in the lush green valley later
to be known as Sodom and Gomorrah. Sometimes what seems good on the
front end turns out to be disastrous later. Such would be the case for Lot and
his family.

The Bible tells us that when we are weak, then we are really strong. To
willingly choose the way of the cross, as Abraham did, becomes our strength.

Question

What do you think Sarah thought when Abraham decided to separate from
Lot and his family? What would you have done if your husband decided to
move away from close family?

*Father, give me the grace to trust you if you lead me or my family to an
unknown place.*

Losing Your Life for His Purposes

*"For whoever wants to save their life will lose it,
but whoever loses their life for me will save it."*
LUKE 9:24 NIV

When the time came for God to fulfill Joseph's dreams, it appears Joseph himself had virtually no interest in it at all. It appears Joseph had given up his life to the purposes of God.

Joseph's day of exaltation had arrived. He was given freedom and an exaltation but the kind he really never asked for. He did not appear to be all that interested in what was about to happen. He watched as the pharaoh took his ring off his finger and put it on Joseph's finger. Joseph never asked for that. All he wanted was to go home. He longed to go back to Canaan, to see his father, and to have his dreams fulfilled.

Here we find an extraordinary paradox, a triumph that was the opposite of everything he could have envisaged. Joseph wanted to go home, but a bus ticket to Canaan wasn't available. Before he knew it, he had Egypt in his hip pocket. He had never prayed for that. But God wanted Egypt. What God wanted is what Joseph got.

Joseph was given something that he could be trusted with because it didn't mean that much to him.

Question

Has God placed you in a situation not of your making where you have no control?

Father, give me the grace to trust you for the circumstances and outcomes of my life.

Perfect Timing

When he heard that Lazarus was sick,
he stayed where he was two more days.
JOHN 11:6 NIV

The Bible says Jesus loved his friends Mary, Martha, and Lazarus. Mary was the woman who came and poured expensive perfume on Jesus, and the disciples rebuked her. Lazarus, who was Mary and Martha's brother, had become terminally ill. Jesus was two miles away in Jerusalem during the time of Lazarus' illness.

His response to the news was "This sickness will not end in death. No, it is for God's glory so that God's Son may be glorified through it" (v. 4). Nevertheless, Lazarus died and was placed in a tomb.

Mary was in deep mourning and cried out to Jesus, "Lord…if you had been here, my brother would not have died" (v. 21). Jesus looked beyond Mary and Martha's current grief and immediate need in order to fulfill God's purpose for this sickness. There was a preordained plan for the purpose of Lazarus' death. But only Jesus knew this. Jesus brought Lazarus back from the dead that day.

When we experience sickness and do not see a breakthrough, we must trust that he knows the answer to our need and the timing for its solution. There are times when we experience supernatural healing and other times when we simply do not know why Jesus chooses not to heal. In either case, our devotion to Jesus must not change.

Question

Do you struggle to believe that God-delays are always preordained for a greater purpose?

Father, I trust you for the timing for every event in my life to be fulfilled in your perfect timing.

Possessions of the Kingdom

"I will punish the nation they serve as slaves,
and afterward they will come out with great possessions."
GENESIS 15:14 NIV

Whenever God brings you through a time of great adversity, you can expect to come out of that experience with great possessions if you have been faithful through the trial. This is a universal truth. Wisdom comes from obedience, not knowledge. When we have been tested and proven, the reality of our faith results in possessions from God that we would never receive if we had not gone through those trials. These trials are precious in his sight and should be valued greatly. Those who know you will be amazed at the wisdom that comes from your mouth. It is one of those mysteries of the gospel that only those who experience incredible testing and hardship can explain.

The people of Israel were enslaved four hundred years, but when the time came to free them from the bondage of slavery, they came out with great possessions. These physical possessions symbolize the spiritual possessions we receive when we come out of being enslaved to those things that have hindered us all our lives. These possessions are to be shared with others so that they also can know how they might become free.

Question

What has God freed you from that allows you to share your possessions with others?

Father, give me an opportunity today to share with someone I work with what God has done in my life.

Unprofitable Anger

Do not be quickly provoked in your spirit,
for anger resides in the lap of fools.

ECCLESIASTES 7:9 NIV

Do you recall the last time someone cut you off in traffic or when you were forced to wait in line because someone held things up at the front of the line? Perhaps your employer did something that was downright unfair.

Anger becomes a warning sign that something is not right, and we need to find the source of our anger. Anger can be traced to a few sources. First, when we lose control of a circumstance that we have placed certain expectations on and those expectations do not result in our desired outcome, we are tempted to get angry. The source of this type of anger is both fear and protection of personal rights. You see, when we believe we have a right to something, we have not given the Lord permission to allow an outcome different from what we want. If an outcome is different from our expectations, this may stimulate fear. You no longer are in control of the circumstance, and this creates fear in you.

Question

The next time you get angry ask the Lord what is the source of that anger? Did the Lord allow that failure to let you see what is "under your hood"?

Father, thank you that you have not given us a spirit of fear "but of power and of love and of a sound mind" (2 Timothy 1:7 NKJV).

Give Me Your Last Meal

*"I am gathering a few sticks to take home
and make a meal for myself and my son,
that we may eat it—and die."*

1 Kings 17:12 NIV

Imagine telling a widow who was about to eat her last meal with her only son to give you a portion of that meal. Imagine you have a need for provision and God tells you to go to the most desperate person in the land to get your provision.

God led Elijah to a poor widow who was ready to prepare her last meal using her last handful of flour. Why would God lead Elijah from one desperate situation into another? He wished to perform yet another miracle and show his faithfulness to those who needed it most. Elijah proceeded to tell the widow:

> But first make a small loaf of bread for me from what you have and bring it to me, and then make something for yourself and your son. For this is what the Lord, the God of Israel, says: "The jar of flour will not be used up and the jug of oil will not run dry until the day the Lord sends rain on the land." (vv. 13–14)

Would you have questioned such logic in the face of a life-threatening situation? The woman demonstrated her faith in God and Elijah by giving him her last meal. This act of faith insured that her provision would be there day after day. Provision followed obedience.

Question

Do you need God to multiply provision for you today?

Father, help to apply my faith to that which you have placed in my hand.

Mustard-Seed Faith in Business

"If you have faith inside of you no bigger than the size of a small mustard seed, you can say to this mountain, 'Move away from here and go over there,' and you will see it move! There is nothing you couldn't do!"

MATTHEW 17:20 TPT

Does God do miracles in business?

J. Gunnar Olson, a Swedish businessman, once told me a story about God performing a miracle in his own business. He owns a plastics company in Sweden. They make huge plastic bags that are used to cover bales of hay in the farmlands across Europe. It was harvest season, and they were getting ready to ship thousands of pallets of these bags to their customers. More than one thousand pallets were ready to ship when an alarming discovery was made. Every bag on the warehouse floor had sealed shut from top to bottom. Scientists declared the entire stock was worthless trash. The company would go out of business.

Gunnar, his wife, and children sought the Lord in prayer about this catastrophe. The Holy Spirit spoke through various family members. Gunnar sensed they were to trust God for a miracle in this situation. They prayed. They took authority over that mountain based on Matthew 17. The following Monday they went to the warehouse and laid hands on every pallet, asking the Lord to restore the bags to their original condition. It took several hours. Later, the employees began to inspect the bags. As they checked pallet after pallet, they discovered that every single bag had been restored to its original condition! An incredible miracle had taken place.

Question

What obstacles have been placed in your life that need a miracle today?

Father, thank you that all things are possible with God.

A Lack of Provision

"You shall drink from the brook,
and I have commanded the ravens to feed you there."
1 KINGS 17:4 RSV

The prophet Elijah pronounced a drought upon the land because of the sin of Ahab and the nation of Israel. There was only one problem. Elijah had to live in the same land as Ahab.

> Now Eli'jah the Tishbite, from Tishbe in Gilead, said to Ahab, "As the LORD the God of Israel lives, before whom I stand, there shall be neither dew nor rain these years, except by my word." And the word of the LORD came to him, "Depart from here and turn eastward, and hide yourself by the brook Cherith, that is east of the Jordan. You shall drink from the brook, and I have commanded the ravens to feed you there." (vv. 1–4)

God provided for Elijah in a supernatural way. The ravens brought bread in the morning and meat in the evening. His water came from the brook.

God often uses money to confirm direction for our lives. Many times, God uses a lack of provision to move us into new directions. It is a catalyst to encourage new ideas and strategies. Many times, the loss of a job becomes the greatest blessing to our lives because it provides the catalyst to do things we simply would never do without taking the step to get out of our comfort zone.

Question

Are you needing supernatural provision?

Father, thank you that you are my provider.

Hearing His Voice

"When he has brought out all his sheep,
he walks ahead of them and they will follow him,
for they are familiar with his voice."

JOHN 10:4 TPT

Jesus said that the key to being able to hear God's voice is first to be one of his children. The shepherd is always representative of Christ. Sheep are representative of God's children. This passage tells us that the shepherd communicates with his children. We are called by name, and we can listen to our shepherd's voice. There is another comforting aspect to this relationship. The shepherd goes before the sheep to prepare the way. Jesus has already gone before us today to prepare our way.

Knowing the Shepherd and his voice allows us to have the assurance that we will not be fooled by another shepherd's voice. The sheep know his voice. It is only when we are dull of hearing that we mistakenly hear another's voice and follow it. Sin can create a poor frequency in our communication with the Shepherd. Make sure your frequency is free of static (sin) today so that the Shepherd can lead you and go before you.

Finally, distractions can also keep us from hearing our Shepherd's voice. When the sheep get entangled in the fence or wander off, they get too far away to hear the shepherd's voice. We must stay in close proximity to the Shepherd to hear his voice. Stay close to the Shepherd today. Listen and follow. He wants to lead you.

Question

How is your frequency to be able to hear the Shepherd's voice?

Father, increase my sensitivity to hearing your voice today.

Understanding the Roadblock

Joshua said, "Alas, Sovereign Lᴏʀᴅ, why did you ever bring this people across the Jordan to deliver us into the hands of the Amorites to destroy us?"

Jᴏsʜᴜᴀ 7:7 ɴɪᴠ

Have you ever felt like you were doing what God wanted you to do but your plans were totally frustrated? This was how Joshua felt.

The Lord had been with the people of Israel as they entered the promised land. They defeated every enemy because of God's blessing and protection. They had just taken the city of Jericho. The next battle was the city of Ai. They scouted the enemy and determined it would require only three thousand men to defeat them. They attacked, and soon the reports came back that they were being routed. Joshua could not understand this. He cried out to God asking why this was happening.

The Lᴏʀᴅ said to Joshua, "Stand up!…Israel has sinned; they have violated my covenant, which I commanded them to keep. They have taken some of the devoted things; they have stolen, they have lied, they have put them with their own possessions. That is why the Israelites cannot stand against their enemies." (vv. 10–12)

Whenever we open ourselves up to sin, God removes his protective shield from our lives in order for the sin in our lives to be purged out. If you feel you are being thwarted in some way, ask God if there is any sin that is the cause of the problem. He will show you.

Question

Is there any sin in your life that might be hindering God's favor in your endeavors?

Father, reveal anything in me that might not be pleasing in your sight.

A Mother's Powerful Prayer

If anyone longs to be wise, ask God for wisdom and he will give it!
JAMES 1:5 TPT

Monika's son Robert graduated from eighth grade with high honors. He was a very good student. There was a computer game that Robert had been asking for all year. Monika got him the game for a graduation gift. Robert was thirteen and on summer break, so he was able to play his game often.

They were getting back to a school schedule when Robert began having nightmares. He would say to his mom, "What's wrong with me? I'm scared."

Each night Robert asked his mom to come into his room and pray over him. It was about the third night when Monika went into his room and Robert said, "I would do anything not to feel this way. God," he prayed, "I would even give up my game if I won't feel this way anymore, God."

Then Monika realized something. "Oh my goodness—that's it! The game!" His game was a "war game," and the violence of the game had given Robert post-traumatic stress. Monika said, "Thank you so much, Lord, for revealing this to us!"

She told Robert, "It's your game that is making you feel this way. You're way too young to be playing this game. I should not have gotten it for you. You're feeling things someone might feel when he or she comes home from war. You have anxiety, and you can't sleep, and you're depressed." She got rid of the game.

Robert never asked for the game back, and from that moment on, he had no more nightmares and no more anxiety and no more post-traumatic stress. She credits God for answering her prayer.

Question

Are your children being exposed to things that are not good for them?

Father, please show me any toys, apps, or games that might be harmful to me or my kids.

Healing before Ministry

After the whole nation had been circumcised,
they remained where they were in camp until they were healed.
JOSHUA 5:8 NIV

Before the nation of Israel could go into the promised land, they had to be circumcised. It was a very personal instruction from God that had spiritual significance. God requires each of us to be circumcised in heart before we are allowed to enter and receive the blessings that await each believer in the promised land.

This circumcision in our spiritual life can often be very painful. Circumcision requires losing our old way of life. The process of spiritual circumcision may mean a loss in areas that have been a part of our lives in order to draw us to the Savior. God understands this. Consequently, like the people of Israel, we must wait until we are healed before we begin to be effective in our calling. If we launch out too early, we will be ineffective and may risk infection and disease and will not be at our full capacity. God wants each of us to walk in his healing grace.

The people of Israel fought only two battles when they were coming out of Egypt. In the promised land they fought thirty-nine battles. Each of us must be prepared to enjoy the benefits of living in the promised land. However, we must also be prepared to wage war against the enemy of our souls. Make sure the Lord has provided the needed healing to your circumcision experience before you enter the promised land.

Question

Have you gone through a circumcision of heart in your life?

Father, heal my heart of any wounds so that I might move forward in my relationship with you.

The Worship Service

"This is why I weep and my eyes overflow with tears.
No one is near to comfort me, no one to restore my spirit."

LAMENTATIONS 1:16 NIV

I walked into the worship service. I pushed my mom's wheelchair into the room among many, many others. This was no ordinary worship service. This wasn't our first time. The organizer recognized us and asked if we would assist in handing out the songbooks.

Only a few of the participants could actually use them. You see, I was in a nursing home unit for residents with dementia and Alzheimer's where my mom resided. A few chairs over sat the father of my older sisters' longtime best friends. Next to him was my brother-in-law's grandmother.

They were all once successful people—doctors, lawyers, business leaders, and stay-at-home moms. They had lived in fine southern homes. But they now lived in one-half of a single room. Some patients could still recognize their loved ones; others could not.

The service began with singing. Only a few voices could be heard among the patients. Then, something remarkable happened. The speaker said they would now close with a well-known song: "Jesus loves me, this I know, for the Bible tells me so." Suddenly, the voices in the room got louder. Patients who were not singing before were now singing. I looked over at my mom. She was whistling the tune. I looked over at my friend whom I had brought with me; tears were streaming down her face.

Sometimes the presence of God can show up in the smallest and simplest acts.

Question

Do you ever wonder why the end of life can seem so cruel sometimes?

Father, give me the grace to love those who need love and can't acknowledge it.

Sweating Outcomes

In vain you rise early and stay up late, toiling for food to eat—
for he grants sleep to those he loves.
PSALM 127:2 NIV

Coming into the promised land in business will change the way you and I view our work. No longer will we see getting up early and staying up late as God's way. Living in the promised land in work means we know that God is the source of our provision and that our work is an act of worship to him. Provision is a by-product, not an end to itself. God has made it clear that obedience is the assurance of provision. Whenever we go beyond the normal workday due to fear of non-provision, we are operating in unbelief. We are saying that it is up to us to make things happen. Sure, there are times when we work longer hours due to a deadline, but we must be sure the motive is not out of fear of loss or fear of non-provision.

If we are obedient to what God has called each of us to, we will not lack. At times it may be less than what we might like; at other times it may be more than we deserve. These are God's ways.

The Bible tells us to come out of Babylon. Babylon is a system of work and philosophy that is contrary to God's ways.

Question

Are you operating from a Babylonian value system in any aspect of your work?

Father, help me to walk in the freedom you have given me to work unto the Lord.

Fears That Keep Us from God

Then all the people of the region of the Gerasenes asked Jesus to leave them, because they were overcome with fear. So he got into the boat and left.

LUKE 8:37 NIV

Jesus did many miracles when he lived on earth. One of those miracles involved the deliverance of a demon-possessed man. The people of the community witnessed this awesome demonstration of God's power when Jesus commanded the demon spirit to come out of the man and go into the nearby herd of pigs. The man was healed and sat at Jesus' feet.

You would expect the people who witnessed this to embrace Jesus as one performing good deeds and to honor him. The opposite was true. Instead, they were overcome with fear. Why? Many of us respond the same way to Jesus when he does an out-of-the-ordinary act among his people. We are fearful because we have never personally experienced this before. So, we draw wrong judgments. The result is that Jesus removes himself from us.

The Lord is able to do far exceeding above what we think. Jesus does not remain in the places where there is fear of his goodness. It is often subconscious fears that prevent us from going to a deeper level with him. The people in Gerasene could not benefit from Jesus' presence because of their fears.

Question

Have you feared Jesus because of what he might require of you?

Father, I embrace you for all the ways you show yourself strong to me.

Forgive This Man?

*"When you pray, make sure you forgive the faults of others
so that your Father in heaven will also forgive you."*

MATTHEW 6:14 TPT

She was sexually molested from age five into her teen years under threat of murder. The pain and trauma led her into a thirty-five-year addiction and prostitution. After trying to commit suicide at twenty-six, she encountered Jesus…although she was still bound.

A wealthy businessman kept wanting to pay her for sex, but she refused. He insisted with, "I'll have you one day!"

She was invited to a party where this man had paid the host to drug her. As she awoke from unconsciousness, she noticed that her friend who had gone with her to the party was not there. She called the friend later on the phone. He said, "I will help you get him!" and told her what happened. The "businessman" organized it all. He and six other men had thrown her friend out of the house before raping her. (She wondered why he did not do more to stop the attack.)

She chose to forgive all the people who had wronged her. She had a dream about that businessman as a child being molested repeatedly. It allowed her to pray for him and forgive. Years later, she encountered the man who had raped her. Stricken with fear, she froze. With tears he said, "I have to ask your forgiveness! I have come to Jesus. Please forgive me."

The prayers that she had prayed over the piece of paper extending forgiveness to him became the catalyst for this man's coming to Christ and of her inner healing.

Question

Do you have someone you need to forgive?

Father, I choose to forgive _____.

Unrighteous Acts

*"Shouldn't you walk in the fear of our God
to avoid the reproach of our Gentile enemies?"*
NEHEMIAH 5:9 NIV

Nehemiah was the cupbearer to King Artaxerxes in Babylon. Jerusalem's walls had been destroyed, and word had come to Nehemiah that the remnant of his people left in Jerusalem were distressed over the plight of the wall.

Nehemiah was grieved over this situation. He appealed to his king for permission to rebuild the wall, and the king agreed. When Nehemiah got to the city, he found many problems among his own people due to an economic crisis in the region. Among the classes affected by the economic crisis were (1) the landless, who were short of food; (2) the landowners, who were compelled to mortgage their properties; and (3) those forced to borrow money at exorbitant rates and sell their children into slavery (see v. 5). It was unlawful for Hebrews to charge interest to other Hebrews.

Nehemiah stepped forward to admonish his people for these wrongful actions not only on the basis that it was wrong but also because God would respond to such action by making them susceptible to his judgment through the gentile enemies.

Whenever we sin, we give God permission to unleash the enemy into our souls to deal with that sin. Nehemiah understood this principle and warned the people of the consequences from God that their actions would bring. The people repented and returned the money gained through usury.

Question

Are there any activities you are involved with that would bring the reproach of God?

Father, is there any unrighteousness in my practices that makes me vulnerable to judgment?

When Service Exceeds Devotion

She had a sister called Mary,
who sat at the Lord's feet listening to what he said.
LUKE 10:39 NIV

Martha was Mary's older sister. Older sisters always think they know best. They tend to mother the younger siblings. So, when Jesus came over to spend an evening at their home Martha wanted to prepare a special meal. She noticed Mary was spending all her time in the living room listening to Jesus. Martha finally felt compelled to appeal to Jesus about the situation.

> But Martha was distracted by all the preparations that had to be made. She came to him and asked, "Lord, don't you care that my sister has left me to do the work by myself? Tell her to help me!"
>
> "Martha, Martha," the Lord answered, "you are worried and upset about many things, but few things are needed—or indeed only one. Mary has chosen what is better, and it will not be taken away from her." (vv. 40–42)

Jesus reveals a danger in this story that each of us must be aware of. When our concern for serving Jesus exceeds our need to be with Jesus, we are in danger of focusing on the lesser thing. The hardest thing for most workplace believers to do is to *sit and listen*. It is easier to be busy and active.

Question

Do you need to spend more time listening before you begin doing?

Father, help me to spend time in your presence every day.

Tests of the Heart

Remember how the LORD your God led you all the way in the wilderness these forty years, to humble and test you in order to know what was in your heart, whether or not you would keep his commands.

DEUTERONOMY 8:2 NIV

Has God performed a heart test on you lately? There are times in our lives when God leads us into the desert in order to let us find out what is in our heart. These times can be very difficult and humbling. They can test our mettle like no other time. Desert times often mean we are living without those things we are normally accustomed to: water, food, supplies, and comforts. In modern terms, it may mean a different environment. God is performing a very important work during these times. He wants to know whether we will be obedient to him when we are in the desert or only when times are good.

These desert times may mean experiencing new ways of provision from the Lord, like manna from heaven. It may mean seeing miracles we've never seen before, like clothing that never wears out. It may mean seeing your normal capabilities expanded, like walking hundreds of miles without pain. Desert experiences provide new lessons and new experiences that only these times can teach us.

Question

What desert experience has God brought into your life lately?

Father, give me grace to pass the test. I want to enter my promised land.

Firstfruits

*"All the silver and gold and the articles of bronze and iron
are sacred to the LORD and must go into his treasury."*
JOSHUA 6:19 NIV

One of the earliest examples of the practice of giving God the firstfruits of the increase was when Joshua and the people entered the promised land for the first time. When they crossed the Jordan River, their first battle was Jericho. God set a precedent with this battle by instructing them not to take any spoils from it.

Unlike future battles, the fruits from this victory were to go into the treasury as a remembrance of their first victory in the promised land. In addition, the city of Jericho was to be a lasting monument to God's faithfulness. God instructed Joshua never to rebuild this city. If they or anyone in the future attempted to rebuild the city, the life of the firstborn would be required. Years later, in the days of King Ahab, Hiel the Bethelite attempted to rebuild this city, and his firstborn died as a result. God never forgets to enforce his Word.

Question

Is your work a lasting monument to the faithfulness of God in your life? Is it bringing glory to the Father? Are you giving the firstfruits from your increase to God?

Father, help me to be faithful in giving the firstfruits of my increase to you as recognition of your provision for me.

Victoria's Friends

For it is not from man that we draw our life but from God as we are being joined to Jesus, the Anointed One. And now he is our God-given wisdom, our virtue, our holiness, and our redemption.

1 CORINTHIANS 1:30 TPT

Victoria grew up like many in middle-income families. She loved school and was even on her homecoming court all four years in high school. After some tragic family deaths during her teen years, she began to experiment with alcohol and drugs. She was raped, underwent multiple abortions, and worked as a dancer at a local strip club for more than four years.

By age twenty-eight, she was homeless, stranded, and fired from her job as a strip-club dancer. She became suicidal. Weighing barely one hundred pounds, she was no longer profitable to the adult industry. Then a Christian gave her a Bible. The first book she read was Job, and something gripped her heart. A church family took her into their home. They surrounded her with love and pointed her to who she was in Christ. Victoria says, "Jesus is the only healer of deep, deep wounds."

Victoria's compassionate heart is now focused on reaching others who are on the brink of life or death. She founded Victoria's Friends, a ministry that goes into the heart of the darkest places of the city—strip clubs. Trained women's ministry volunteers bring baskets full of gifts to the dancers in their dressing rooms with no motive other than to show they care.

Hundreds of young women have come out of this lifestyle because one woman decided to do what others had done for her—rescue her from the pit of darkness.

Question

What type of rescue mission might God call you to lead or support?

Father, help me be a source of freedom for others.

Avoiding Self-Based Faith

We live by faith, not by sight.

2 CORINTHIANS 5:7 NIV

Over the years I have run into many business leaders who make the statement, "Whenever I get things in order in my business, I want to get more involved in ministry." What are these leaders really saying? They are saying that as soon as they can get the amount of money that creates security, they will trust God. They are saying that what they have been doing to date has not been ministry. This separation of work from faith is common among our culture. We fail to understand that all of life should be ministry.

I would love to hear one workplace believer say, "The Lord has blessed me with great resources. But now God has told me to give away my wealth and to trust him to provide for me through new ways." That is exactly what C. T. Studd, the great cricket player in the 1800s, did. He was reared in a wealthy home, but his deep conversion experience led him to take actions that forced him to trust God in ways he never had to before. He became one of the great missionaries of all time.[26]

Faith that bears fruit is faith that is born from experience with a living God. It is faith that says, "I don't know where the next check is coming from. All I know is that God told me to do this and trust him for the next step."

Question

Are you called to something that requires stepping out in faith?

Father, I trust you to lead me into wherever you call me to go.

Being Given over to Death

We consider living to mean that we are constantly being handed over to death for Jesus' sake so that the life of Jesus will be revealed through our humanity. So, then, death is at work in us but it releases life in you.

2 CORINTHIANS 4:11–12 TPT

It is the great mystery of the gospel of Jesus Christ. Death gives life. Jesus' death on the cross gave life. The death of a vision brings new vision. The death of a seed gives new life. It is the central focus of God's requirement for experiencing him—death to the old nature.

When Jesus extended us an invitation to experience salvation and a relationship with him, it came with a great cost—our very lives. Yet what we don't realize is that until we relinquish our total lives, we really aren't living at all. Without this death we will continue to strive, manipulate, and fret over every detail of life. It is when we finally say, *Yes, Lord, I am yours completely*, that we experience real freedom for the first time. This is the only time when Christ is fully seen in and through our lives. Christ describes our lives as vessels— vessels through which he can reveal himself and become visible to others.

Question

How is your vessel today? When people look inside, will they see a life that is dead to all things except the life of Christ revealed?

Father, today I lay my life down so that you might live fully through me.

Forgiveness Ensures Freedom

"If you do not forgive others their sins, your Father will not forgive your sins."
MATTHEW 6:15 NIV

Corrie ten Boom (1892–1983) was born in Amsterdam and raised in the Dutch Reformed Church. When the Nazis came to power in the late 1930s, Corrie and her family hid Jews in the basement of their home. In 1944, Corrie's family was arrested, and she and her sister were sent to Ravensbrück concentration camp in Nazi Germany, where her sister died. Corrie was released shortly before the end of World War II because of a clerical error.

Corrie concluded that God had saved her for a purpose. She committed her life to preaching the good news of Jesus Christ. At one meeting in Germany in 1947, she taught on God's forgiveness. Afterward, a man came up to her who was a former Ravensbrück guard—but Corrie needed no introduction.

"I've become a Christian since the war," he said. "I know God has forgiven me for the cruel things I did there, but I would like to hear it from your lips as well…will you forgive me, too?" He put out his hand.

All she could think about were the horrors this man had committed. Then she remembered the words of Jesus that required her to forgive any sin. She silently prayed, *Jesus, help me!* Then she took the man's hand and cried out, "I forgive you, brother!" She later recalled, "I had never known God's love so intensely as I did then."[27]

Corrie would take the gospel to more than sixty countries around the world and change hundreds of thousands of lives through her speaking, writing, and the motion picture *The Hiding Place*, based on her autobiography.

Question

Is there someone who needs your forgiveness today?

Father, help me see people the way you see them, people in need of forgiveness.

Ability versus Availability

His pleasure is not in the strength of the horse,
nor his delight in the legs of the warrior;
the LORD delights in those who fear him,
who put their hope in his unfailing love.

PSALM 147:10–11 NIV

Do you ever feel so skilled in what you do that you require little help from others? Perhaps you may feel that you are more skilled than any other in your field. Does God need your skills and abilities in order to accomplish his purposes on this earth? The answer is no.

One thing God does not need is our skills and abilities. However, he does give us the privilege to exercise our gifts and abilities for his service. That service may be as a computer technician, a secretary, an ironworker, a lawyer, or whatever position where God has placed you. God calls each of us to our vocations to work unto him. The psalmist tells us that his pleasure is not in our strength and ability, but his pleasure is in the attitude of the heart. It is what we find in the heart that helps determine whether our ability translates into availability. You see, God is looking throughout the earth for a man or woman who is fully committed to him. "For the eyes of the LORD range throughout the earth to strengthen those whose hearts are fully committed to him" (2 Chronicles 16:9). When our agenda becomes his agenda, we can expect God to fully support all that we do.

Question

Where are the opportunities in which God is calling you to be available to him?

Father, thank you for allowing me to be used in your service to build your kingdom.

Our Labor in the Lord

So now, beloved ones, stand firm, stable, and enduring. Live your lives with an
unshakable confidence. We know that we prosper and excel in every season by
serving the Lord, because we are assured that our union with the Lord makes our
labor productive with fruit that endures.

1 CORINTHIANS 15:58 TPT

There is a paradigm shift going on among a remnant of workplace believers today. That paradigm shift is a focus on using our work life as a platform for ministry versus a platform solely for material success. There is a remnant of workplace believers throughout the world today who understand their birthright in the workplace is to reflect Christ fully in and through their work. It is reflected by a commitment to use their resources and skills to provide a product of excellence with the overall motive to affect people for Jesus Christ. The difference is that these individuals have an overriding ministry objective to their work.

When the apostle Paul tells us to fully work unto the Lord, he does not mean we must be working as missionaries in "full-time vocational Christian effort." He understands that all of life is holy and sacred to God. If our motive is to serve God where we are, then our labor in the Lord is not in vain.

Question

Are you working with the primary motive of reflecting his life and character through your work?

Father, let nothing move me from making you central to reflecting your life
through me every day.

Impossible Tasks

He answered, "You give them something to eat."
MARK 6:37 NIV

Has anyone ever asked you to do something that seems totally ridiculous?

I imagine that the disciples may have felt this way when Jesus responded with this comment after they asked him how they were going to feed the five thousand who had stayed around to hear him speak. The disciples suggested a logical answer to the problem: "Send the people away so that they can go to the surrounding countryside and villages and buy themselves something to eat" (v. 36).

That wasn't the answer Jesus wanted. He saw the need of the people. He had compassion on them. He wanted to solve the problem with a kingdom response, not logic. He asked the apostles what they had in their hand.

So often what we already have in our hand is what Jesus wants us to use to solve our problems. We must add faith to what we already have in our hand. Then we will see the gospel of the kingdom manifested to solve problems in a supernatural way. Jesus wanted to meet a need in which God would receive the glory. Sending the people away did not meet the need, nor did it bring glory to the Father.

Do not settle for the gospel of salvation only. Jesus came that we might experience the gospel of the kingdom in its fullest sense. Our job is to look past our logical reasoning and see how God might want to solve our problem in a supernatural way.

Question

Is there a problem you need to bring a kingdom breakthrough?

Father, I believe you can solve any problem when I invite you into it.

When God Seems Far Away

Lord, why do you seem so far away when evil is near?
Why have you hidden yourself when I need you the most?
PSALM 10:1 TPT

One of the great mysteries of God is his ways. Some of his ways almost appear to bring us into the most difficult places, as if he were indifferent to our circumstances. It might even seem that he is turning his head from our sorrows. "Yet when I hoped for good, evil came; when I looked for light, then came darkness" (Job 30:26 NIV).

When we are taken into these dark periods, we begin to see light that we never knew existed. Our sensitivities become heightened, and our ability to see through spiritual eyes is illuminated. Unless we are taken into these times, our souls never develop any depth of character. We do not gain wisdom, only knowledge. Knowledge is gained through understanding; wisdom is gained through the experience of darkness.

It does not feel or appear that he is there when we are in the midst of the dark periods. However, he is there walking with us. God says he will never leave us. However, when we are in those dark periods, it does not feel like he is there because he does not rescue us from the circumstances. He does this for our benefit in order that we might become more like Jesus. Jesus learned obedience from the things he suffered (see Hebrews 5:8).

Question

What does that say about how you and I will learn obedience?

Father, help me embrace the dark times and gain the wisdom that you intend for me from these times.

The Value of Words

"Just let your words ring true.
A simple 'Yes' or 'No' will suffice.
Anything beyond this springs from a deceiver."
MATTHEW 5:36–37 TPT

Imagine for a moment that you are living in Jesus' time. It is before Jesus has begun his public ministry. He is a carpenter in your local town of Nazareth. You have asked Jesus to make a table for you. You're on a deadline, and you must have it in a week. You agree on the price of $100 for the table and the time of one week for completion. A week later you arrive to pick up the table. You lay your money down on the table, and Jesus says, "Ms. Johnson, I am sorry, but the table is not ready. I ran into complications. Also, I can no longer honor the price I gave you. It is now $150 instead of $100."

Two years later you hear about this same Jesus who is preaching to the local townspeople. How are you going to view this Jesus? You probably won't give much credence to his message because of your personal experience. In the same way, our lives have the ability to reinforce the message we stand for, or they can violate it and make it totally ineffective.

If we are unable to fulfill a commitment or pay a bill on time, we must communicate with those we owe and make a good faith effort to resolve the matter within our means.

Question

Do your words mean anything to those who hear them? Do you make commitments and fail to follow through on them? What would others say about how you follow through?

Lord, show me how I am doing in following through with my commitments to others. Help me be a person of my word.

Changing Habits: The Ten-Dollar Challenge

*Jesus replied, "I tell you the truth,
everyone who sins is a slave of sin."*
JOHN 8:34 NLT

I hate that I am always running late," my friend lamented. "It has been a problem for me all my life."

"Do you really want to change that?" I asked.

"Yes, I do."

"All right. Every time you are late to work or anywhere else where you have committed to be at a particular time, you must give me twenty-five dollars."

"No way!" my friend responded. "I would go broke! But I will do ten dollars."

"All right, ten dollars it is. It has to be a large enough amount of money for it to hurt your pocketbook."

"Believe me, that will hurt," my friend said. In order for my friend not to be resentful of me for the money she had to give, we put it in a jar to be given to a Christian cause. This ensured my motive was only for her best interest.

About a month later, my friend found great motivation to be on time to every place she had to be. In the first week, the jar got only ten dollars from my friend. The next week, twenty dollars. The third week, nothing. By the fifth week, my friend had changed a lifelong habit that had hindered her all her life.

Psychologists tell us that it takes twenty-one days to form a habit. So, if you need to change some habit, you need to be actively engaged in that new behavior at least twenty-one days. My friend needed an individual to hold her accountable, and it took a potential loss of something to provide the added incentive.

Question

What are the habits that keep you from becoming all that God may want you to become?

Father, help me to change behaviors that hinder me from experiencing you.

Choked by Wealth

Whoever loves money never has enough;
whoever loves wealth is never satisfied with their income.
ECCLESIASTES 5:10 NIV

Workplace believers are especially susceptible to a trap in their spiritual lives, one to which others may not be so susceptible. That trap is wealth. Scripture tells us that if we are having our basic needs met for food and clothing, we are considered to have riches (see 1 Timothy 6:6–10). Jesus cautioned us against living a lifestyle that requires more than our basic necessities.

However, it is clear that Jesus was not against wealth but against a dependence on wealth. Jesus continually taught that a dependence on anything other than God is evil. Often when Jesus determined that money was an issue for an individual, he addressed it and found that the individual could not let it go. This was true for the rich young ruler. When talking about what he must do to inherit the kingdom, Jesus told him to do the one thing that would be the most difficult—to give away his wealth and follow him. Jesus was not saying this was what every person must do but only the rich young ruler because Jesus knew this was his greatest stumbling block. For others of us, it could be something else Jesus would ask us to give up (see Matthew 19:16–30).

Much like the frog in the boiling pot that does not recognize the heat until it's too late, if we are not careful, we gradually begin to acquire and walk the treadmill of material gain before we recognize it becoming part of our nature. This leads to a leanness in our soul.

Question

Do you have the same hunger for God that you once had? Has financial blessing had an adverse effect on your passion for Jesus Christ?

Father, keep my heart hungry for more of you.

Using Jerry Springer to Preach

"It is not the healthy who need a doctor, but the sick.
But go and learn what this means: 'I desire mercy, not sacrifice.'
For I have not come to call the righteous, but sinners."
MATTHEW 9:12–13 NIV

A friend of mine once told me the story of Linda Rios Brook, a businesswoman who desired to impact the culture with the good news of Jesus Christ. Linda lived on the front lines of the fast-paced world of media. She was forced to resign her position after making comments about her faith in her local newspaper.

Linda was approached by a Christian foundation with the opportunity to purchase a television station in her local market. The idea of managing a "religious" television station did not appeal to her in the least because she knew that such a format would not sustain a for-profit business model.

After losing hundreds of thousands of dollars every month in an attempt to attract a "Christian audience," she realized that the station could not survive without a more mainstream programming lineup. An opportunity arose to get the Rush Limbaugh program from a competitor, but she would also have to take *The Jerry Springer Show*. Linda struggled with what to do with this program, knowing the religious community would criticize this decision. Then, the Lord gave her an idea.

She decided to place a rolling statement across the bottom of the page that said, "Need a friend? Call…" She decided to use the controversial *The Jerry Springer Show* to minister to those who might be watching the program, who, she concluded, represented a ripe field for the gospel. Her insight proved true. The phones began to ring off the hook, and many came to Christ as a result.

Question

Do you need to think outside the box to reach those who need Christ most?

Father, use my skills and abilities to reach the lost.

The Flight of Geese

In Judah the hand of God was on the people to give them unity of mind to carry out
what the king and his officials had ordered, following the word of the LORD.

2 CHRONICLES 30:12 NIV

A major corporation conducted a study on the flight of geese. They found that geese fly in a *V* formation with one goose in the lead. After a short time, this goose relinquishes the lead to another goose. The researchers noticed that during flight, head movements of the lead goose seem to give signals to the other geese to let them know how he was doing. They concluded that the formation flight pattern reduces wind drag due to the lift the other birds receive and believe it increases their performance by up to 70 percent.[28] Whenever one goose drops out of the formation, another goes with it. These two geese join another group later.[29]

Independence is one of the strongholds of the workplace. However, our dependence on others is a good thing. It can bring us into a unity of spirit that accomplishes much more with less effort while meeting needs for each of us. Jesus said that others would know we are Christians by our love for one another and by our unity (see John 13:34–35). By walking together, we increase our strength. By going it alone, we must carry a load we were never intended to carry.

An old African proverb says, "If you want to fast, go alone. If you want to go far, go together."

Question

Do you value working with others to accomplish something greater?

Father, please reveal if there is an independent spirit within me that prevents me from joining others in the mission you have called me to.

Entitlements

He humbled himself and became vulnerable,
choosing to be revealed as a man and was obedient.
He was a perfect example, even in his death—
a criminal's death by crucifixion!
PHILIPPIANS 2:8 TPT

Society today has duped many of us into believing that the world owes us. It owes us a good living, a loving spouse, good health throughout our whole life, sexual pleasure whenever we want it, and paid vacations the rest of our lives. The world has told us if we work hard and do right, we are entitled to these things. This is the Esau perspective on life. For a mere meal, he sold his own birthright for a simple pleasure to which he felt entitled.

Jesus said he came only to do the work of the Father. I am sure that Jesus had times of refreshment in his life that allowed him to get recharged for the mission God called him to. However, he understood the balance of maintaining work, mission, and play. When we view life with an attitude of entitlements, we are susceptible to becoming disappointed, resentful, and even bitter when our expectations go unmet.

Question

What are the motives for your work life? Is it only to gain increased pleasure and leisure time?

Father, reveal to me if I need to relinquish any rights that may be hindering my freedom to experience your love and grace.

An Encounter with God

I was left alone, gazing at this great vision;
I had no strength left,
my face turned deathly pale and I was helpless.
DANIEL 10:8 NIV

Daniel received a vision that troubled him greatly. He wanted understanding of this vision. He set himself out to understand the vision by fasting for three weeks. Three days after his three weeks of fasting, a messenger of God appeared to Daniel. The messenger explained that heaven had heard his prayer from the first day, but the angel was temporarily prevented from coming by the prince of Persia, a demon angel, who sought to thwart God's messenger from coming to Daniel.

There are times in our lives when we must set ourselves to seeking God with all our hearts. It is in these times that we hear from heaven in ways we may never have experienced before. Daniel's perseverance in prayer was rewarded with a personal encounter with heaven. However, in order to receive from God, Daniel had to be left alone, have his strength removed, and be placed in a helpless condition. When we have no ability in our own strength to move heaven or the events around us, we are in position to hear from heaven. It is the acknowledgment of our humanity and our frailness that places us in a position to have a personal encounter with the living God.

Question

Do you need a personal encounter with God today? Do you need God to intervene on your behalf?

Father, reveal yourself to me today in a personal and powerful way.

A Fleeting Shadow

Man is nothing but a faint whisper, a mere breath.
We spend our days like nothing more than a passing shadow.
PSALM 144:4 TPT

Every time I fly over a large body of water, I imagine opening the window of the jet and pouring out my coffee into the immense body of water below. I imagine the time that I spend on this earth compared to eternity is no more than that cup of coffee in the ocean. The incredible size of the ocean compared to one small cup of coffee is what eternity is like compared to our life. Why, then, do we invest so much in temporal pursuits when we know that our investment here can have so much impact on our eternity? It is the great paradox of human behavior, especially for Christians.

Do not let the worries and cares of this life keep you from having an eternal impact on the lives of those you meet each day. Satan has a way of keeping our focus on the problems of today rather than the spiritual opportunities before us. He is master of the urgent, not the important.

Question

Does your life have an overall ministry objective to it? This does not mean we must be constantly involved in "Christian activity." It only means that we should be about what God has called us to do with the motive of being obedient to this mission.

Father, I pray today that all that I do in work and play will bring glory to you.

Faith in Times of Despair

"Arise, cry out in the night, At the beginning of the watches;
pour out your heart like water before the face of the Lord."

LAMENTATIONS 2:19 NKJV

Our small group was playing Bible Challenge, a Bible trivia game. A question was presented, "Who is the author of Lamentations?"

Betty shouted out "Jeremiah!" I thought it was someone else, but she spoke with such conviction, I went with her answer. It turns out she was right.

Betty laughed and said, "You know you're bad off when you're looking for comfort in the book of Lamentations!" Betty had been walking through three years of medical challenges and felt like she was still no closer to a resolution than when she started her journey. At times she had been discouraged to the point of despair and felt totally abandoned by a God she knows loves her. And yet, in the midst of all of it, she found comfort in Jeremiah's words in Lamentations 3.

Because of the LORD's great love we are not consumed,
for his compassions never fail.
They are new every morning;
great is your faithfulness. (vv. 22–23 NIV)

If you are at the point of despair, do what Jeremiah did and pour out your heart to God. And then call to your mind the fact that great is God's faithfulness. He has not abandoned you, and he loves you. Don't allow Satan to deceive you into thinking anything else. God will be faithful in your life.

Question

Do you ever question God's love and care for you?

Father, help me overcome feelings of despair and rejection and realize you will never leave me nor forsake me.

The Plans of Tomorrow

You don't have a clue what tomorrow may bring. For your fleeting life is but a warm breath of air that is visible in the cold only for a moment and then vanishes!
JAMES 4:14 TPT

I once had a group of workplace believers meet at my office every week for fellowship, study, and prayer. One man attended our group for several years. Jim was well liked and in good health. One Thursday he showed up as usual. The next morning, I received a call: "Jim is dead! He died in his easy chair last night!" Jim had no prior problems, and there was no indication he was about to go be with the Lord. Naturally, it came as a shock to us all.

A friend of mine told me that someone challenged him to do an experiment. He challenged my friend to live his life for one year as if it were the last year he would live. My friend responded to the challenge and did as proposed. It changed his life forever. He began to focus on different priorities and people when he viewed life in these terms.

Life is fragile. Consider where you are investing your time and energies. Someone once said they had never heard anyone on his deathbed say that he wished he had made more money in his lifetime or that he wished he had made a certain business deal. Usually they say something like, "I wish I had spent more time with my kids."

Question

Who are the people in your life you need to appreciate more before they are gone?

Father, give me your priorities for my life today.

A Two-Way Relationship

He wakens me morning by morning,
wakens my ear to listen like one being instructed.

ISAIAH 50:4 NIV

The prophet Isaiah describes his relationship to God as a relationship that has two-way communication. Have you ever felt that your communication with God was only one way—you talking to him only? Isaiah tells us, "The Sovereign LORD has given me a well-instructed tongue, to know the word that sustains the weary...The Sovereign LORD has opened my ears; I have not been rebellious, I have not turned away" (vv. 4–5).

The key to Isaiah's relationship with God lies in four important principles:

1. He had an instructed tongue. Isaiah had given rule of his life completely to God's purposes.
2. He knew the Word of the Lord, which allowed him to sustain and encourage others.
3. He took time to listen.
4. He did not flee from the tough assignments. He didn't shrink back.

If we are to be able to listen to God, we must follow the same principles. Knowing and spending time studying God's Word allows the Holy Spirit to bring to mind his instructions for what he wants for us.

Question

Are you hearing God consistently in your life?

Father, may you develop in me a greater sensitivity to your voice.

Overcoming Our Past

Then the Spirit of the LORD came on Jephthah.
JUDGES 11:29 NIV

We've all heard stories of individuals who have overcome extreme hardship during their childhood years. Children whose parents are alcoholics, orphans who never have parents, those who have lost their parents to a fatal crash, those who suffered from a serious childhood disease: these are all people with difficult circumstances to overcome.

Jephthah was a man who overcame his obstacles and refused to allow his circumstances to prevent him from becoming great in God's sight. He was born to Gilead, a result of his father's adulterous encounter with a prostitute. Jephthah's half-brothers decided to reject Jephthah and drove him away from their home saying, "You are not going to get any inheritance in our family… because you are the son of another woman" (v. 2). Imagine the rejection this young man felt as he was cast away from his own family.

This experience taught Jephthah to become a hardened warrior. As he got older, his reputation as a warrior became known to those in his country, so much so that when the Ammonites made war on Israel, the elders of Gilead went to Jephthah and asked him to be their commander. Jephthah had to fight off those feelings of rejection from previous years. He overcame his hurt and pain and responded to the call God had on his life.

The Lord prepares each of us in similar ways. The Lord knows our struggles and will make our life an instrument in his hand if we will follow him with an upright heart.

Question

Have you had to overcome some painful experiences in your life?

Father, I pray you heal my heart of the wounds that were inflicted. You are my healer.

Sowing in Tears

Those who sow their tears as seeds
will reap a harvest with joyful shouts of glee.
PSALM 126:5 TPT

The most difficult place to keep moving in faith is the place of extreme pain. Extreme pain, especially emotional pain, can become immobilizing to the human spirit if it is allowed to overcome us. The psalmist tells us there is only one remedy for overcoming painful circumstances that will result in joy. We are to sow in the midst of these times. You cannot do this if you live by feelings alone. It is an act of the will. This act requires that we go outside ourselves in pure faith.

I learned this principle during one of the deepest periods of my life. I had lost much that was dear to me. A mature man in the faith admonished me to reach out to others in spite of my own pain. "Invest in someone else," he said. I did not realize what a place of healing and comfort that would become.

"Those who go out weeping, carrying seed to sow, will return with songs of joy, carrying sheaves with them" (v. 6 NIV). Pain can become a source of joy if we take the first step by planting seed. There is a harvest that will come if we sow in the midst of tears.

Question

How are you handling your pain?

Father, help me go outside myself and serve someone else today.

Being a Person under Authority

"Truly I tell you, I have not found anyone in Israel with such great faith."
MATTHEW 8:10 NIV

The centurion came to Jesus and told him of his servant who was paralyzed and in terrible suffering. He came to Jesus because he believed Jesus could heal him. He told Jesus of the matter, and Jesus was willing to come with the centurion. But the centurion would not have it. He knew that Jesus, being under the authority of heaven itself, did not have to see the servant to help him. The centurion understood authority. He understood that he himself had certain rights that his position granted him to have power over situations and people. He also was a man under authority. The centurion understood Jesus' position and what power that position held in heaven—the power to heal his servant if he chose to exercise that authority.

When Jesus saw that the centurion understood this principle of authority and that he did not have to visit the servant to heal him, he acknowledged the centurion's faith.

Today, we find few who understand this system of authority God has ordained. It requires great faith to operate in this realm. Yet Jesus said that when we understand this, we demonstrate the kind of faith that he rarely sees.

Question

Do you recognize the authorities God has placed in your life as those God is using to protect you?

Father, I will honor and respect those who are in authority over me.

You Think That?

If you consider yourself to be wise and one who understands the ways of God,
advertise it with a beautiful, fruitful life guided by wisdom's gentleness.

JAMES 3:13 TPT

I can't believe you think I said that," I complained to my wife. "I was simply trying to explain that I don't have the same feelings about that issue as you do." Her response left little empathy for my position because of the tone with which I responded to her. We resigned ourselves to agree to disagree.

We all see things through our own set of glasses at times. Men view things differently than women. Bosses see things differently than employees. One ethic group will see a situation totally different than another. Our life experiences, our past treatment of circumstances, and our personalities all contribute to how we view situations in daily life.

Perception is often each person's reality whether that reality is true or not. Your perception of a situation is going to dictate your response more than the actual reality of the circumstances.

Whenever conflict arises from viewing things differently, there is really only one way to resolve the difference. Usually, the other person is offended by the tone of the other more than the position that is taken. If the other person is offended, offer a few words: "I'm sorry. Will you forgive me for my tone?"

Humbling ourselves is the only way to resolve the relational breach.

Question

Is there someone you need to seek forgiveness from for taking an adversarial position?

Father, help me to walk in humility in my relationships.

Building a Solid Foundation

"Everyone who hears my teaching and does not apply it to his life can be compared to a foolish man who built his house on sand."
MATTHEW 7:26 TPT

There were two kinds of people in the days of Jesus. Some heard the words that Jesus spoke and were awed by his wisdom and understanding but did nothing about what they heard. Others heard those words and acted on them. Jesus said that those who heard the words but failed to put them into practice were foolish and likened them to someone who builds a house on sand. The person who followed what Jesus taught was a person who would be sure to weather life's storms (vv. 24–25).

You never know how well your house is built until it is tested by the elements. Torrential rains reveal the quality of your roof. Wind and cold reveal how well your home is insulated. Heat and sun reveal the quality of your paint and siding. All these elements reveal whether a solid foundation has been laid to make your home a secure and lasting place to live.

Many of us find that we have given only lip service to God's commands. We are faced with the reality that our foundations are not strong enough to weather life's storms.

Question

How do you react when trials come? Do you fret and worry?

Father, thank you for being my rock I can build life upon.

Forgiving Those Who Judge You

The LORD restored Job's losses when he prayed for his friends.
Indeed the LORD gave Job twice as much as he had before.
JOB 42:10 NKJV

Have you ever been wrongly judged? Have you ever had people assume there was sin in your life because of the troubles you may have experienced? Or perhaps they judged your motives as wrong. What if the people judging you were your closest friends?

This was exactly what happened in the life of Job. His friends did not understand how a godly person could ever go through his degree of adversity unless God was judging him for his sin. However, his friends were wrong, and God intervened. "I am angry with you and your two friends, because you have not spoken the truth about me, as my servant Job has," said God to Job's three friends (v. 7 NIV).

Nothing has really changed after thousands of years. I recall going through a seven year "Job" experience. Friends in the marketplace could not understand why I would experience such calamity unless I had made poor choices. Those in the church often wrongly equated trouble with sin. Sometimes this can be true, but often, trouble is simply a consequence of a call on one's life such as Joseph and the apostle Paul experienced.

This forgiveness is often *the* most important step in gaining restoration in our own lives. The Scripture verse above reveals that it was not until Job prayed for his friends that God restored Job in the things he had lost.

Question

Is there someone in your life you need to forgive? It may be the missing piece of your puzzle for restoration.

Father, help me to forgive those who wrongfully judge me.

Becoming a Mighty Woman

All those who were in distress or in debt or discontented gathered around him, and he became their commander. About four hundred men were with him.

1 SAMUEL 22:2 NIV

Have you ever felt that you could accomplish a whole lot more if you had more talented people around you? Imagine what David must have thought in the years following his anointing by the prophet Samuel as the next king of Israel. He spent the next many years running from King Saul. Now God was beginning to bring men to support David. But what kind of men? God gave David not the elite or the sophisticated; instead, he gave him those who were in debt and discontented with life. The down-and-outs. David turned those men into the best fighting men of their day. In fact, David never lost a battle during his entire reign as king of Israel—quite a feat for a bunch of no-name lowlifes!

Jesus took a few men who weren't exactly the cream of the crop either. He built his life into these men, which resulted in twelve men who turned the world upside down.

Question

Are you one of God's mighty women? Are you investing your life to build other mighty men and women? David and Jesus set the example of what can be done when we invest in others.

Father, make me a mighty woman of prayer for a cause greater than myself.

Becoming Aware of God

"Surely the LORD is in this place,
and I was not aware of it."
GENESIS 28:16 NIV

Jacob was forced to flee his family after receiving the blessing of God from his father, Isaac. He fled because of his broken relationship with his brother, Esau, who threatened to kill him. He was alone after leaving his family and was sleeping in the wilderness area at Bethel. It is here that Jacob encountered God personally for the very first time. He had a dream in which heaven was opened to him. The Lord spoke to him there and gave him a promise to give him the very land on which he was lying.

This encounter with God made him realize that God was in this place even though he had not been aware of it. God had to remove Jacob from all that was of comfort to him in order to reveal himself to Jacob. What began as a crisis that forced him to be removed from his family and friends led to an encounter with the living God and a fresh vision of God's purposes for his life.

God often must do radical things in the life of the servant in whom he has special plans: separation from family, removal of physical and emotional resources, an encounter with God. These are often the hallmarks of ownership by God that build a vision into a life.

Question

Do you see your place of work as a place where God resides?

Father, I invite you into my workplace today. Help me experience you in my own Bethel.

God's Preparation for Moving Out

In this way the man grew exceedingly prosperous and came to own large flocks,
and female and male servants, and camels and donkeys.

GENESIS 30:43 NIV

When Jacob left his family because of a breach in his relationship with his brother Esau, he went to work for his uncle Laban, where he stayed for twenty years. It came time for him to leave, but he had no physical assets to show for those years under Laban. Laban had taken advantage of his nephew in every way. God's hand was on Jacob, and God had plans to prosper him. However, Jacob had one problem: he had no resources of his own. For Jacob to launch out on his own, he would need resources. In those days, resources often meant large flocks of animals. God gave Jacob a dream that resulted in a strategy for creating wealth by multiplying his sheep.

There are many important lessons for us in this story. First, when God decides it is time to move you into a larger place of his bidding, he can provide the resources you need to support the call. God gave Jacob a dream that resulted in a strategy never used before to build wealth. It was totally from God's hand. It was creative and new. God called Jacob to move out after he had demonstrated his faithfulness in twenty years of serving Laban.

Question

Do you need God to give you a strategy in your work-life call?

Father, thank you that you know how to bring breakthrough in my own situation.

Getting a Haircut

"There I will give her back her vineyards,
and will make the Valley of Achor a door of hope."

HOSEA 2:15 NIV

I walked into the local hair salon for only the second time and sat down to get a haircut. "Hello, Donna, how are you?" I said pleasantly. All of a sudden, she looked at me sadly and began to cry uncontrollably with her head on my shoulder. "Donna, what's wrong?"

Donna said how her marriage was in a crisis and her husband was being abusive. She told me tale after tale of years of drug use by her husband. The other customers were all quietly sitting in their chairs as this was taking place. As Donna began to settle down, we talked, and eventually, we prayed together right there in the hair salon.

I gave Donna a few books to read and invited her to our house for a prayer gathering. Donna slowly gained strength. She became free of the abusive relationship when they divorced.

God revealed himself to Donna through different people. First, he sent me to sit in her chair, then God sent ladies who invited her to a Bible study. She soon invited Jesus into her life and became baptized.

Today Donna has broken free of the harmful, codependent, abusive relationship. She has entered a new love relationship with her Savior. Today, Donna is a servant of Jesus masquerading as a hairstylist.

Question

Do you find yourself in a crisis? God loves to show himself faithful in such times.

Father, I invite you into my crisis to help me be an overcomer.

Perseverance for Success

Even in times of trouble we have a joyful confidence, knowing that our pressures will develop in us patient endurance. And patient endurance will refine our character, and proven character leads us back to hope.
ROMANS 5:3–4 TPT

Perseverance is the key to every great accomplishment because nothing of lasting value has ever been achieved without it. Industrialist Henry Ford is one of the great success stories of American history, but he failed in business five times before he succeeded. A Ford Motor Company employee once asked his boss the secret of success, and Henry Ford is often credited with replying, "When you start a thing, don't quit until you finish it."

The path ahead of you is strewn with obstacles. People will oppose you. There will be financial setbacks, time pressures, illnesses, and misfortunes. Some of the biggest obstacles will be inside of you: self-doubt, insecurity, procrastination, and worry. You must give yourself permission to succeed.

When we persevere through adversity, we win the approval of our Lord Jesus Christ, who told the suffering church at Ephesus, "I know your works, your labor, your patience, and that you cannot bear those who are evil…and you have persevered and have patience, and have labored for My name's sake and have not become weary" (Revelation 2:2–3 NKJV).

Life is a marathon, not a sprint. The race doesn't go to the swiftest but to those who don't give up. We need endurance in order to deal with the stress of adversity. People give up or give out when they feel depleted—when they physically, emotionally, and spiritually run out of gas. Spend time with optimists and encouragers. Seek out people of faith. Persevere to the end.

Question

Do you need to persevere right now?

Father, thank you for the grace to persevere through every trial.

Working versus Striving

He said to me, "This is the word of the L<small>ORD</small> to Zerubbabel:
'Not by might nor by power, but by My Spirit,' says the L<small>ORD</small> Almighty."
ZECHARIAH 4:6 NIV

Your greatest obstacle in fulfilling God's purposes in your life is the skills you have acquired to perform well in your work life. One of the great paradoxes in Scripture relates to our need to depend on the Lord, yet at the same time, we're instructed to use the talents and abilities God gives us to accomplish the work he gives us to do.

When we reach a level of excellence and performance in our fields, it actually becomes an obstacle to seeing God's power manifest in our work. What we naturally do well becomes the object of our trust. When this happens, God retreats. You see, God allows us to develop skills, but these must be continually yielded to God's Spirit. There will be times when God will use these skills to accomplish his purposes. There will be other times when God will not use any of our skills just to ensure that we know it is by his power that we can do anything.

Question

Are you balancing trust and obedience with your skills and ability?

Father, teach me what it means to walk according to the power of the Holy Spirit in my life.

The Goal of the Christian Life

"Let me make this clear: A single grain of wheat will never be more than a single grain of wheat unless it drops into the ground and dies. Because then it sprouts and produces a great harvest of wheat—all because one grain died."
JOHN 12:24 TPT

The goal of the Christian life is death, not success—death to our old nature, life to our new self. A popular teaching says that if we follow God, we will prosper materially. God may, in fact, bless his people materially, but few can make this claim among third-world countries. Wealth must never be the goal of a person's life, only a by-product.

Jesus' obedience did not gain him popularity among the heathens or the religious. It did not win him financial success or a life of pleasure. His obedience resulted in his death on the cross. This is the same goal Christ has for each of us—death of our old nature so that he might live through us.

The Christian life is a paradox. The first will be last, death in return for life, and praise to God to overcome a spirit of heaviness.

Question

Have you died to your old nature?

Father, I willingly lay down my old life for my new life in you.

Hearing the Father Speak

"My sheep listen to my voice;
I know them, and they follow me."
JOHN 10:27 NIV

An Englishman wanted to share the gospel with a Muslim man but knew little of Muslim beliefs. The two men talked as they walked and agreed they would each share their beliefs with one another. The Muslim went first. As the Englishman listened, he asked the Holy Spirit to show him how to share his faith with the Muslim man. "Do you consider your god your father who speaks?" the Englishman asked the Muslim.

"Certainly not," replied the Muslim man.

"That is one of the big differences between your god and my God. My God speaks to me personally."

"You cannot prove that," stated the Muslim man.

The Englishman again prayed, *Lord, how do I prove this to this man?* A few moments later the two men began walking toward two young ladies on the other side of the road coming toward them. As they approached, the Englishman spoke to the ladies said to one woman, "I believe you are a nurse. Is that correct?"

The woman was startled and said, "How would you know that? I have never met you before."

He replied, "I asked my Father, and he told me." The Muslim had his proof.

Question

Are you hearing God daily in your relationship with God?

Father, give me a listening ear so that others might know that I have a heavenly Father who speaks.

The Greatest Test

*"I know, my God, that you test the heart
and are pleased with integrity."*
1 CHRONICLES 29:17 NIV

God tests his children to know what is in their hearts. God's desire for each of his children is for them to walk in relationship with him, to uphold his righteousness and integrity. It is a high calling that we will fail to achieve without complete dependence on him.

The greatest tests come not in great adversities but in great prosperity. For it is in prosperity that we begin to lose the sensitivity to sin in our lives. Adversity motivates us to righteousness out of a desire to see our adversity changed.

Hezekiah was a great godly king. He was a faithful, God-honoring king most of his life, but toward the end, he became proud. God wanted to find out if he would still honor him and recognize his blessings in his life. So God sent an envoy to his palace to inquire about a miracle that God had performed on behalf of Hezekiah. Would Hezekiah publicly acknowledge the miracle God had performed on his behalf? No. Instead he bragged about his own riches and treasures and failed to acknowledge God's blessing in leading his nation.

Prosperity can be our greatest test.

Question

Do you regularly acknowledge the Lord's blessing in your life?

Father, give me the grace to be a faithful follower during times of prosperity. May I give you the glory for all you do in my life.

Abraham, Isaac, and Jacob

"God will surely come to your aid and take you up out of this land to the land he promised on oath to Abraham, Isaac and Jacob."

GENESIS 50:24 NIV

I was traveling with my mentor when he said to me, "I would like you to consider why God referred to himself as the 'God of Abraham, Isaac, and Jacob.' Why didn't he simply say, 'the God of Jacob'?" For the next hour of our flight, I racked my brain to answer this question. I had never read it in a commentary, and the Scriptures do not really say why this is so. We both had some interesting observations, one from my mentor and one from my own insight.

After a while, my friend asked, "So, what did you discover?"

I shared my observation: "Could it be that the Lord has given us a 'type of trinity' in Abraham, Isaac, and Jacob? Abraham was considered a father figure to the nation of Israel. Isaac was the son who had to be sacrificed on the altar. Jacob was the man who had to learn to walk according to the Holy Spirit instead of his flesh. Each of these patriarchs had a particular relationship with God to fulfill."

"Hm. That is interesting. I also believe the Lord has given us three distinct personalities in whom he performed his work. Each of us can identify with one of these men in how God has related to them."

Question

Which of the patriarchs do you identify with most in your Christian pilgrimage?

Father, help me to learn from others who have gone before me.

One of the Twelve

He died for all, that those who live should no longer live for themselves
but for him who died for them and was raised again.

2 CORINTHIANS 5:15 NIV

It is believed that there were about five thousand believers during the time of Christ. Among those believers, it was thought there were three types. The largest number of believers were those who came to Jesus for salvation. They served him little beyond coming to him to receive salvation. A much smaller number, say five hundred, actually followed him and served him. Then, there were the disciples. These were those who identified with Jesus. They lived the life that Jesus lived. Each of these ultimately died in difficult circumstances. They experienced the hardships, the miracles, and the fellowship with God in human form.

Which of these categories best describes you? Jesus has called each of us to identify with him completely. "This is how we know we are in him: Whoever claims to live in him must live as Jesus did" (1 John 2:5–6).

Question

Which of the above descriptions of followers of Christ best exemplifies your walk with Jesus?

Father, allow me to walk as Jesus did to experience his power and love in my life so that others will see the hope that lies in me.

God's Motives

"He brought me out into a spacious place;
he rescued me because he delighted in me."

2 SAMUEL 22:20 NIV

Wrong motives can result in broken relationships, poor business decisions, and falling out of God's will. Sometimes we do not know the motive of another person's actions. It is wrong for us to assume what their motive is until we have confidence that we know their intentions. If we are not careful, we become judge and jury over them.

God's motives are always the best for us. His desire is to bring us into a spacious place. Sometimes he wants us to go beyond our borders of security so that we might experience life at a level that goes beyond ourselves. Sometimes we need to be rescued by the Lord like Peter when he stepped out of the boat to walk on water.

Peter didn't have complete success in his venturing out, but it was a process that would lead him to the next victory in his faith walk with Jesus. Sometimes failure is what is needed in order to move to the next level of faith with God. However, we must be willing to fail and let God rescue us.

Question

Have you ever questioned the motive behind God's activity in your life?

Father, thank you for having only the best intentions for my life.

The Cost of Broken Covenants

During the reign of David, there was a famine for three successive years;
so David sought the face of the LORD.

2 SAMUEL 21:1 NIV

There was a famine in the land, and David equated that famine to the blessing or lack of blessing from God. He sought God to know why. The Lord did not take long to answer: "It is on account of Saul and his blood-stained house; it is because he put the Gibeonites to death" (v. 1). Years earlier, when Joshua entered the promised land, the Israelites were tricked by the Gibeonites into believing they were travelers when they were actually enemies of Israel. The Gibeonites tricked Israel into making a peace treaty with them. It was one of the first major mistakes Israel made after entering the promised land. As a result of the peace treaty, the Gibeonites were kept as slaves to Israel. This was never God's intention for Israel. He had wanted Israel to destroy all their enemies, but they made an error in judgment that required that they honor a covenant with the Gibeonites.

Saul disregarded this covenant with the Gibeonites and sought to annihilate them. David sensed there was something preventing God's blessing on Israel. As a nation, they had violated a covenant made before God. Now they were reaping the consequences.

Question

Are you failing to walk in God's blessing due to some failed commitment?

Father, reveal any issue in my life that might be preventing me from experiencing your blessing.

Preparation for Greatness

*"He trains my hands for battle;
my arms can bend a bow of bronze."*

2 SAMUEL 22:35 NIV

David was a mighty warrior, and God described him as man fully devoted to his purposes after he learned important lessons from his failures. God took David through a training ground that could be looked on as cruel and unusual punishment by many a person. God chose him at a young age to be the next king, yet King Saul rejected him and hunted him down. David was a fugitive for many years. He had uprisings in his own family, and he had relationship problems. He certainly did not have a life free of trouble; he made many mistakes. He was human like all of us, yet he learned from his mistakes and repented when he failed.

Toward the end of David's life, he recounted his relationship with God. It is a sermon on God's ways of dealing with a servant leader.

"You have given me your shield of victory; your help has made me great. You have made a wide path for my feet to keep them from slipping" (vv. 36–37 NLT).

God was David's source for everything.

Question

Is God your source for everything in your life?

Father, I acknowledge you today as Lord over all areas of my life. Thank you for your faithfulness.

Those in Whom God Delights

His people don't find security in strong horses, for horsepower is nothing to him.
Manpower is even less impressive! YAHWEH shows favor to those who fear him,
those who wait for his tender embrace.

PSALM 147:10–11 TPT

Mammon and power are the ruling strongholds of the workplace. If you possess either of these, then you will be courted by those who serve the workplace in hopes of increasing market share. It is a competitive environment that often gives way to decisions and actions that are dictated by the financial bottom line. More often, it is becoming a common business practice for employers to require workers to put more time into their jobs, often requiring weekend work in order to be more competitive. For the Christian worker, this brings pressures on the family and will result in "lost market share" in the spiritual realm.

The Lord is not impressed with your abilities. Only one thing delights him: those who fear him and put their hope in his unfailing love. He is the one who gives us the ability to work, plan, and execute. He does not want us to look to our abilities but to his abilities. Sometimes it is difficult to balance these two perspectives. However, if we ask God to show us how to maintain this balance, he will do it.

Question

What does it mean to fear God and place our hope in his love? It means we acknowledge that God is the source of all that we are.

Father, I put my hope in your unfailing love today.

Performing Miracles with Your Staff

*"Take this staff in your hand
so you can perform the signs with it."*
EXODUS 4:17 NIV

What is the staff God has put into your hand? Is it being an office worker? Is it being a doctor? Is it being a builder? Moses' staff represented his vocation as a shepherd. God had something in mind for his vocation—to perform miracles and bring freedom to those enslaved. And awesome miracles he did! God turned the Nile River into blood with the touch of the staff. He turned the staff into a snake. He parted the Red Sea with it. He delivered a nation from slavery. These are just a few of the miracles God did with that staff. What is God doing through your staff?

When we yield our talents and abilities to the Lord, God can perform miracles through them. First, Moses had to yield what he had in his hand to God. Only after this took place could God use that staff. As long as Moses held on to it, God could not and would not perform miracles through it.

Question

Have you yielded your staff to the Lord?

Father, I submit my staff to you to see what you might want to do through it.

A New Remnant of Priests

Strangers shall stand and feed your flocks,
and the sons of the foreigner shall be your plowmen
and your vinedressers.

ISAIAH 61:5 NKJV

God is calling forth a remnant of workplace believers whom he will use mightily to bring good news to those who have never heard the gospel. The "10/40 Window" is a name given to the geographic areas of the world where few have heard the name of Jesus Christ: between ten- and forty-degrees north latitude. This region represents many of the Muslim nations in the Middle East, India, China, and the former Soviet Republic.[30]

God is mobilizing his workplace believers around the world to be the vessels who will bring the good news to these peoples. The "Joshuas and Calebs" are spying out the land. This class of workplace believer has a pioneer spirit that is seeking ways of penetrating strongholds of spiritual darkness in these countries. God is raising them up. They see the risks, but they see the awesomeness of God that enables them to accomplish something for his kingdom by using their resources and talents. The wealth of these nations are the souls who are precious in God's sight. Salvation for many souls will be their true reward for their efforts.

Question

Has God called you to be such a vessel? Has he called you to be a catalyst in some way?

Heavenly Father, I pray you affect nations through my life.

Persecuted for Christ

Blessed are ye, when men shall revile you, and persecute you, and shall say all manner of evil against you falsely, for my sake. Rejoice, and be exceeding glad: for great is your reward in heaven: for so persecuted they the prophets which were before you.

MATTHEW 5:11–12 KJV

Meena and Sunita were Hindu sisters living in India. They embraced a newfound faith in Jesus and began to live for him, but it came with much persecution. Their neighbors severely beat them for sharing their faith. In fact, they beat Sunita until she was unconscious, dragged her to the edge of town, and left her to die. When she regained consciousness, her wrist was broken so badly that a bone was protruding from her body. More upsetting, Sunita did not know the whereabouts of her sister, Meena. Hiding in a goat shed, Sunita cried out to God, "I can die, or I can witness. Make me a witness for you, Lord."

The courageous sisters eventually found each other and refused to renounce their faith. They moved to a different village and started a small stationery shop to support themselves.[31]

Sometimes life can throw the most difficult and life-threatening circumstances our way. Our sisters in other countries often live persecuted lives for their faith in Christ. Their faith is an inspiration to us all.

Question

Are you willing to suffer hardship for the name of Christ?

Father, help me to be a witness for you, no matter the cost.

Tamar's Payback

Judah acknowledged them and said, "She has been more righteous than I, because I did not give her to Shelah my son." And he never knew her again.
GENESIS 38:26 NKJV

In Genesis 38, we read about Judah, one of Joseph's brothers. Judah would not give his son to Tamar, Judah's daughter-in-law, so she could have children in memory of her dead husband. It was the custom in that time for a brother to father children for his brother's wife if the woman's husband died. Under the law, Judah did a great injustice to Tamar.

So, Tamar devised a plan. Hearing that Judah planned to go to the town of Timnah, she disguised herself in a veil and, posed as a Canaanite prostitute, waited for Judah to pass by. Soon, Judah propositioned her and gave her his personal seal and staff as a pledge of future payment.

Time passed, and Judah discovered Tamar was pregnant. He knew that there was only one way this could have happened—she had prostituted herself! Enraged, Judah said, "Bring her out and have her burned to death!" (v. 24 NIV)

As the people brought Tamar out to be executed, she cried out, "I am pregnant by the man who owns these" (v. 25 NIV). She held in her hands the seal and staff of Judah.

Seeing them, Judah knew he stood convicted. He broke down and confessed, "She is more righteous than I" (v. 26 NIV).

Tamar took a bold action to force her father-in-law to do what God's law required to ensure the family would continue through her (see Deuteronomy 25:5). In today's culture, we might disagree with her method, but this story reveals the courage of Tamar to confront an injustice and to uphold the law of God.

Question

Are you called to address injustices?

Father, help me be a catalyst to address injustices where I see them.

Disobedience Rooted in Fear

Moses said to them,
"No one is to keep any of it until morning."
EXODUS 16:19 NIV

Have you ever seen God do something really good in your life only to find that you have abused the blessing he gave you? Such was the case of the Israelites as they were traveling through the desert on their way to the promised land. God was providing for them in miraculous ways. He provided manna for them as their bread each day. God said each one was to gather only what he or she needed for that day. No one was to keep it until the next morning.

"However, some of them paid no attention to Moses; they kept part of it until morning, but it was full of maggots and began to smell. So Moses was angry with them" (v. 20). God was teaching the Israelites daily trust in his provision for them. God put a self-destruct feature in the manna. Yet God also told them to gather two days' worth on the sixth day so that they would have manna to eat on the seventh day and, therefore, would not have to gather on the Sabbath. Interestingly, this manna did not spoil.

When we operate out of fear, we can expect the Lord to lovingly discipline us in order to help us learn to trust him. There is a danger when we seek to "insure ourselves" against calamity. If your actions are born from fear, you can expect God to demonstrate his loving reproof so that you might not live in fear.

Question

Do you ever feel like you need to hoard for fear of not having enough?

Father, I trust you for my daily provision.

Your Testimony

*The beautiful message you've heard right from the start
is that we should walk in self-sacrificing love toward one another.*

1 JOHN 3:11 TPT

Over the last several years, I have seen two distinct types of Christian workplace believers. One type enthusiastically teaches their Bible knowledge to others. These people, though they may be genuine in their motive, often lack one essential ingredient to being effectively used by God: a testimony. The second type of people I have encountered has a genuine testimony of what God is doing and continues to do in their lives. This was the case in the early church. Men and women were able to give powerful testimony of events and experiences that could only be explained as a work of God.

God desires to build a testimony in each of us. Each of us is one of God's chosen vessels to reflect his power in and through us. When others see this power reflected, they are impacted because they cannot explain that power. God desires to frame your life with experiences designed to reflect the character and nature of Christ. Sometimes these events can be very devastating, but they are designed to reveal his power in and through us.

Question

What would others say your testimony is today? Can others see God's work in your life?

Father, reveal your life through my activities so others can see my life as a testimony of your grace and power.

Learning from Failure

Then Peter came to Him and said, "Lord, how often shall my brother sin against me, and I forgive him? Up to seven times?" Jesus said to him, "I do not say to you, up to seven times, but up to seventy times seven."

MATTHEW 18:21–22 NKJV

The apostle Peter was one of three disciples who walked with Jesus closer than the other nine. He was the most enthusiastic and the one man who was willing to step into territories where others would not dare. He was the first to step out of the boat and walk on water. His ardent desire to protect Jesus led to Jesus rebuking him for having a demon influence him. As Peter matured, the Holy Spirit harnessed his many extreme emotions.

The greatest trial for Peter was when he denied the Lord just before Jesus was crucified. Three times he denied knowing Jesus. Jesus predicted that the cock would crow after the third time just to reinforce the prophecy to Peter. Peter was crushed when he realized he had failed his Lord so badly.

The Lord forgave Peter for his denial. However, gaining forgiveness from Jesus was not the most difficult part for Peter. The hard part was forgiving himself. As we mature in the faith, we begin moving in victory after victory with our Lord. Then out of nowhere, an event happens that reveals our true sin nature. We cannot believe that we are capable of such sin.

Question

What is the root of our inability to forgive ourselves? It is pride at its deepest level. We are making an assumption that we should never have sinned and that we are too mature to sin.

Father, help me forgive myself whenever I fall short.

May It Be

Mary responded, saying, "Yes! I will be a mother for the Lord! As his servant, I accept whatever he has for me. May everything you have told me come to pass." And the angel left her.

LUKE 1:38 TPT

Have you ever had a boss give you an assignment that had rules you never used before? That must have been the way Mary, the mother of Jesus, felt.

God was about to do something so extraordinary that it required a face-to-face meeting with Mary and his messenger angel, Gabriel. What God was about to do was so foreign that it needed detailed explanation.

Mary was going to become pregnant while yet unmarried, something totally taboo in her culture. In fact, unmarried women were stoned to death if found to be with child. So, when Mary heard the assignment and responded by saying, "May it be done" (Luke 1:38 HCSB), this tells us what a courageous woman of faith she must have been.

She did not understand the implications. She would have to trust the explanation to Joseph, who was not going to understand. In fact, he immediately considered divorce proceedings when he found out she was pregnant.

God sent an angel to Joseph to explain the situation through a dream. I am sure the time between Mary telling him about her pregnancy and his dream must have been a difficult time for both of them. Mary did not know God was going to solve the problem. This is another example of her faith and courage. I would imagine most women might have responded to the angel like this: "I won't do it unless you tell my husband!"

Question

Do you have an assignment from God that seems impossible?

Father, give me the grace to obey things I cannot understand or outcomes I cannot control.

Power of the Tongue

Your words are so powerful that they will kill or give life,
and the talkative person will reap the consequences.

PROVERBS 18:21 TPT

Words have the power to motivate or destroy, energize or deflate, inspire or bring despair. Many successful executives can remember the time their parents failed to give affirmation to them as a child. The result was either overachievement to prove their worth or underachievement to prove their parents were right.

Words have the ability to define us. When we allow others to define us by the words they speak, we make them an idol. Your identity must always be in Christ.

Many a wife has lost her ability to love because of a critical husband. Many a husband has left a marriage because of words of disrespect and ungratefulness from his wife. Stories abound regarding the power of words. There are just as many stories of those who have been encouraged, challenged, and comforted with words that made a difference in their lives.

Jesus knew the power of words. He used parables to convey his principles of the kingdom of God. He used words of forgiveness and mercy. He used words to challenge. He used words to inspire his disciples to miraculous faith.

Question

Do your words give life? Do they inspire and challenge others to greatness?

Father, help me use words to encourage and inspire others instead of tear down.

Not by Sight

For we live by faith,
not by what we see with our eyes.
2 CORINTHIANS 5:7 TPT

When I married my wife, Pamela, in 2016, she had five dogs. I had two cats, and eventually, we made the decision to give up the cats because of the turmoil. One of our dogs passed away recently.

The smallest of the dogs, Gabriel, is blind, so we built a ramp that they could all use to go down to the yard from the deck. It took Gabriel one day to figure out how to use the ramp. He's so familiar with the environment that you wouldn't know he's blind. If someone moves something out of place, he will hit it though.

Gabriel is a shadow to Pamela. Everywhere she goes, he goes. She's his security. When he's next to Pamela, he is very protective. He has an extreme sense of smell and hearing. He can sense when anyone is close to him and when someone comes into the room, and he growls at them to protect Pamela. Amazingly, he is the alpha male among all the other dogs.

Gabriel has to live by his senses and faith. He has to sense where he is going and what is in front of him. So, too, do you and I have to live by faith, not knowing what is ahead of us at times.

Question

What are you needing to trust God with today to live by faith?

Father, I choose to live by faith not knowing all that might be ahead of me.

God's Authority

"I won't speak with you much longer, for the ruler of this dark world is coming. But he has no power over me, for he has nothing to use against me. I am doing exactly what the Father destined for me to accomplish, so that the world will discover how much I love my Father. Now come with me."

JOHN 14:30–31 TPT

There is a constant war going on between our flesh and the spirit. As Christians, the Holy Spirit seeks to move us under the authority of his domain in order for us to fulfill all that we were created for. Every person was designed to be under some form of authority. Jesus modeled this in his own life. He lived under the authority of his heavenly Father. He made no independent decisions. He, unlike us, was sinless and always remained in complete submission to his Father. He acknowledged that the prince of this world has a hold on many but did not have a hold on Jesus.

The prince of this world does have his hold on many in our world, even among our brothers and sisters. The one thing most of us want the most is the freedom to make our own decisions. It goes all the way back to the garden of Eden when the decision was made to exercise a personal right: freedom to decide, freedom of choice, freedom from hindrances, freedom from pain. However, Jesus chose to live under the authority of the Father's desire for his life. He was the ultimate model of someone under authority.

Question

Under whose authority are you living today?

Father, help me to live under your authority so that I might fulfill all you call me to do.

When Planting Yields No Fruit

*"You have planted much,
but harvested little."*
HAGGAI 1:6 NIV

Have you ever worked and worked only to yield very little from your efforts? Such was the case for the workplace believers during the time of the prophet Haggai. Finally, God spoke through the prophet Haggai to inform the people why their efforts were not yielding any fruit.

"You expected much, but see, it turned out to be little. What you brought home, I blew away. Why?" declares the LORD Almighty. "Because of my house, which remains a ruin, while each of you is busy with your own house." (v. 9)

Zerubbabel was governor of Judah at the time. He was a godly man who sought to do God's will. He responded to the people after hearing God's words.

Then Zerubbabel son of Shealtiel, Joshua son of Jozadak, the high priest, and the whole remnant of the people obeyed the voice of the LORD their God and the message of the prophet Haggai, because the LORD their God had sent him. And the people feared the LORD. (v. 12)

Sometimes God has to stir up the spirit of one to initiate needed change. God is stirring up the spirit of workplace believers throughout the world today. They are seeing what breaks God's heart, and they're responding.

Question

Are you one who will make a difference for the kingdom, or are you concerned about building bigger and better barns?

Father, make me the person you want me to be so I might be a reformer like Zerubbabel.

Reasons for Adversity

*He said, "My child, don't underestimate the value of the discipline
and training of the Lord God, or get depressed when he has to correct you.
For the Lord's training of your life is the evidence of his faithful love."*

HEBREWS 12:5–6 TPT

Do you ever wonder why we go through adversity? I've discovered four primary reasons any believer can go through adversity.

1. *Consequence of the Call*: Joseph went through adversity as a consequence of the call God had on his life. "You meant evil against me, but God meant it for good," said Joseph to his brothers (Genesis 50:20 ESV). His adversity saved the lives of a nation.

2. *Sin*: If there are any open doors of sin in our life, the devil has a legal right to sift us. There are many examples in Scripture where sin prevented God's blessing, such as Gehazi trying to gain money for Elijah's healing of the army commander, Naaman (see 2 Kings 5). He lost his job and got leprosy.

3. *Sonship*: The above Scripture verse reveals that God will send reproofs because he is treating us as sons and daughters who need correction from time to time.

4. *Warfare*: We live in a spiritual battle on earth with principalities and powers. Satan wants to steal, kill, and destroy from our lives (see John 10:10).

Question

Are you in the midst of adversity right now and need clarity on the reasons for your adversity?

Father, reveal to me the source of my adversity so I can respond in your power.

Humility in Relationships

God resists you when you are proud but multiplies grace and favor when you are humble.

1 Peter 5:5 tpt

I'll never forget the first time I discovered what a feeling was. It was in my early forties. *Surely not!* you may be thinking. Yes, it is true. Since then, I have discovered many men still live in this condition. It took an older mentor to help me understand the difference between information and a feeling. Many wives are frustrated because their husbands share information but not their feelings. They want to know what is going on inside their men. The fact is, most men have not been taught to identify feelings, much less how to share them. It is something that men must learn to do because it is not a natural trait.

Emotional vulnerability is especially hard for men. Author Dr. Larry Crabb states:

> Men who as boys felt neglected by their dads often remain distant from their own children. The sins of fathers are passed on to children, often through the dynamic of self-protection. It hurts to be neglected, and it creates questions about our value to others. So to avoid feeling the sting of further rejection, we refuse to give that part of ourselves we fear might once again be received with indifference.[32]

Perhaps you have a father, husband, or son who struggles with understanding feelings. You might be God's catalyst to help them recognize their feelings and be able to better share them with you or others with whom they are in relationship.

Question

Does the man in your life struggle with sharing his feelings?

Father, help me open the door to the men in my life who need to better understand how to share their feelings.

Perception Is Not Reality

"The lions may roar and growl,
yet the teeth of the great lions are broken."
JOB 4:10 NIV

In the advertising business, we often say that "perception is reality" for the person who views our advertising message. It does not matter whether the audience believes the message to be true, only that they *perceive* it to be true. Their actions will be the same whether they believe it or only perceive it.

The enemy of our souls is very good at this game. He may bring on us what we perceive to be true when it is a lie. It may appear that there is no way around a situation. He may bring great fear on us. When we buy into his lie, we believe only what we have chosen to perceive to be true. It usually has no basis of truth. Such was the case when Peter looked on the waters during a night boat journey with the other disciples. At first glance, he and the disciples screamed with fear, thinking that what they saw was a ghost. It was Jesus (Matthew 14:26).

Satan's name means "accuser." He travels to and fro to accuse the brethren. Behind that front is a weak, toothless lion with a destination that has already been prepared in the great abyss. He knows his destination, but he wants to bring as many with him as possible, so he often has a big roar but little bite.

Question

Have you ever perceived something that wasn't true?

Father, help me discern the difference between perception and reality.

When God Speaks

"The LORD is with you,
mighty warrior."

JUDGES 6:12 NIV

Has God ever spoken directly to you in such a way that you knew it was actually his voice speaking to you specifically? I don't mean just an appropriate verse of Scripture or a circumstance that seemed probable that it was coming from God. I am talking about a situation when you knew that you knew it was the God of the universe speaking directly to you.

In the book *Experiencing God*, authors Henry Blackaby and Claude King say that one of seven important steps to experiencing God in everyday life is knowing how God speaks to us. "God speaks by the Holy Spirit through the Bible, prayer, circumstances, and the church to reveal Himself, His purposes, and His ways."[33] You can examine the life of every major character in the Bible and see this principle expressed in the way God worked in each of their lives.

One of the ways God speaks is through others. Throughout history, God often used others to speak to individuals, especially in the Old Testament, when God often spoke through the prophets. This is still one of the ways he speaks today.

God desires to encourage us by speaking to us. He does this in many ways. The next time someone speaks into your life, prayerfully consider whether God is using that person to convey something important he wants you to know.

Question

Is your heart open to hearing God's voice in your life?

Father, help me to discern your voice in my daily activities.

Receiving Your Inheritance

The Danites failed to conquer their territory,
so they went up and fought with Leshem and captured it.
They put the sword to it, took possession of it, and lived in it.

JOSHUA 19:47 NET

What is the spiritual inheritance God has reserved for you? When God told the Israelites they were going to receive the promised land, it was not given to them on a silver platter. In fact, they would encounter thirty-nine battles while taking the land God promised to them. It took a joint effort between God and the Israelites to engage and battle the enemy that maintained control of the land.

God has given you and me a spiritual inheritance that must be won in the heavenlies and the natural world. A dear friend and mentor once counseled me after watching my life over a period of time, and he said, "The Lord has given you a spiritual inheritance. That inheritance lies in relationships, and because it lies in relationships, that is the place the enemy has attacked you most. The enemy always attacks us in the area where we are to receive our inheritance. You must walk in faithfulness and obedience to his righteousness in how you deal with relationships." These were words of wisdom that have since guided my path. The Lord has proven these words to be true.

Question

What is the spiritual inheritance he has reserved for you? What areas of your inheritance must you take possession of?

Father, give me the grace to contend for my inheritance.

Being Fully Persuaded

He never stopped believing God's promise, for he was made strong in his faith to father a child. And because he was mighty in faith and convinced that God had all the power needed to fulfill his promises, Abraham glorified God!

ROMANS 4:20–21 TPT

Why did God consider Abraham a righteous man? It was because Abraham looked beyond his own limitations of age and strength and considered God as the one who could accomplish his own goals. Abraham came to a place in his life where he realized it had little to do with him and all to do with God. His part was initiating the faith within himself.

> Against all hope, Abraham in hope believed and so became the father of many nations, just as it had been said to him, "So shall your offspring be." Without weakening in his faith, he faced the fact that his body was as good as dead—since he was about a hundred years old—and that Sarah's womb was also dead. Yet he did not waver through unbelief regarding the promise of God, but was strengthened in his faith and gave glory to God. (Romans 4:18–20 NIV)

Question

What are the things in your life that seem impossible? What are the mountains in your life? Are these there in order to build your faith in the one who can enable you to ascend to the peak?

Father, help me to walk in faith so that you will accomplish great things through me, just like you did Abraham.

Faithfulness in Our Calling

"The LORD is with you when you are with him.
If you seek him, he will be found by you,
but if you forsake him, he will forsake you."

2 CHRONICLES 15:2 NIV

Asa was the king of Judah from 912–872 BC. He reigned for forty-one years and was known as a good king who served the Lord with great zeal. He reformed many things. He broke down idol worship to foreign gods; he put away male prostitutes and even removed his own mother from being queen because she worshiped an idol. The Scriptures say that as long as he sought the Lord, the Lord prospered Asa's reign.

However, Asa was not totally faithful in his calling. There came a time in his life when he made a decision to no longer trust in the God of Israel. The prophet Hanani came to Asa to inform him that God's blessing was no longer on his life because of an ungodly alliance he had made. "You have done a foolish thing, and from now on you will be at war" (16:9).

Even if we began well, there are no guarantees that we will finish well. It is only through God's grace that we can be faithful to our calling. Each of us is capable of falling away from God. However, he strengthens those whose hearts are fully committed to him.

Question

Are you confident that God is behind your plans?

Father, help me be faithful to the purposes you have for my life.

For Better or Worse

*For this reason a man is to leave his father and his mother
and lovingly hold to his wife, since the two have become joined as one flesh.*
EPHESIANS 5:31 TPT

I always admired the marriage of Ronald and Nancy Reagan. *Time* magazine published a story on seven marriage lessons that we can learn from the Reagans' marriage:

1. *Be each other's best friend.* They genuinely liked being with each other, and their children often recalled their times alone when sharing a meal in front of the TV.
2. *Always have each other's back.* Nancy defended President Reagan when the media or political enemies attacked him.
3. *Show respect for each other's opinions.* The Reagans genuinely valued each other's opinions and perspectives.
4. *Encourage one another's dreams.* They shared in what each other's dreams were and how they might achieve them together.
5. *Participate in each other's struggles.* There were many struggles in their lives. Most noteworthy was when President Reagan got Alzheimer's. Nancy cared for her husband for many years before his passing.
6. *Have fun together.* They often rode horses together on their ranch. They loved doing things that were fun together.
7. *Never give up on your partner.* No matter how tough the situation or great the challenge, the Reagans were committed to each other.[34]

Question

If you are married, are you fully committed to each other?

Father, help me to be a faithful woman in my relationships.

Deborah, God's Judge

Now Deborah, a prophet, the wife of Lappidoth,
was leading Israel at that time.

JUDGES 4:4 NIV

Have you ever had to mobilize others to keep your enemies from destroying your people and their livelihoods? That is the story of Deborah, a prophet and national judge for Israel. Her story is found in the book of Judges.

Deborah was more than a judge. She was a wife, a prophetess, and a defender of Israel. When enemies were threatening her nation, she kicked into action. The nation was in a crisis with powerful enemies seeking to destroy them. They greatly outnumbered Israel and had many armored chariots. Israel had no such weapons.

Deborah saw the crisis situation of her people and decided to act at God's direction. So she summoned a warrior named Barak, the son of Abinoam, and delivered a firm instruction: "The LORD, the God of Israel, commands you: 'Go, take with you ten thousand men of Naphtali and Zebulun and lead them up to Mount Tabor'" (v. 6). Deborah had a plan to try to draw King Jabin's general, Sisera, out to meet the challenge of Barak and his men. But Barak was not quite sold on the idea. He required Deborah to join him in the battle, which she courageously did.

God gave Deborah and Barak victory that day, so much so that not a man on the enemy's side was left standing. Like Moses and Esther, Deborah was chosen by God to stand in the gap for her nation in a time of crisis.

Question

Has God ever required you to take up a cause on behalf of others?

Father, may I have the courage to respond when you call me to stand in the gap for others.

Fear Keeps Us from Our Destiny

The believers were wonderfully united as they met regularly in the temple courts in the area known as Solomon's Porch. No one dared harm them, for everyone held them in high regard.
ACTS 5:13 TPT

Every workday in thousands of offices across the globe, Christians testify of God's grace in their lives in some way. Sometimes it comes through a subtle performance of their duties with a smile and peace that nonbelievers cannot understand. In other cases, there might be more visible, unexplainable examples of God's work. This was the defining difference in believers in the early church. They lived a life that followed Christ's example with signs and wonders that could not be humanly explained.

> The apostles performed many signs and wonders among the people. And all the believers used to meet together in Solomon's Colonnade. No one else dared join them, even though they were highly regarded by the people. Nevertheless, more and more men and women believed in the Lord and were added to their number. (vv. 12–14 NIV)

How often we have heard nonbelievers acknowledge their respect for the Christian workplace believer, but they dare not join them in their persuasion. It is this fear of the unknown that keeps many a nonbeliever on the path to hell.

Question

Whom has God placed in your path today for you to help detour from a path of eternal torment to a path of freedom and eternal life?

Father, give me a divine appointment that might be the turning point for someone who is lost.

Divine Appointments

*"When they arrest you, don't worry about how to speak or what you are to say,
for the Holy Spirit will give you at that very moment the words to speak.
It won't be you speaking but the Spirit of your Father speaking through you."*
MATTHEW 10:19–20 TPT

Os is now taking over this division. He will be managing all of these activities from now on. You should know that he has a different management philosophy than what you may have experienced before. He has a biblical management philosophy. Os, would you like to explain what they could expect from you in this regard?"

These were the words spoken about me by a non-Christian CEO when he decided to increase my responsibilities in the company. We had never spoken of spiritual issues before.

Each business day, you and I will have the opportunity to stand before presidents, marketing directors, secretaries, or other coworkers to create a defining moment. When that happens, there is a good chance you will be thought of as someone to avoid. You might be considered "religious" or "fanatical." If so, consider this a great compliment because it says you are standing apart from the crowd.

You may never be flogged for your faith. However, you may very well be brought before others to give account for what you believe. It may be at a water cooler, or it could be during lunch with a coworker. In whatever situation you find yourself, the Holy Spirit awaits the opportunity to speak through your life to that person who needs to hear.

Question

Are you available to God to testify of God's work in your life?

Father, use me to speak to someone about you today.

Living an Obedience-Based Life

"They trusted in him and defied the king's command and were willing to give up their lives rather than serve or worship any god except their own God."
DANIEL 3:28 NIV

Have you ever known someone who lived an outcome-based Christian experience? This means that their decisions are made based on the positive or negative outcome, not on absolute obedience.

Shadrach, Meshach, and Abednego were three men who lived an obedience-based life. When King Nebuchadnezzar passed a law that said all were to worship his idol, these young men determined they would not worship anything other than God. You can be sure these men did not make this decision at the time of the decree. Their decision had been made years earlier. Their convictions were already in their hearts.

Each of us must come to a place of knowing what our boundaries are in given situations. What will you tolerate from your employer? What situation crosses the line for you? Where are the boundaries for questionable practices in your life? If you do not work these out ahead, you will live a life of situational ethics, determining what decision to make based on the merits of the situation.

Shadrach, Meshach, and Abednego were willing to die for what they believed. In this case, they were delivered from the fiery furnace. God used their faithfulness to impact a king, and they were promoted to higher positions. And, in this case, God delivered them.

Question

Are you an obedience-based Christian? Or are there situations that can move you based on the outcome?

Father, help me stand firm on the issues that are important to you, no matter what the outcome may be.

My God Shall Provide

I am convinced that my God will fully satisfy every need you have, for I have seen the abundant riches of glory revealed to me through Jesus Christ!
PHILIPPIANS 4:19 TPT

Have you ever gone through a time of complete dependence on God for your material needs? Perhaps you lost a job and could not generate income on your own. Perhaps you got sick and could not work. There are circumstances in our lives that can put us in this place.

When God brought the people of Israel out of Egypt through the desolate desert, they had no ability to provide for themselves. God met their needs supernaturally each day by providing manna from heaven. Each day they would awake to one day's portion of what they needed. This was a season in their lives to learn dependence and the faithfulness of God as provider. By and by, they entered the promised land. When they did, God's "supernatural provision" was no longer required. The manna stopped the day after they ate this food from the land, but that year, they ate of the produce of Canaan (see Joshua 5:12). In both cases, God provided for their needs.

For most of us, we derive our necessities of life through our work. Sometimes it appears it is all up to us; sometimes it appears it is all up to God. In either case, we must realize that the Lord is our provider; the job is only an instrument of his provision. He requires our involvement in either case.

Question

Can you acknowledge the Lord as the provider of every need you have today?

Father, thank you for being my faithful provider.

Remaining Vertical with God

*When he was verbally abused, he did not return with an insult;
when he suffered, he would not threaten retaliation.
Jesus faithfully entrusted himself into the hands of God,
who judges righteously.*

1 PETER 2:23 TPT

Have you ever been wrongfully accused? Oh, the need to defend and justify becomes so great. *What will people think if they believe these things are true?* we reason. Imagine what Jesus thought as they hurled insults and threats upon him. The God of the universe had visited earth only to be slandered and accused of blasphemy.

Jesus could have done two things in response. He could have used his power to put the people in their place. In other words, he could have responded "horizontally" and fixed the problem right then. However, he chose to respond in a different way. "He entrusted himself to him who judges justly" (1 Peter 2:23 NIV).

It requires great faith to entrust ourselves to God in the midst of personal assault. However, if we can do this, we will discover a level of grace and wisdom that will be birthed from this experience that we never thought possible. We will discover a freedom in God that we never knew before. Whenever we suffer for righteousness without seeking to protect our reputation and rights, we are placing our total faith in the one who can redeem us. This activates God's grace in our lives and enables us to experience God's presence like never before.

Question

Are you being persecuted for what you believe?

Father, help me to keep a vertical relationship with you today and to trust you to solve any problem I may have.

Labor Alone Will Not Satisfy

All the labor of man is for his mouth,
and yet the soul is not satisfied.
ECCLESIASTES 6:7 NKJV

How would you feel about yourself if your job were removed from you tomorrow? Let's imagine that your income wouldn't change, just what you did every day.

One of the schemes that Satan uses in the life of the Christian worker is to get her to view her value solely based on the type of work she does and how well she does it. We call this performance-based acceptance. It says, "As long as I have a good job and I do it well, I have self-esteem."

This is a "slippery slope" and can be used by Satan to keep our focus on our performance versus Christ. We are never to find our value in what we do. Instead, our value is solely based on who we are in Christ. The apostle Paul wrestled with this after he came to faith in Christ. He had grown to the top of his field as a Jewish leader.

If anyone else thinks he may have confidence in the flesh, I more so: circumcised the eighth day, of the stock of Israel, of the tribe of Benjamin, a Hebrew of the Hebrews; concerning the law, a Pharisee; concerning zeal, persecuting the church; concerning the righteousness which is in the law, blameless. But what things were gain to me, these I have counted loss for Christ. (Philippians 3:4–7)

You'll never really know the degree to which your self-esteem is rooted in your work until your work is removed. Unemployment, illness, or a financial crisis that leads to job loss can bring this to light.

Question

Is your value in life dependent on your work?

Father, thank you that my identity is in knowing you and you only.

Pleasing to the Lord

"It must be prepared with oil on a griddle;
bring it well-mixed and present the grain offering
broken in pieces as an aroma pleasing to the LORD."

LEVITICUS 6:21 NIV

There is a requirement to be blessed at a deeper spiritual level by God. Christ requires it of each of his servants. He required it of Paul when he struck Paul down on the Damascus road. He required it of Joseph when his brothers left him in the pit and then sold him into slavery. He required it of Jacob when he left his homeland penniless and needy. He required it of most every major leader that he used significantly: brokenness.

Brokenness cannot be achieved on your own. It is something God does himself. We cannot determine that we are going to be broken, but we can refuse to become broken. When God begins this deeper work in our lives, we can kick and scream and refuse the process. We can manipulate and strive to stay on top, but this only delays his work.

Pride and mammon are ruling strongholds of the workplace. Brokenness is considered a weak position in the workplace. However, God says until we are broken, we cannot be an aroma pleasing to the Lord. God wants you to be an aroma in the workplace. In order for this to happen, you and I must be a broken vessel in his hand.

Question

Is God taking you through a time of brokenness? If so, embrace it.

Father, make me a pleasing aroma to you no matter the cost.

Settling Disputes

A coin toss resolves a dispute and can put an argument to rest between formidable opponents.

PROVERBS 18:18 TPT

We prayed about it. We discussed it. My friend had one desire; I had a different one.

"Okay, let's settle the issue the way the early church settled matters when an agreement could not be achieved. Let's flip a coin."

"You must be joking!" my friend lamented.

"No, the early church cast lots often to determine a course of direction and even to select the disciple who would take Judas' place."

"Okay," my friend agreed.

We flipped the coin, and the matter was quickly settled.

In the Old Testament there are many examples of casting lots for determining a decision. We hear little of this method today. Most of us do not want to release the decision process to this seemingly "flippant" process, yet the Lord says, "The lot is cast into the lap, but its every decision is from the LORD" (Proverbs 16:33 NIV).

Flipping a coin is the equivalent to casting a lot. It removes our own opinions and leaves the final outcome to the Lord. Pray before you take such an action.

I believe the Lord would first have us make decisions through agreement and continued prayer for the decision. However, there are times when this approach can be the quickest and simplest. It removes each person's temptation to lord it over the other. Cast the lot and settle the dispute.

Question

Do you have disputes with someone close to you?

Father, help me to work through disagreements with others with grace.

Seekers of God

The Lord looks down in love, bending over heaven's balcony. God looks over all of Adam's sons and daughters, looking to see if there are any who are wise with insight—any who search for him, wanting to please him.

PSALM 53:2 TPT

Are you a woman who is a seeker of God? The Lord delights in seeing those children of his who truly understand the meaning of life and why there is only one thing worth seeking, God himself.

I can always tell when I have not been seeking God. The cares of this life, the urgent over the important, and the petty irritations—these are the symptoms of a life that has not been in the presence of God. Do we understand, really understand? That is the question God raises to each of us. If we understand, then why do we spend day after day toiling and fretting over what doesn't matter? Can we set proper boundaries in our lives that don't allow our time with him to be continually stolen away? It is a challenge in a world that screams, "Activity, activity!"

Be intentional about your time with your Lord. Make it a priority time in your life.

Question

Do you have a consistent time for seeking him in your life? Are you committed to developing that intimacy with your Lord that he so desires?

Father, make spending time with you a longing of my heart.

Proving the Word of God

His feet were bruised by strong shackles and his soul was held by iron.
God's promise to Joseph purged his character until it was time
for his dreams to come true.

PSALM 105:18–19 TPT

God spoke to Joseph as a young boy through a dream and vision regarding his future. He could not understand its complete meaning at the time, but he knew it had great significance. Joseph knew God had a destiny for his life. However, the proving of that word from God was filled with thirteen years of waiting, rejection, pain, sorrow, and, on occasion, questioning God's faithfulness.

His life was all but a life of influence and impact as a prisoner and slave. No doubt he wondered whether that dream was simply some vain imagination. David must have felt the same when he was anointed king over Israel as a young man only to spend years fleeing from King Saul.

God's preparation for greatness in his kingdom is often filled with difficulty. God is more concerned about developing the inner life of his servant. That inner life can only be prepared by removing all self-confidence and replacing it with God-confidence. God-confidence is only developed in the furnace of life. This is the place where the foundations of your soul mature. Let him prove your faith.

Question

Is the Lord proving his word in your life? Perhaps he is using circumstances and events to move you into a place of patient waiting as he puts you in the place he desires for you.

Father, thank you for allowing me to be tested for greater use in your kingdom.

The Effect of One

The people that do know their God shall be strong, and do exploits.
DANIEL 11:32 KJV

What does it mean for workplace believers to live for a cause greater than themselves in our day and time? In 1857, Jeremiah Lanphier was a businessman in New York City who was asked by his local church that was on Fulton Street—one block from today's Ground Zero—to start a prayer meeting for those in the workplace. His personal prayer was, *Lord, what wilt thou have me to do?*

Lanphier was a man approaching midlife without a wife or family, but he had financial means. He made a decision to reject the "success syndrome" that drove the city's businessmen and bankers. God used this businessman to turn New York City's commercial empire on its head. He began a prayer meeting on September 23, 1857. The meetings began slowly, with only six who showed up for the first meeting, but within a few months, many noonday meetings began convening daily throughout the city. After six months, more than fifty thousand were meeting for daily prayer. The movement spread to other nations. It is estimated that over one million conversions resulted from this awakening.[35]

This was an extraordinary move of God through one person.

Question

Could God do something extraordinary through you? Take a step. Ask God to do mighty things through you.

Father, make me a catalyst to bring revival in our nation.

Your Epitaph

He will bless them that fear the Lord,
both small and great.
PSALM 115:13 KJV

George Washington Carver grew up at the close of the Civil War in a one-room shanty on the homestead of Moses Carver—the man who owned his mother. The Ku Klux Klan had abducted him and his mother, selling them to new owners. He was later found and returned to his owner, but his mother was never seen again.

Carver would overcome all these obstacles to become one of the most influential men in the history of the United States. However, after he recommended to farmers that they plant peanuts and sweet potatoes instead of cotton, he was led into his greatest trial. The farmers lost even more money due to the lack of market for peanuts and sweet potatoes. Carver cried out to God, "Mr. Creator, why did you make the peanut?" God led him and worked with him to discover some three hundred marketable products from the peanut. Likewise, he made over one hundred discoveries from the sweet potato. These new products created a demand for peanuts and sweet potatoes, and they were major contributors to rejuvenating the Southern economy.

As he made new discoveries, he never became successful monetarily, but he overcame great rejection he felt during his lifetime because he was black. He was offered six-figure income opportunities from Henry Ford, and he became friends with the presidents of his day, yet he knew what God had called him to do. His epitaph read: *He could have added fortune to fame, but caring for neither, he found happiness and honor in being helpful to the world.*[36]

Question

What problem might God want to solve through you?

Father, thank you for giving me problems that I might solve.

Play to Your Strengths

Now there are diversities of gifts,
but the same Spirit.
1 CORINTHIANS 12:4 KJV

Have you ever tried to do anything that you were not gifted to do? I am not a handyman. If there is a household project, like a plumbing leak or anything mechanical—forget it. God has not given me any "natural" gifts for such things. And I'd prefer not buying anything that requires assembly!

I have a friend who can fix or assemble anything. It comes naturally to him, and he loves to help me. This same person looks at some of my abilities, and he marvels. We appreciate the gifts God has given to each of us. These differences have created a need for one another. God wants each of us to need one another. The Scriptures describe the body of Christ in the same way. Each person is a member of Christ's body with gifts and talents designed to make his body perform as a multitalented group, all playing to the same tune. It is when one member is "out of tune," decides he doesn't like his gifts, or decides to do something he is not designed to do, that the orchestra begins to sound off key. Imagine if the parts of the human body decided they didn't want to fulfill their purposes any longer. That body would no longer function effectively because one or more of its members were not performing the functions they were designed for.

Question

What has God equipped you for? What role has he called you to play in God's kingdom?

Father, help me fulfill the role you gifted me to fulfill in my life and for others.

Beware of the Thief

This know, that if the goodman of the house had known what hour the thief would come, he would have watched, and not have suffered his house to be broken through.
LUKE 12:39 KJV

What are the times when you and I are most vulnerable to being caught off guard by the enemy of our souls?

Leisure time is the place in which Satan seeks to take us off our normal routine of personal quiet times. In the normal routine of life, our senses are tuned to the need to draw upon God's Spirit to see us through the activities of each day. However, when we get away from our schedules and go on vacation, we can often drop these routines. We wrongfully think that we do not need to spend time with the Lord during leisure times. This is a grave mistake. The vacation becomes a test of character. During vacations, we turn freely to what we love most. This test reveals to us what is at the core of our existence.

Jennifer is a teacher in a large school. She explains that the greatest difficulty she and the other teachers encounter is the summer vacation. Just when they have brought a student to a certain discipline in their study habits, they lose them. She says, "When they come back, we have to begin all over again." It is the same in our spiritual lives. It only takes a small crack in the door of our heart to lose our spiritual focus.

Question

Do you keep up your disciplines when you're away from your normal routines?

Father, help me to keep my focus on knowing you and to keep growing in intimacy with you, no matter where I am.

Born to Pray

Those who suffer he delivers in their suffering;
he speaks to them in their affliction.
JOB 36:15 NIV

Bradley was born with cerebral palsy in South Africa. He barely survived birth. He did not walk until he was four years old. One leg was longer than the other, and he could not speak well. For most of his life, his hands shook uncontrollably. Feelings of rejection and bitterness at his plight were common.

When Bradley was seventeen, his father took his son to a healing service. That night, the young boy's leg miraculously grew two inches. Now he no longer walks with a limp. His shaking is gone. Bradley met the Savior and began to grow in his intimacy with him. God began to speak to him and develop his ability to hear and see things and to share them with others to bless their lives. Today, this young man travels around the world as an internationally known teacher and founder of a school of intercessory prayer.

One evening, Bradley walked forward at a Christian business conference with a written prophetic word for someone in the room. He didn't know who. It was the last day of a forty-day fast I had undertaken. The message Bradley shared gave a specific description of what I had been experiencing during the two years leading up to that night. Nobody would have known such details. It was a miraculous "telegram from God" that provided confirmation and encouragement of where God was taking me. God used one broken man to speak to another broken man.

Question

Do you ever question the ways of God and attribute qualities to him that are not true?

Father, thank you for taking the difficult circumstances in life and making something good from them.

Death Works in You

*We would not, brethren, have you ignorant of our trouble which
came to us in Asia, that we were pressed out of measure, above strength,
insomuch that we despaired even of life.*

2 CORINTHIANS 1:8 KJV

Have you ever gone through a very difficult time in your life? These times make us value life. They make us appreciate the simple things that we took for granted before the crisis. Perhaps for the first time, we can identify with others who find themselves in a similar trial.

I recall having an attitude of superiority over those who went through a difficult financial crisis. Because I had never experienced any financial crisis in my life, this pride kept me from identifying with such people. Then the Lord brought such a financial loss into my life. I learned a great deal during that period. I learned that the world and even Christians often treat such people as lepers. Like me, they didn't know how to relate. The experience taught me greater dependence on God, faith in the provision area of my relationship with God, and compassion for others.

When God brings death to one area of life, he resurrects it in a new way. Death works in us to bring new life and new perspectives. These are designed to press us forward to places where we never would have moved without the experience. God knows how much this is needed in our life to gain the prize he has reserved for each of us. It is his strategic mercy that motivates him to bring such events into our life.

Question

Do you know someone going through a difficult time that needs your encouragement?

Father, help me to identify, pray for, and encourage those who are experiencing hardship.

Our Work versus Our Value

*The LORD God took the man and put him in the Garden of Eden
to work it and take care of it.*

GENESIS 2:15 NIV

Man was created to have seven basic needs. Each of us has a need for dignity, authority, blessing and provision, security, purpose and meaning, freedom and boundary, and intimate love and companionship. When we go outside God's provision to meet these needs, we get into trouble.

Every woman has a need to work and can gain satisfaction in caring and seeing something come from her efforts. Many of our basic needs are derived from our work; it is one of the first gifts God gave to man in the garden of Eden. He gave him responsibility to care for and work the garden. God knew men and women needed to be productive. They needed to gain satisfaction from their work.

The danger of this is when we allow our work to be our complete source of purpose and meaning in life. This leads to a performance-based life. A performance-based life says, "As long as I perform in my work well, I am acceptable to myself and others." This is a subtle trap for all of us.

Our value must be centered in Christ, not in what we do. If we lose our job or our business, this should not devastate us if we are centered in him. It will certainly create difficulties, but God is the orchestrator of all the events in our lives for his purposes. Even difficult times have purposes.

Question

Where do you find meaning and purpose in life?

Father, help me to have a proper balance in my work and my life.

The Consequences of Faith

Therefore we are buried with him by baptism into death:
that like as Christ was raised up from the dead by the glory of the Father,
even so we also should walk in newness of life.

ROMANS 6:4 KJV

If you commit yourself to live for Christ in and through your work life, there will be a consequence of faith. You could avoid much hardship and take a much easier road in life if you do not choose to live an obedient life of faith in Christ. This is a spiritual law. None of us is excluded from identification with the cross.

When we commit ourselves to fully follow Christ, he begins a "circumcision" process in each of us designed to rid our lives of all that is of the world system. This circumcision is required of every believer.

Moses had much preparation from God for his calling to free the people of Israel from Egypt. He spent years in training as a young boy in the family of Pharaoh. He tried to free the people through the flesh by killing an Egyptian. That cost him forty years in the desert of loneliness and toil before God said he was prepared to free the people from their suffering. God invested much in Moses; however, that preparation was not enough. Experience and preparation had to be mixed with obedience. God required his family to be circumcised.

Question

Are there any areas in your life that have not come under the lordship of Christ? Is there any lack of obedience that will prevent you from being used fully by the Lord?

Father, show me any area of disobedience today so that I might repent to be used by you.

The Post-it Note

Things never discovered or heard of before, things beyond our ability to imagine—
these are the many things God has in store for all his lovers.
1 CORINTHIANS 2:9 TPT

In 1973, Spencer Silver, an inventor at 3M, created a "low tack," reusable, pressure-sensitive adhesive. For five years, the company wondered if this had any application. It became known as the product that provided a "solution without a problem" within 3M.

However, in 1974, Art Fry, a fellow scientist at 3M, was singing in the choir at his church. He'd been experimenting with the new adhesive that would allow one to adhere paper to a surface without being too attached so it could be removed easily. His adhesive paper worked well as a hymnal bookmark.[37]

Alan Amron, the credited inventor of the Post-it Note, explained how the product came about when he wanted to leave a note for his wife on the refrigerator. He looked around the house for Scotch tape and couldn't find it, but he saw some gum on the counter. He took the gum, put a piece in his mouth, and started chewing. While he was chewing, he thought about how tacky the gum was, so he took piece out of his mouth, got a little dust off the counter, put the dust in the gum, kneaded it, and stuck the note to his wife onto the refrigerator with the gum mixture. It stayed on the refrigerator all day, and his wife commented that this adhesive would make a great product. An international product was born![38]

Question

Has God given you an invention you need to pursue?

Father, thank you for giving me ideas that solve real problems in the world.

Becoming a Valued Draft Pick

*"These seven eyes of the LORD…will rejoice
when they see the plumb line in Zerubbabel's hand."*

ZECHARIAH 4:10 HCSB

We often played pick-up football as children in grammar school. Two captains would alternate making the best choices among schoolmates to make up the two teams. I was often chosen first because I was a good athlete. It felt good to be valued by others for what they perceived I could contribute. Conversely, it must have felt crummy to be the last chosen or not chosen at all.

Such was the case for Zerubbabel. He was a man chosen by God to rebuild the temple. God saw something in Zerubbabel that he could use for his purposes. The people also recognized that Zerubbabel was a man in whom they could place their faith. "So the LORD stirred up the spirit of Zerubbabel son of Shealtiel, governor of Judah, and the spirit of Joshua son of Jozadak, the high priest, and the spirit of the whole remnant of the people" (Haggai 1:14 NIV).

God made each of us to solve a problem.

Question

Are you someone God considers a choice pick in these days to accomplish his purposes or to solve a particular problem? Is there an assignment God may want you to consider for which you are uniquely qualified?

Father, may I be a woman worthy of being used for your purposes. Show me the assignment you have for me.

Walking in the Anointing

Samuel took the horn of oil and anointed him in the presence of his brothers,
and from that day on the Spirit of the Lord came powerfully upon David.

1 SAMUEL 16:13 NIV

Has the Spirit of the Lord rested on your life? Can you cite the time when God's Spirit began demonstrating his power through you?

David knew the day the Spirit of the Lord began a special work in him. That Spirit was different from most leaders. Instead of seeking power and control, David led in response to a need. Instead of being a perfect person, he learned from mistakes and acknowledged them among those he led. Instead of placing confidence in his own abilities, he sought wisdom from the only real commander in charge. David never lost a battle through his many years of leading Israel. He failed God by sinning with Bathsheba and by numbering the troops, but he learned from those failures, and he had to pay a price for them. However, God's Spirit never left David. He never left because of David's willingness to keep a soft heart toward God, even when he failed.

God wants to do the same in you and me, but he will not allow that Spirit to rest on us if we seek to control outcomes and manipulate out of our need for power. Servant leaders know that they are only a tool in the master's hand. They do not value themselves more than they ought. David's heart was fully the Lord's.

Question

Is your heart fully the Lord's to do with what he wills?

Father, thank you for helping me become the leader you desire me to be.

Independence That Leads to Sin

He arose, and came to his father. But when he was yet a great way off, his father saw him, and had compassion, and ran, and fell on his neck, and kissed him.

LUKE 15:20 KJV

The two young men had worked for many years in their family business. One day, one of the sons decided he wanted to venture out on his own. He had been under the employment of his dad's business long enough. He felt he had learned all he needed to know. He wanted his independence. He wanted to take his stock options early, which would allow enough capital to begin on his own. The other son remained behind, working day in and day out, faithfully doing his job.

The first son went out on his own only to find it was more difficult than he had ever imagined. The immediate cash gained from the advance from his dad's business was a temptation that was too great for him. He spent all of the money, failed to invest it in another business, and fell into sin. Finally, he came crawling back to his dad, seeking to be taken back as a mere laborer. The father took him back with open arms, fully restoring him to his original place. The son experienced grace and love in a way he had never known before.

When we desire independence so much that we launch out without God's full blessing, we can expect to fall on our face. Pride discourages us from dependence on anyone but ourselves, yet God says that we are to depend on him alone.

Question

Is there any pride that is encouraging independence from total trust in God?

Father, reveal any pride in me that might prevent you from using me.

Being a Woman Firefighter Hero

In every battle, take faith as your wrap-around shield, for it is able to extinguish the blazing arrows coming at you from the evil one!

EPHESIANS 6:16 TPT

Brenda was not a typical girl growing up playing with dolls. She grew up with other aspirations, like being a firefighter. In 1977, the New York City Fire Department first allowed women to take the test to become firefighters. She was a third-year law student at NYU at the time she learned of this. She passed the written portion but failed the physical fitness portion. The other eighty-nine other women who took it also failed the physical component. She believed the physical exam was designed to keep women out of the fire department. Berkman filed a lawsuit claiming the exam was discriminatory. She won the case.

Berkman served as a New York City firefighter for almost twenty-five years before retiring in 2006 at the rank of captain. In the aftermath of the 9/11 tragedy, the force lost 343 members of the FDNY in one day. Three female members of the force died on that tragic day. Berkman struggled with the deaths of close friends and colleagues, the disarray within the ranks of the department, and the renewed sexism toward women in the rescue and recovery efforts.

What motivated Berkman to fight? "For women of my generation, having grown up in the 1950s, we'd reached a point where we were tired of people saying to us, 'You can't do that because you're a girl.' We saw that women ahead of us had struggled to get women the right to vote, the right to practice law and practice medicine, the right to go to college and follow their dreams."[39]

Question

Has God called you to stand in the gap for an injustice?

Father, show me if I am to stand in the gap for those who do not have a voice.

Living as if You Were Dead

Likewise reckon ye also yourselves to be dead indeed unto sin,
but alive unto God through Jesus Christ our Lord.
ROMANS 6:11 KJV

What are the things that arouse the strongest emotions in you? Perhaps it is a rude motorist who cuts you off in traffic. Perhaps it is the anger you feel when you are wrongfully accused. Perhaps it is frustration that results from not having enough money to meet needs. When do emotions turn into sin? Anger itself is not sin. Jesus had righteous anger when they sold doves in the temple.

Whenever our peace is upset over events and circumstances in life, we have moved past emotions into sin. Sin says that circumstances of life now dictate anxiety, worry, fear, or anger. Consider the attributes of a dead man. He does not get angry when slandered. He does not worry about the future. He does not fear what can be done to him. Why? Because he is dead. Nothing can harm a dead man.

Christ said we are to live as if we were dead—dead to the temptation of responding to stimuli in our life that are designed to stir up the sinful nature that resides in each of us. We do not have to respond to that nature; we can consider it dead. This does not mean we cannot have strong emotion about our circumstance, but it means we must not sin. Christ had strong emotions in the garden of Gethsemane, yet he did not sin.

Question

Is there any circumstance in your life that is causing a reaction in your flesh?

Father, reveal any areas in my life I have not yielded to you.

The Training Ground of God

Praise be to the LORD my Rock,
who trains my hands for war,
my fingers for battle.

PSALM 144:1 NIV

David was a man skilled in war. From his days as a shepherd boy to the days of serving in Saul's army to leading his own army, David learned to be a skillful warrior. How does one become a skillful warrior?

The only way one can become a skillful warrior is to be trained and placed in the middle of the battle. It is only when we are placed in the furnace of battle that we truly learn to fight the real battles. Practice doesn't make you battle ready. War games won't prepare you for facing your real enemy in the battlefield. The stark reality of being in the midst of the battle makes us effective warriors.

Simply reading your Bible will not make you a warrior for the kingdom. Knowledge without experience is mere folly. Only when you are placed in situations where there is nothing or no one but God who can save you will you learn the lessons of warrior faith.

This is the training ground of God, which will make you into a soldier for Christ. Do not shrink back from the battle that God may be leading you to today. It may be a training ground that is necessary for the calling he has on your life.

Question

Has God placed you in his training ground right now?

Father, may I become a woman trained for battle.

What We Will Become

"The Lord is with you,
mighty warrior."
JUDGES 6:12 NIV

God always looks at his children for what they will be, not what they are now. The Lord already had seen Gideon as a leader of others, not just a laborer who threshed wheat.

Gideon was an Israelite who lived during a time of oppression from the Midianites. God had allowed Israel to be oppressed because of its rebellion. However, the Israelites cried out to God, and he heard their cry for help. He decided to free them from the oppression of their enemies. God chose a man with little experience in such matters to lead an army against Midian.

When God came to Gideon through a visit by an angel, the angel's first words to him were, "The Lord is with you, mighty warrior." God always looks at his children for what they will be, not what they are now. The Lord had already seen this man as a leader of others, not just a laborer who threshed wheat.

The apostle Paul said, "I can do all things through Christ who strengthens me" (Philippians 4:13 NKJV). God has reserved an inheritance for you and me. He has foreordained that we should accomplish great things in his name—not so that we will be accepted or become more valued but to experience the reality of a living relationship with a God who wants to demonstrate his power through each of us.

Question

What does God want to accomplish through you today?

Father, thank you for using me to build your kingdom.

It's Time for a Funeral

I have been crucified with Christ
and I no longer live,
but Christ lives in me.
GALATIANS 2:20 NIV

There's nothing wrong with you that a good funeral won't solve," I said to the woman. "I'll even send you flowers!" She smiled in response. I was speaking figuratively to the woman who was stressing out about an issue in her life.

Her problem was the same problem most of us have—too much of "me" and not enough of Jesus and the cross. Many of the daily problems in life can be solved by coming to an end of ourselves so Jesus can take over. The psalmist said, "Precious in the sight of the LORD is the death of His saints" (Psalm 116:15 NKJV).

The apostle Paul recognized the need for a funeral, too, when he penned these words:

What shall we say then? Shall we continue in sin that grace may abound? Certainly not! How shall we who died to sin live any longer in it? Or do you not know that as many of us as were baptized into Christ Jesus were baptized into His death? Therefore we were buried with Him through baptism into death, that just as Christ was raised from the dead by the glory of the Father, even so we also should walk in newness of life. (Romans 6:1–4 NKJV)

Whenever we stress over a matter, get angry over a daily circumstance, or seek to have our own way, it is a sign there is still life in the grave.

Question

Do you need to have a good funeral? Send yourself some flowers today.

Father, help me to die to self so only Christ lives through me.

Making the Lord Our Banner

Moses built an altar and called it
The LORD is my Banner.
EXODUS 17:15 NIV

The Amalekites came and attacked the Israelites at Rephidim. God instructed Moses to stand on top of the hill with the staff of God in his hand. Moses' staff represented something that God said he would use to bring glory to himself. The staff represented what Moses had done for most of his life—shepherding. It was his vocation. When God first called Moses at the burning bush, he told him to pick up the staff; God would perform miracles through it.

God wants to perform miracles through each of our vocations. At Rephidim, God defeated the Amalekites only when Moses held his staff to heaven. It was a symbol of dependence and acknowledgment that heaven was the source of the Israelites' power. When Moses dropped his hands, they began to lose the battle.

Each day we are challenged to reach toward heaven and allow God to be the source of victory in the workplace or else be defeated. God calls us to let his banner reign over our work so that others may know the source of our victory. "Then the LORD said to Moses, 'Write this on a scroll as something to be remembered'" (Exodus 17:14). The Lord wants those behind us and around us to know that he is the source of our power and success. With each victory is a testimony that is to be shared with our children and our associates.

Question

Is the Lord your banner today?

Father, I ask for your favor and power over all I put my hand to.

The New Employee

We are like common clay jars that carry this glorious treasure within,
so that this immeasurable power will be seen as God's, not ours.

2 CORINTHIANS 4:7 TPT

What would happen if Jesus took your place for a year in your workplace? Let's consider some hypothetical things that he might do.

He would do his work with excellence. He would be known around the office for the great work he did (Proverbs 22:29).

He would develop new ideas for doing things better (Ephesians 3:20).

He would hang out with sinners so he could develop a relationship with them in order to speak to them about the Father (Matthew 9:10).

He would strategically pray for each worker about their concerns and their needs. He would pray even for those who disliked him (Matthew 5:44).

He would rally the office to support a needy family during Christmas (Jeremiah 22:16).

He would offer to pray for those who were sick in the office and see them get healed (Matthew 14:14).

He would honor the boss and respect him or her (Titus 2:9).

He would consider the boss as his authority in his workplace (Romans 13:1).

He would be truthful in all his dealings and never exaggerate for the sake of advancement (Psalm 15:2).

He would be concerned about his city (Luke 19:41).

He would always have a motive to help others become successful, even at his own expense (Proverbs 16:2).

Hmm. Sounds like some good ideas we could each model.

Question

How many of these things are you doing?

Father, help me manifest God's presence and power in my workplace.

A Faithful Woman

Life's blessings drench the honest and faithful person,
but punishment rains down upon the greedy and dishonest.
PROVERBS 28:20 TPT

There is a distinct difference between the worker who operates based on living in the promised land versus the one who operates in Egypt. In Egypt, the worker sweats and toils to generate an outcome. The final objective is foremost in her mind. Outcome is everything.

In the promised land, we learn that obedience is the only thing that matters. We are called to execute and leave the outcome to God. Sometimes that outcome is very positive, yielding a return. In other cases, we may not yield a corresponding return. We may even get a negative outcome. The difference is that we know that we have been faithful to what God has called us to, and we yield results to God. God often blesses obedience beyond what we deserve. If God brings wealth to your life, it should come as a fruit of our obedience, not an end in itself.

God may call each of us to be obedient to situations that may not yield immediate, positive results. It is in these times that our faith must be obedience-based versus outcome-based.

Question

What if Jesus had considered the immediate ramifications of whether he would go to the cross? Based on the immediate outcome, the decision would have been an easy one. Who wants to die on a cross?

Father, make me a faithful woman today.

Expectations

No matter what, I will continue to hope and passionately cling to Christ, so that he will be openly revealed through me before everyone's eyes. So I will not be ashamed! In my life or in my death, Christ will be magnified in me.

PHILIPPIANS 1:20 TPT

Have you ever had expectations that did not get fulfilled? Perhaps a coworker let you down. Perhaps you were trusting God for something in your life that never materialized. Expectations can be a difficult trap for each of us if we are not fully committed to God's purposes in our lives.

Paul wrote this verse from prison to the people of Philippi. He had an expectation that his life would bring glory to God, whether through his continued ministry or his death. His joy in living was not based on his expectations getting fulfilled but on remaining true to the purpose for which God made him.

When we react to circumstances with bitterness and resentment due to unmet expectations, we're saying that we know better than God.

Once we yield our expectations to the Lord, this will allow God to work in our hearts the grace that is needed to walk in freedom from the disappointment of the unmet expectations. If we do not do this, we will allow the seed of bitterness and resentment to enter in. This seed of bitterness will create leanness in our soul and eventually will spread to others.

Question

Do you have any unmet expectations? How have you responded to them? Have you processed this with the Lord and others who may be involved? These are the steps to freedom from unmet expectations.

Father, I release all my expectations to you.

Second Chances

He prayed to the Lord, and said, "Ah, Lord, was not this what I said when I was still in my country? Therefore I fled previously to Tarshish; for I know that You are a gracious and merciful God, slow to anger and abundant in lovingkindness, One who relents from doing harm."

JONAH 4:2 NKJV

Have you ever gone through a time of disobedience with God? Jonah was a prophet of God who decided he didn't want to prophesy for the Lord. God wanted him to deliver a message to Nineveh to warn them against impending destruction if they didn't turn from their ways. Because the Ninevites were his enemy, Jonah didn't really want them to repent, so rather than travel to Nineveh and deliver the message, he hopped on a boat going the opposite direction. You probably know the rest of the story. He was eaten by a fish and spent a few days thinking about his decision.

There is a place where we all will obey. What circumstances must take place for you to become obedient? For some of us, it requires a good shake-up. For Jonah, it required a big shake-up because he was the man God had chosen to save 120,000 people. He was chosen by God to be used by God, and God didn't give up on him.

God gave Jonah a second chance. He gave the people of Nineveh a second chance. It is a lesson of love from a heavenly Father who specializes in second chances.

Question

Have you blown it? Have you disappointed someone close to you? God is the God of second chances. All we have to do is acknowledge our waywardness. He will restore.

Father, thank you for second chances.

Finding Meaning in Our Labor

I said, "I have labored in vain; I have spent my strength for nothing at all.
Yet what is due me is in the LORD's hand, and my reward is with my God."
ISAIAH 49:4 NIV

Have you ever felt like you're spending your life using your talent for nothing? Life is often spent doing mundane activities that seem to have little eternal purpose.

The great prophet Isaiah was struggling with his own purpose. He knew he was chosen to be a voice for God, yet life became purposeless for Isaiah. We all go through periods when our purpose seems to be clouded with the mundane. We see little meaning in life. On the other hand, Isaiah didn't stay in this place. We read in this passage that he knew the truth of his existence. He could look past his present circumstance and know that his real reward and purpose would be revealed in eternity. He knew that God was just and fair, so he placed his faith on this truth.

When life appears to lack meaning and purpose, remember that if you devote your life to the purposes he has for you, the fruits of your labor will be manifested in due time. "The one who calls you is faithful, and he will do it" (1 Thessalonians 5:24).

Question

Do you sometimes feel like life is purposeless?

Father, help me see that all of life has meaning and purpose.

Experiencing God in Your Business

Now faith brings our hopes into reality and becomes the foundation needed to acquire the things we long for. It is all the evidence required to prove what is still unseen.

HEBREWS 11:1 TPT

The CEO walked into the president's office after reviewing the president's new marketing plan for the next year. It was a well-prepared, thoughtful plan.

"This will not do!" exclaimed the CEO. "This plan describes how you will achieve these objectives through your own planning. I am certain you can achieve these objectives through normal business operations; however, you have allowed no room for faith in your plan. Now you must determine what God wants us to trust him to accomplish through this business. You must go beyond what you can naturally achieve."

What was this CEO saying? If you and I want to experience God in business at the practical level, we must be willing to trust him for more than what our natural abilities can accomplish. God likes to show himself in the midst of unlikely circumstances. This is the place where God receives the glory. This is how glory was brought to the Father. It is no different in our lives.

The world is looking for real faith. Perhaps you are the instrument that he wants to use to demonstrate real faith to the unbelieving business world. It will require courage, faith, and action; also, it will require risk. You may risk finances, reputation, and being misunderstood. This was the risk of all leaders in the Bible. It was a risk worth taking.

Question

Are you willing to see God move in your business life?

Father, show me how to express the power of God in my work life.

A Faithful Number Two

Jesus sat down, called the twelve disciples to come around him, and said to them, "If anyone wants to be first, he must be content to be last and become a servant to all."
MARK 9:35 TPT

Sometimes the greatest accomplishments come from the number two person in a story, whose name may never be known. Such was the case for Biddy Chambers, wife of famed devotional writer Oswald Chambers. *My Utmost for His Highest* became one of the most loved devotionals in Christianity, with more than thirteen million copies sold. But his most famous work was not published until ten years after his death, and it was only published because of Biddy.

Gertrude (Biddy) Hobbs studied Pitman shorthand as a young woman, and by the time she was old enough to work full time, she could take dictation at the phenomenal rate of two hundred fifty words per minute. She met Oswald in 1908 on a ship bound for America. When the voyage ended, they began to write to each other. They soon realized God brought them together, and they married in 1910.

Oswald and Biddy served in the World War I YMCA camp in Egypt. She took detailed notes of every talk Oswald gave. Chambers would tragically die in 1917 from a pulmonary hemorrhage after an emergency appendectomy at age forty-three. He was buried in Cairo with full military honors.

The compilation of her husband's sermon notes became a book known as *My Utmost for His Highest*. She would publish twenty-nine other books with her husband's name on the covers. She refused any compensation for her work.[40]

Question

Is there someone in your life you are supposed to support without regard for credit for yourself?

Father, make me a servant of others for your kingdom purpose.

Being an Overcomer

"Everything I've taught you is so that the peace which is in me will be in you and will give you great confidence as you rest in me. For in this unbelieving world you will experience trouble and sorrows, but you must be courageous, for I have conquered the world!"

JOHN 16:33 TPT

Why does it seem that those involved in Christian enterprise find the way so hard? It seems as though it is harder for those who are committed Christians in business. Have you found this to be true?" This was the comment from a business associate recently. My answer was a definite yes. In fact, if you were not a Christian and sought to do a similar business without regard to maintaining a biblical philosophy, the way would be much smoother sailing. It makes us think of the prophet who asked, "Why does the way of the wicked prosper?" (Jeremiah 12:1 ESV).

When the Israelites crossed the Jordan before they entered the promised land, they fought only two battles. Then after they entered the promised land, they fought thirty-nine battles. The way of the cross is not paved with lilies; it is paved with grace.

Do not be surprised when you find the way harder as a believer than you did when you were a nonbeliever. You now have more at stake among the spiritual forces that desire to defeat you.

Question

Do you recognize that you are in a spiritual war?

Father, help me stand firm against the evil forces that desire to keep me from walking in freedom in the promised land.

Small Things

Who despises the day of small things?
ZECHARIAH 4:10 CSB

Life is filled with a series of small things that can amount to something big. Have you ever considered why the God of the universe came to earth and spent thirty-three years identifying with mankind through work? Jesus grew up as a carpenter's son and, no doubt, learned the trade from his daily routine of helping his father, Joseph. For thirty years he worked. When it was time for him to begin to fulfill his purpose for mankind, he told countless stories of people and their work. He told stories of landowners, farmers, fishermen, tax collectors, and so on. He related to the everyday man because he himself was one. This is why it was important for him to have some personal work experience.

Life is filled with daily routines. Every now and then, God takes us to the mountaintop to experience his presence in a dramatic way. This is not the norm. It was not the norm for those in the Bible either. Moses spent forty years in preparation. Paul spent a great deal of his life working toward the wrong purpose until a dramatic event changed his life. Jacob spent twenty years working for Laban.

God uses work to develop character qualities that he plans to use at the appropriate time. In the small things, we develop trustworthiness with God. The day-in and day-out grind of working life molds us and makes us into what God desires. God may still be preparing you for something far greater. For now, however, you are learning the daily lessons of small things.

Question

What character qualities is God working on in you right now?

Father, help me to become more like Christ every day.

When the Lord Tarries

"For the vision is yet for an appointed time; but at the end it will speak, and it will not lie. Though it tarries, wait for it; because it will surely come, it will not tarry."

HABAKKUK 2:3 NKJV

God has a storehouse of blessings that he has reserved for you and me. However, our timing to receive those blessings may not be the same as our Lord's. God has a specific timetable that he requires to accomplish his purposes. Sometimes that timetable seems excruciatingly cruel and painful, yet it is needful.

Joseph remained a slave in Egypt and was then placed in prison after being wrongfully accused. In such circumstances, it would be easy to second-guess the God of the universe. Joseph thought he was going to be delivered from prison when he interpreted a dream for a court official, but then he was forgotten another two years. Why? An early release would have disrupted God's perfect plan.

God takes time to develop character before anything else. God could not afford to have a prideful thirty-year-old managing the resources of an entire region of the world.

We can sometimes delay this timetable if we refuse his correction. Although it is sometimes difficult to understand, the Lord is just and gracious in his dealings with his children. When he does decide to move on our behalf, we will appreciate the delay and will often understand the reason it was necessary. "Blessed are all who wait for him!" (Isaiah 30:18 NIV).

Question

Are you are awaiting the fulfillment of a vision in your life?

Father, thank you for your grace to sustain me in all you call me to do.

Living a Life of Faith

*Then the anger of the LORD was aroused against Uzza,
and He struck him because he put his hand to the ark;
and he died there before God.*

1 CHRONICLES 13:10 NKJV

A life of faith often requires us to leave God's work alone. Responding to a need out of a desire to help move a vision along can be the greatest challenge for a Christian entrepreneur. There is a fine line between presumption and faith.

Uzzah learned that presumption could cost him his life. He was part of the crew that was to move the ark with the help of a team of oxen. When the way became rough, Uzzah responded in a natural way. He grabbed the ark to steady it. When he did, he was immediately struck down. God had said it was forbidden to touch the ark.

King David mourned the death of his servant and argued with God about this loss. Walking with God in the workplace requires sensitivity to balancing our God-given talents and operating in the power of the Holy Spirit in and through our work life.

You can only grow in your understanding of this balance by being accountable to others in the process. By having other committed Christians walking close to you, you establish a safety net to keep you from presumption and the deceit of the heart. God also gives godly spouses to help many in this area.

Question

Can you recognize the activity of God in your work-life calling?

Father, show me how to work through the power of the Holy Spirit.

Bad Alliances

"Woe to the rebellious children," says the LORD, "Who take counsel, but not of Me, and who devise plans, but not of My Spirit, that they may add sin to sin; who walk to go down to Egypt, and have not asked My advice, to strengthen themselves in the strength of Pharaoh, and to trust in the shadow of Egypt!"

ISAIAH 30:1–2 NKJV

Have you ever entered a working relationship with someone you knew you were not supposed to? Throughout the history of Israel, the people were called to come out of an old way of life. Egypt represented that old way; when things got tough, the Israelites reverted to what was comfortable. They always knew they could take a trip to Egypt and find what they lacked. Perhaps this was their reasoning: "If we can't get it accomplished under the new way, why not go back to the way we used to do it? At least we know we can get it there."

When God calls us into a walk of faith, we can expect to be tested in this walk. If we enter into alliances that God has not ordained, it will only bring heartache. Such was the case for Israel. "But Pharaoh's protection will be to your shame, Egypt's shade will bring you disgrace" (Isaiah 30:3 NIV).

Question

Are you in an alliance that may advance your business but at a spiritual cost?

Father, guide me in all my alliances to insure your blessing upon them.

Waiting for the Lord

Wait on the LORD; be of good courage,
and He shall strengthen your heart;
wait, I say, on the LORD!

PSALM 27:14 NKJV

Hearing and doing God's will are two important steps that often get confused as one step. When we hear God's voice, this is only 50 percent of the process. The next important step is to know when to move. It is one thing to hear; it is another to know when to act.

There was a time when the Lord showed me I was to write. This was a major change in my life from what I was doing. As I began to write, I attempted to find a publisher for my work. This became a real frustration. I encountered many false starts, and many well-intentioned people wanted to assist, but their efforts resulted in further delays.

Finally, a close friend asked me, "Os, have you completed the book you are working on?"

"No," I replied.

"When you complete the book, God will provide a publisher if he has called you to write. You need to complete the book."

A few months later, I was in discussions with a publisher about my work. They were going to be in my city and wanted to meet with me. The day we met, they offered me a contract on my book. It also was the exact day that I had completed the book. I thought back to the words my friend had said.

God is always on time. He is never late, and he is seldom early.

Question

Are you waiting on God to answer a prayer?

Father, I pray for the wisdom to discern your will and your timing for the events in my life.

Being a Vessel to Bless Others

Generosity brings prosperity, but withholding from charity brings poverty.
Those who live to bless others will have blessings heaped upon them,
and the one who pours out his life to pour out blessings will be saturated with favor.

PROVERBS 11:24–25 TPT

One of the reasons God entrusts money to us is to bless other Christians by meeting their needs. God uses the transfer of money within the body of Christ to build unity among Christians. Sometimes we withhold money that God has designated for someone else. He wants to bless through us, but his will cannot be accomplished through us if we are disobedient.

This was the case for a business owner who tells of the time when God told him to forego a company bonus one year. God directed him to share his year-end bonus with an employee to show his appreciation for him. He wrestled with God for three full days before obeying the Lord on the matter. When he finally met with the employee to give him his check, the man said he had been praying about a financial need he had three days earlier. He had decided to borrow the money to meet his need. The amount of money he borrowed was the exact amount the business owner gave him.

God had already planned to provide for the employee through the business owner, but because he was hesitant, he almost missed the opportunity to be an instrument of God in this man's life.

Question

How many people do we let down because we feel the "harvest" God provides is all ours?

Father, help me to have an open hand when it comes to finances.

The Door of Full Surrender

We see our difficulties as the substance that produces for us an eternal,
weighty glory far beyond all comparison, because we don't focus our attention
on what is seen but on what is unseen. For what is seen is temporary,
but the unseen realm is eternal.

2 CORINTHIANS 4:17–18 TPT

I was recently sitting with a woman leader of a workplace organization as she described a question she poses to women leaders. "What if there were two doors to choose from; behind one door was the complete will of God for your life, and behind the other door was how life could be according to your own preference. Which door would you choose?"

The struggle for most of us lies in the desire to follow God completely and the fear of what might be behind the door of full surrender. Most of us desire to follow God, but few of us will do it at any cost. We do not really believe that God loves us to the degree that we are willing to give him complete permission to do as he wills in us.

If we desire to fully walk with Christ, there is a cost. We may give intellectual assent and go along with his principles and do fine; however, if we are fully given over to him and his will for our life, it will be a life that includes the assurance of his rewards in heaven.

Do not fear the path that God may lead you on. Embrace it. For God may bring you down a path in your life to ensure the reward of your inheritance.

Question

Which door would you choose?

Father, give me the courage to choose your will, no matter the cost.

Angels in the Workplace

God sends angels with special orders to protect you wherever you go,
defending you from all harm. If you walk into a trap, they'll be there for you
and keep you from stumbling.

PSALM 91:11–12 TPT

For years Sergis ran his small retail business from his store in a local shopping center. Every week a visitor would drop by to collect a percentage of his sales. The visitor wasn't his landlord; the mafia had taken control of businesses in his small country.

Through the ministry of a workplace Christian, Sergis came to faith in Christ, and God began a deep work in his life. One day Sergis decided he could no longer give God's money to the mafia.

A few days later his "friends" paid him a visit. They kidnapped him, blindfolded him, and placed him in a jail cell located in the middle of a mafia-controlled house. During the night, Sergis sat in the jail cell discouraged. Two locked doors with guards separated Sergis from his freedom. Suddenly, in the middle of the night Sergis awoke to a voice: "Sergis, get up. Follow me." Sergis awakened to a real angel of God sent to deliver him. The angel opened the doors while the guards remained asleep. Sergis and the angel walked quietly past the guards to freedom. Sergis immediately went to his Christian brothers to share the miracle that had just taken place.

This true story is living proof that we serve a God who still does miracles on behalf of his servants.

Question

Do you believe God could deliver you if you were in the same situation?

Father, I trust you for the miracle I need from you today.

Blessing God's Chosen

"The LORD bless you and keep you; the LORD make his face shine on you and be gracious to you; the LORD turn his face toward you and give you peace."
NUMBERS 6:24–26 NIV

Recently, a friend from London sent this personal account of an experience he had: "I was walking past the stock exchange in the city of London when I overtook an Orthodox Jew with his black hat and long gray beard. Even though he was a stranger, I put my arm on his shoulder and gave him the blessing which God gave to Moses to give to Aaron with which he was to bless the Jews.

"'The LORD bless you and keep you; the LORD make his face shine on you and be gracious to you; the LORD turn his face toward you and give you peace.'

"The Jewish gentleman turned around with a smile. 'God said to Abraham, "Those who bless the Jews will be themselves blessed." You will be blessed!'"

History tells us that nations that support Israel are quantifiably more prosperous than nations that do not. Conversely, nations that oppose Israel are less prosperous. This is a principle revealed in God's Word. Make a decision to be a friend to Israel.

Question

Is there an opportunity to bless a Jew today? You will fulfill God's instruction to bless God's nation.

Father, help me be a blessing to Israel and its people today.

Secret Places

"I will give you the treasures of darkness and hidden riches of secret places,
that you may know that I, the LORD, who call you by your name,
am the God of Israel."

ISAIAH 45:3 NKJV

When God takes you to a depth of soul experience, be alert to new truths and new perspectives. During these times God often leads us to amazing new discoveries.

Bible teacher F. B. Meyer once observed,

Whenever you get into a prison of circumstances, be on watch. Prisons are rare places for seeing things. It was in prison that [John] Bunyan saw his wondrous allegory [*The Pilgrim's Progress*] and Paul met the Lord and John looked through heaven's open door and Joseph saw God's mercy. God has no chance to show His mercy to some of us except when we are in some distressing sorrow. The night is the time to see the stars.[41]

I began writing *TGIF: Today God Is First* daily devotionals in the middle of a seven-year period of darkness. Today, the devotionals are read daily by hundreds of thousands of people around the world in 105 countries. God revealed to me secret things that have benefited countless others. Writing has become a central focus of God's work in me. If I had not gone through that dark time, I wouldn't be an author today.

When we go through a trial of adversity, we need to understand that God is performing radical surgery on our life designed to give us a new heart. He will reveal treasures from these secret places if we are willing to walk through the process patiently.

Question

Has God placed you in a season of isolation?

Father, I pray you reveal secret things in hidden places so I may know you better.

May I Pray for You?

Don't be pulled in different directions or worried about a thing.
Be saturated in prayer throughout each day, offering your faith-filled
requests before God with overflowing gratitude.

PHILIPPIANS 4:6 TPT

I walked into my client's office. The secretary seemed to be physically struggling with her breathing, and her countenance was different than normal. "Are you okay?" I asked.

"Allergies," she replied. "Sometimes it gets so bad I can hardly breathe."

"May I pray for you?" I asked.

"Oh, I don't want to take up his time with something as trivial as my allergies. I'd rather not waste it on me. You should pray for someone much less fortunate than me. My mother always taught us to pray at the dinner table for those less fortunate than us," she replied. The woman was touched that I would offer to pray for her. The next day I told her my prayer group was praying for her. She could not believe that I would do such a thing for her.

It is interesting what happens when you offer to pray for someone. Offering to pray for someone can be the most genuine and loving thing you can do for another person. It can be the one means of getting a conversation on a spiritual plane that cuts across religious stigmas and gets to the root of the problem—the person's real need.

Question

Is there anything too small to pray about? Do we, in fact, bother God when we make any request that is not dealing with only the poor in Calcutta?

Father, I pray today you open a door to allow me to pray for a coworker.

Being a Shelter for Those in Need

Each one will be like a shelter from the wind and a refuge from the storm, like streams of water in the desert and the shadow of a great rock in a thirsty land.
ISAIAH 32:2 NIV

Have you ever walked in a dry, hot climate for an extended time? The sun beats down, sweat begins to pour off your brow, and your throat and mouth are parched with thirst. A little shade, a slight breeze, or a cool drink becomes the greatest thing one could receive at that moment.

When you and I walk with Christ in the workplace, we become that kind of oasis for non-Christians. However, they may not recognize it at the time. Let's face it, the workplace is pretty tough, especially when Christ is not in the center of it.

When a person becomes aware of his or her need of Christ through you or me, we have become a shelter from the wind. We become their refuge from the storms of life.

Someone once said that you and I might be the only Bible someone ever reads, so we need to be something worth reading.

"Then the eyes of those who see will no longer be closed, and the ears of those who hear will listen" (v. 3).

Question

Are you available to be that shelter for a nonbelieving friend? If so, then you may open the eyes of someone who has been blind her whole life.

Father, help me to share the good news of Christ with others I may come in contact with today.

Sing to the Lord

Sing to the LORD a new song!
Sing to the LORD, all the earth.
PSALM 96:1 NKJV

She was born in Lake Charles, Louisiana. Her mother described her child as one who was a living "music box" because she was always singing. At age fifteen, she was diagnosed with mononucleosis, which kept her out of school for two years. This allowed her time to take voice lessons.

Later she attended a college prep school and decided to enter the medical field to do mission work. She completed a year and a half of prep school in six months and decided to take a year off to do mission work in Brazil. Later she would enroll in Louisiana State University and sing in the choir and even lead the choir. She tried out for *American Idol* in 2010 and 2012. In 2010, she was cut before the final twenty-four, and in 2012, she made it to Hollywood but was cut in the first round.

However, in 2015 she made her debut on an album produced by North Point Church, a large church in North Atlanta. It was here that her career began to skyrocket, leading to many awards.

Her song "You Say" peaked at No. 29 on the *Billboard* Hot 100 chart and has broken the record for the number of weeks at No. 1 on the *Billboard* Hot Christian Songs chart for any solo artist at 129 weeks. As of this writing, God honored her with two Grammy Awards, seven GMA Dove Awards, five *Billboard* Music Awards, two American Music Awards, and four No. 1 singles on the *Billboard* Christian Airplay and Hot Christian Songs chart.

Her name is Lauren Daigle, God's "Music Box."

Question

Has God given you a gift you need to pursue?

God, give me the faith and courage to pursue my dream.

Embracing the Mess

The only clean stable is an empty stable. So if you want the work of an ox and to enjoy an abundant harvest, you'll have a mess or two to clean up!
PROVERBS 14:4 TPT

I used to walk through a new home subdivision. I would often see the street filled with red clay from the land as bulldozers cleared it to lay a foundation. The job site was littered with lumber and all sorts of trash from workers, and it was generally a mess. Each house under construction looked ugly; it had all its insides exposed as it was being pieced together, yet this process was necessary to get to the finished product. When completed, the home was beautiful. The landscaping looked like it came out of a home design magazine. Everything was clean and perfect in order for the new homeowner to move in.

Our walk with God is much the same process. Often, we must go through a messy period of our lives in which all aspects of it are in disarray. It is in these times that God builds a new structure. He might remove some structural timbers in our lives and replace them with new ones. He might even add on another room. And unless this process takes place, we will never see the end product.

It would be impossible to keep oxen in a barn without having to clean up the mess from time to time. It just comes with the territory, but the result of the oxen is an abundant harvest. God may be allowing a mess in order to ensure a fruitful harvest in your life.

Question

Is there are construction process taking place in your life right now?

God, I pray you construct something beautiful in my life.

Special Callings

Nevertheless, each person should live as a believer in whatever situation the Lord has assigned to them, just as God has called them.

1 CORINTHIANS 7:17 NIV

Each of us is called to relationship with God through Jesus Christ. We are called by him, to him, and for him. Once we enter that relationship with Christ, we are called into the physical expression of that relationship. This is where our vocations are manifested as a result, not as an end in themselves.

Additionally, there are examples of special callings in the Bible in which individuals have a direct communication from God to do a specific task for him. Moses, Paul, Peter, and many others had direct communication about what God was calling them to do. Not everyone receives this "special" calling. This is not to say God is not personal with each of us. Some have had extraordinary supernatural encounters with God that led to their calling being specific to a task ordered by God.

Calling goes beyond our work and includes our relationships to others: our spouse, our children, our neighbors—and our coworkers. Therefore, the next time someone says, "I was called into the ministry" or "I am in full-time Christian work," stop that person and tell him or her we are all in full-time Christian work. There is no secular and religious in the economy of God. I have a dear friend who often says, "I am a servant of the living God masquerading as a dentist." Are you also first a servant of the living God?

Question

Do you understand that your calling through your work is a holy calling from God?

Father, I worship you in all I do. Make all of my life a ministry unto you.

"I've Seen Your Tears"

He will achieve infinitely more than your greatest request,
your most unbelievable dream, and exceed your wildest imagination!
EPHESIANS 3:20 TPT

My daughter would soon turn eighteen. She and her mom were having to make some decisions that caused her great fear and uncertainty. My relationship with my daughter had been strained as a result of our divorce seven years earlier that tore our family apart. We were having dinner that night, and the pain of the last seven years was more than I could handle. When I returned home that night, I wept uncontrollably.

A few weeks later I had to speak at a church conference in Minneapolis. A friend invited me down to the basement to have prayer with another man he knew. So, I agreed to have prayer.

"The Lord shows me you have a daughter. She has great creativity even in poetry (she won a poetry contest). The Lord says she has been in a stronghold for many years of her life. But the Lord says he is returning the daughter's heart to the father's heart. And he is going to bring her home," said the man with my friend.

Then, when I got up to leave, he said, "And the Lord says he saw you in your bedroom crying over your daughter."

A few months later, my daughter got saved on her eighteenth birthday. God began a huge work in her life. She said, "Dad, what would you think about me coming home to live with you?" Not only did she live with me, but she also came to work with me for eight years. She became a writer. Our relationship was completely restored. Today she has a great marriage and successful career.

Question

Do you need a breakthrough in a family situation?

Father, I pray for those in my family to have an intimate relationship with you.

Reflecting His Glory

They will tell the world of the lavish splendor of your kingdom and preach about your limitless power. They will demonstrate for all to see your miracles of might and reveal the glorious majesty of your kingdom.

PSALM 145:11–12 TPT

How do you measure your effectiveness in God, or should you even be thinking like this? The early church turned the world upside down in that first century. What made them so effective? Was it their theology? Was it great preaching? Was it due to one man's influence apart from Jesus?

The Scriptures are clear as to what made the early church effective. It is at the core of God's heart, and it is quite simple. God desires to reflect his nature and power through every individual. When this happens, the world is automatically changed because those who reflect his glory affect the world.

His desire is to reflect his glory through you and me, so that all men may know of his mighty acts and the glorious splendor of his kingdom.

The apostle Paul understood this principle: "My message and my preaching were not with wise and persuasive words, but with a demonstration of the Spirit's power, so that your faith might not rest on human wisdom, but on God's power" (1 Corinthians 2:4–5 NIV). If you do not see his glory being reflected through your life, then you need to ask why. He has promised to do so if we will walk in obedience to his commands.

Question

Are you seeing the activity of God working in and through you?

Father, I pray you will manifest your love and power through me today.

The Faithfulness of God

You are the Lord who reigns over your never-ending kingdom through all the ages of time and eternity! You are faithful to fulfill every promise you've made. You manifest yourself as kindness in all you do. Weak and feeble ones you will sustain. Those bent over with burdens of shame you will lift up.

PSALM 145:13–14 TPT

Have you ever had a friendship with someone who was faithful? You knew you could depend on that person to do what she said. You learned that her word was completely trustworthy. If she said she would call you, she would. If she said she'd be somewhere at a certain time, she'd be there. In fact, if she was late, you began to wonder if she had an accident because it was so contrary to her nature. It's great to have friends who are faithful.

We must remember that God is more concerned about accomplishing his ultimate purpose in the life of every believer than in giving us the desires of our heart. Sometimes this results in hardship.

The Bible is full of accounts of God's faithfulness that were often accompanied by hardship. He brought Joseph out of slavery to be greatly used in a nation. He delivered the people from Egypt and brought them into the promised land. He gave Abraham the son of promise late in his life. He delivered David from his enemies and made him a king. In story upon story, we learn of God's faithfulness.

Question

Are you a faithful woman?

Father, make me a faithful friend to others and to you.

Things I Cannot Understand

"Surely I spoke of things I did not understand,
things too wonderful for me to know."
JOB 42:3 NIV

If there was anyone on earth who had reason to question God's love, it was Job. He lost his family, his health, and his wealth—all at the same time. His friends came to his side only to question his spirituality. God had already answered the question of his integrity. Job was described in the opening verses of the book as "blameless and upright" (1:1). His calamities were not born from sin. Job acknowledged God's right to do anything in his life until one day, he could take it no longer. He questioned God's motives.

God answered Job, but not in the way Job wanted to hear. God answered him with a series of questions that represents the most incredible discourse of correction by God to any human being. Three chapters later, Job realized that he had questioned the motives of the author of the universe, the author of love. He fell flat before his Creator and realized his total depravity. "Surely I spoke of things I did not understand, things too wonderful for me to know."

Question

Have you ever questioned God's activity in your life? Have you questioned his love for you based on circumstances that came your way? The cross at Calvary answers the love question.

Father, forgive me for ever doubting your complete unconditional love for me.
I trust you for things I do not understand.

Blameless

For the Lord God is brighter than the brilliance of a sunrise! Wrapping himself around me like a shield, he is so generous with his gifts of grace and glory. Those who walk along his paths with integrity will never lack one thing they need, for he provides it all!

PSALM 84:11 TPT

If you were running for political office, what approach would your opponent take against you? If she wanted to launch a smear campaign, would there be any ammunition for her to use? Think how you would feel if the director of the opposing campaign came to you afterward and said, "Ma'am, we tried to find something negative to play up in our campaign against you, but we couldn't."

What does it really mean to be a person who is blameless before God? Being blameless before God does not mean we are perfect. No human being is perfect. It means that we so fully trust in God that we are willing to make things right when we fail. We are willing to humble ourselves continually before the throne of God. "Blessed is the one who trusts in you" (v. 12 NIV). God has a specific plan for the people who fully trust in him. He promises to be their shield, to bestow honor on them. He will not withhold any good thing from them. What a promise! What motivation to be all that we can be in God.

Question

Are you living a life that God views as blameless, which allows him to withhold no good thing?

Father, make me a person who is blameless before you.

A Woman of Good Understanding

She was a woman of good understanding and beautiful appearance;
but the man was harsh and evil in his doings.

1 SAMUEL 25:3 NKJV

There was a man in Carmel named Nabal, who was very wealthy. The Bible says he was harsh and evil in his doings. He was married to Abigail, who was an intelligent and beautiful woman. David and his fighting men had been traveling from battle to battle, and they were tired and hungry. They needed food and materials. David's men approached Nabal about acquiring supplies. They were willing to pay for them.

But Nabal flatly refused, and his refusal angered David. David's immediate response was to prepare for an attack against Nabal with his four hundred men. When Abigail heard what David was intending to do, she took it upon herself to appeal to David. Even though she had been abused by her husband, she attempted to appease David by taking food and supplies for David and his men. She did not tell her husband she was doing this. When Abigail met David, she fell on her knees and said, "On me let this iniquity be!" (v. 24). She asked for David's forgiveness for the mess her husband's behavior had caused. David was impressed with Abigail. Then Abigail went back to her husband Nabal, where he was having a dinner party, and he was drunk. The Lord struck Nabal, and he died.

David quickly moved in and proposed to Abigail, and she accepted. This could be fastest engagement in the history of mankind.

Question

Are you a woman who stands up for righteousness even at the cost of your own hurt?

Father, make me a woman who stands up for righteousness no matter the cost.

Waiting on God

The Lord longs to be gracious to you;
therefore he will rise up to show you compassion.
For the Lord is a God of justice. Blessed are all who wait for him!

ISAIAH 30:18 NIV

Have you ever noticed that God is not in a hurry? It took forty years for Moses to receive his commission to lead the people out of Egypt. It took seventeen years of preparation before Joseph was delivered from slavery and imprisonment. It took twenty years before Jacob was released from Laban's control. Abraham and Sarah were in their old age when they finally received the son of promise, Isaac. So why isn't God in a hurry?

God called each of these servants to accomplish a certain task in his kingdom, yet he was in no hurry to bring their mission into fulfillment. First, he accomplished what he wanted in them. We are often more focused on outcome than the process that he is accomplishing in our lives each day. When we experience his presence daily, one day we wake up and realize that God has done something special in and through our lives. However, the accomplishment is no longer what excites us. Instead, what excites us is knowing him. Through those times, we become more acquainted with his love, grace, and power in our lives. When this happens, we are no longer focused on the outcome because the outcome is a result of our walk with him.

Question

Are you willing to wait for God's timing and embrace God's process?

Father, give me contentment and peace to trust you for every activity in my life.

The Jezebel Spirit

It came to pass, as though it had been a trivial thing for him to walk in the sins of Jeroboam the son of Nebat, that he took as wife Jezebel the daughter of Ethbaal, king of the Sidonians; and he went and served Baal and worshiped him.

1 KINGS 16:31 NKJV

Two of the most notorious leaders who exercised evil power in Israel's history were Jezebel and Ahab. Jezebel promoted adherence to the cult of Baal, a demonic false god whose worship involved sexual degradation and baby sacrifices. Ahab, king of Israel, married Jezebel and led the nation into Baal worship. Ahab and Jezebel's reign is one of Israel's darkest chapters.

Jezebel wanted to destroy all evidence of worship of God in the nation. Ahab was a weak leader who feared Jezebel and was controlled, manipulated, and shamed into satisfying her every desire.

One of her most wicked acts was against a righteous man named Naboth, who refused to sell to Ahab land adjoining the palace, rightly declaring that to sell his inheritance would be against the Lord's command. After deriding Ahab, Jezebel had Naboth and his heirs killed so the land would revert to the possession of the king.

Beware, this spirit is rampant in movies and anywhere power exist, especially in government. Interestingly, it took a prophet named Jehu to kill Jezebel by commanding two eunuchs to throw her from the window, signifying that it required someone not controlled by sex to destroy her. Today, stand for righteousness in our culture by being a woman of integrity, grace, and truth. Take a stand against this spirit that seeks to destroy our families and our nation.

Question

Are you or someone you know being influenced by the Jezebel spirit?

Father, I pray against the spirit of Jezebel that operates in our culture, our government, and our workplaces.

Rejected for Christ

They took offense at him.
MATTHEW 13:57 NIV

Jesus taught in the synagogue in the community he grew up in. He was raised as a local carpenter's son. No one saw any miraculous powers in this young boy's life, at least none that have been recorded. But something changed as he became older. Locals would say, "Where did this man get this wisdom and these miraculous powers?" (v. 54). Those in the community could not reconcile God's work in someone they thought they knew simply as the carpenter's son. God brings every person who is committed to him out of their normal routine into a new revelation of himself that impacts others.

Jesus confronted the issues of his day without fear of being rejected. A life of obedience will be an affront to the systems of this world. When God begins his deeper work in you, it will be a stumbling block to those around you. When you are rejected for Christ, consider that Christ is affirming his call on your life and you are becoming a threat to the kingdom of darkness. How many of Satan's workers do you suppose have been assigned to thwart God's activity in your life? Those who sit in a pew from week to week and never speak the name of Christ in the workplace require few opponents because they represent no threat to the kingdom of darkness. He has placed you where you are for this time to extend life to those who live in darkness.

Question

Is the move of God so evident in your life that it invites scrutiny from friends or coworkers?

Father, I pray you will use me to impact the kingdom of darkness.

Mixing Faith with Commerce

"Your servant has nothing there at all," she said,
"except a small jar of olive oil."

2 Kings 4:2 niv

Her husband had died. There was no way to pay her debts. Her creditors decided to take her two sons as slaves for payment of the obligations that still remained. She pleaded for assistance with the only man of God she knew.

"Tell me, what do you have in your house?" Elisha asked (v. 2 NIV).

"Your servant has nothing there at all," she said, "except a small jar of olive oil."

Elisha then instructed her to go and collect all the empty jars that her neighbors might possess. He instructed her to borrow "as many as you can" (v. 3 CEV).

When the jars were collected, he instructed her to pour what little oil she had into the jars. The oil was more than enough to fill the jars. In fact, there was more oil than jars to fill. "Go, sell the oil and pay your debts. You and your sons can live on what is left" (v. 7 NIV).

God often mixes faith with the tangible. The widow believed she had no resources to meet her need. God said she had more than enough resources. She did not see the one jar of oil as a resource. It did not become a resource until it was mixed with faith. Her need was met when her faith was mixed with the practical step of going into the workplace to sell what she had in order to receive her needed income.

Question

Do you have a problem that is perplexing to you? What do you have in your hand?

Father, thank you for the wisdom to know how to solve my problem.

The Response of Faith

"Everything is all right."
2 Kings 4:26 NIV

The prophet Elisha would often travel through the town of Shunem, and in that town was a well-to-do couple who extended hospitality to him. At first, they simply offered Elisha a meal when he came through town. Then, seeing that Elisha needed a place to stay and study, they built a room for him above their house so that each time he came through town, he had a place to stay. He was so appreciative of their kindness that one day he asked the wife what he could do for her. His servant Gehazi later informed Elisha that the woman was barren and her husband was old. "About this time next year," Elisha said, "you will hold a son in your arms" (2 Kings 4:16). A year later, the son arrived.

One day the father was working in the field, and the son became ill and died. The woman ran to meet Elisha to inform him. When Elisha asked what was wrong, she did not panic and react in fear. Her response to Elisha seemed almost unnatural. "Everything is all right," she said. Elisha went to the boy and raised him from the dead. It was a glorious miracle.

Faith looks at situations through God's eyes, not the eyes of our limited understanding. This woman did not panic, for she knew something more than the current circumstance. Put your faith in God to solve any problem.

Question

Do you need to find the Lord in your circumstance today?

Father, I choose today to exercise my faith and trust you for the outcome I need.

Overcoming All Odds

"Because you have prayed to Me."
ISAIAH 37:21 NKJV

Have you ever had your back against the wall so badly that if something didn't happen to change your situation, you were sunk? King Hezekiah was one of Israel's greatest godly kings. One of the greatest challenges to his reign came when the king of Assyria threatened to attack Israel and wipe them out. The Assyrians were the local bullies of the region and had wiped out all other enemies in their region.

They mocked the idea of having a God who could save them.

"Do not let Hezekiah deceive you. He cannot deliver you! Do not let Hezekiah persuade you to trust in the LORD when he says, 'The LORD will surely deliver us; this city will not be given into the hand of the king of Assyria'" (36:14–15 NIV).

The workplace is full of "Assyrian kings" who mock the idea of a living God who delivers. Without God's help, Israel would not overcome. Their backs were against the wall. They would be destroyed.

King Hezekiah saved Israel because of one act. He prayed, and because he prayed, God moved on his behalf. In fact, God moved so powerfully that Hezekiah did not even have to fight the battle.

"Then the angel of the LORD went out and put to death one hundred and eighty-five thousand in the Assyrian camp. When the people got up the next morning—there were all the dead bodies!" (37:36 NIV).

Question

Does your workplace know that God is a living God who can deliver them from a crisis?

Father, thank you for the grace that is sufficient to overcome all the obstacles in my life.

New Things

I forget all of the past as I fasten my heart to the future instead.
I run straight for the divine invitation of reaching the heavenly goal
and gaining the victory-prize through the anointing of Jesus.
PHILIPPIANS 3:13–14 TPT

Our past can be a hindrance or a help in moving toward God's purposes for each of us. For some, the past has meant pain and heartache, and grace is required so that we do not let our past dictate our responses to the future. If we allow our past to make us a victim, then we have not entered into the grace that God has for us. If we live on memories of past successes and fail to raise our vision for new things, we again are victims of our past.

"See, I am doing a new thing! Now it springs up; do you not perceive it? I am making a way in the wilderness and streams in the wasteland" (Isaiah 43:19 NIV). Our past should only be viewed for what we can learn from it. We must move forward and avoid viewing the negative or the positive for more than what we can learn.

Someone once said, "When your memories are bigger than your dreams, you're headed for the grave."

Question

How have you viewed your past? Has it hindered you in some areas of your life? Have you relied on past successes to dictate what you will do in the future?

Father, I choose to forget the past and allow you to do a new thing in my life. Help me see the new things you want to do in and through me today.

The Real Thing

*For the devious are an abomination to the L*ORD*; but He is intimate with the upright.*
PROVERBS 3:32 NASB

Years ago, Coca-Cola had an advertising slogan that said, "It's the real thing." The world is desperately looking for the real thing. We live in a day when technology can make us believe something that isn't, actually is. Animation in movies today is so advanced they can make you believe actors are achieving the most extraordinary feats. It is an amazing deception.

There was one thing that caused Jesus to get angry more than anything else. It was when religious people did things inconsistent with what they taught. Hypocrisy is a form of deception designed to make you believe something isn't reality. Being devious is a form of deceit. God said you can't violate God's ways through deceit and hypocrisy and expect to have an intimate relationship with God.

> Woe to you, teachers of the law and Pharisees, you hypocrites! You clean the outside of the cup and dish, but inside they are full of greed and self-indulgence. Blind Pharisee! First clean the inside of the cup and dish, and then the outside also will be clean. (23:25–26 NIV)

Believers in the workplace have an opportunity to demonstrate to the world the real thing. The apostle Paul prayed that our faith may be proved genuine and "may result in praise, glory and honor when Jesus Christ is revealed" (1 Peter 1:7 NIV).

Question

Are you true to who God created you to be?

Father, make me a follower of Jesus who is genuine in all I say and do.

Drawing Near to Darkness

The people remained at a distance,
while Moses approached the thick darkness where God was.
EXODUS 20:21 NIV

Like the nation of Israel, we are each called to the mountain of God, but few are willing to pass through the darkness to get there. God wanted to reveal his glory to the children of Israel, but they were afraid to enter into his presence. They only wanted to know about God, rather than know him personally like Moses did. This grieved the heart of God.

Why wouldn't the people of Israel risk entering the darkness if it meant being in the presence of God? What did the people fear?

Perhaps they had fears like each of us. The fear of the unknown. The fear of what might happen. The fear that God might not like what he sees. Or perhaps even the greatest fear: the fear of darkness itself and what lies behind that darkness.

Many of us have been satisfied to hear about God from God's messengers. But there is a greater calling for each of you—a calling to enter into his presence. Sometimes entering into his presence means we enter through an unexpected door—a door that appears to have nothing good behind it.

Above all else, we must believe that God is a God of love. If he calls us into darkness in order to enter his presence, then that darkness will become an entry to new levels of relationship with a God who longs for fellowship with you and me.

Question

Do you ever fear entering God's presence?

Father, I desire to be in your presence every day and every hour no matter where it may lead.

The Art of Waiting

By day the L ORD went ahead of them
in a pillar of cloud to guide them.
E XODUS 13:21 NIV

How are you at waiting on God? How do you determine if God is giving you the green light to move forward? Many workplace believers make the mistake of adding up all the pluses and then concluding that God has given them the green light. Several factors go into making a decision from the Lord.

It is important to do three things before you make a decision on a matter. First, you should gather facts. Fact gathering allows you to determine all the realities of a given situation. However, this does not ultimately drive your decision, but it can put a stop to it if it violates a scriptural principle.

Second, you should ask yourself whether the Holy Spirit is guiding you in your decision. "When Yahweh delights in how you live your life, he establishes your every step" (Psalm 37:23 TPT). George Mueller cites that the stops are also by the Lord.[42] God puts hedges around us, but many times we bull our way through the hedges under the guise of tenacity and perseverance. This, too, is unrighteousness.

Third, you should discern whether your decision has been confirmed. God has placed others around us to be used as instruments in our lives to confirm decisions and keep us from the deceit of our own heart. "Every matter must be established by the testimony of two or three witnesses" (2 Corinthians 13:1 NIV). This is God's way of keeping us within the hedge of his protection.

Question

Are you using these three steps in making your decisions?

Father, thank you for leading me through this process for gaining the right decision.

Work as a Calling?

*Put your heart and soul into every activity you do,
as though you are doing it for the Lord himself
and not merely for others.*

COLOSSIANS 3:23 TPT

Martha's wedding-day program was themed "In His Time" from Ecclesiastes 3:11. Little did she know it would become a theme in their marriage. Through the years, God has continued to show Jim and Martha that events happen *in his time* and not their own. As teenagers, they had both made a commitment to full-time vocational ministry. They believed that after college, they would become pastors or missionaries.

Failed attempts to attend seminary led them to pursue business ventures and earn a good living so they could volunteer at church and give their money to church ministries. They often failed to see their own staff, customers, and vendors as ministry. For years they felt that they were neglecting their calling but later got a revelation about their work. When they began reading *TGIF: Today God Is First* devotionals and the book *Halftime*,[43] God started showing them that their work mattered and had a kingdom purpose. Reading the Bible through the lens of work as a calling was life-giving. God led them into a whole new journey *in his time*. Through conversations with friends and other business owners, God began changing their thinking about their own workplace and seeing it as a mission field. Those conversations ultimately turned into the *iWork4Him*[44] national radio show and podcast that has been going for nine years now. He makes all things beautiful *in his time*.

Question

What was the primary revelation Jim and Martha had about their work? What has God revealed to you about the role of your work in his kingdom?

Father, thank you that all of life is sacred and a ministry unto you, including our work.

True Repentance in a Nation

When the king heard the words of the Law,
he tore his robes.

2 CHRONICLES 34:19 NIV

Josiah was a godly king in Israel. However, before he came to power, the nation had fallen into all kinds of evil. One man, Manasseh, had brought the nation to a condition of inexorable evil. God finally had enough.

"I am going to bring such disaster on Jerusalem and Judah that the ears of everyone who hears of it will tingle" (2 Kings 21:12).

Josiah came into power just before this judgment. He began to clean up the evil by burning all the idolatrous temples, ridding the streets of prostitution and sexual sin, and destroying occult shrines. Then one day he discovered the ancient Scriptures in the temple that had lain dormant for years. He gave these orders to Hilkiah the priest:

> Go and inquire of the LORD for me and for the remnant in Israel and Judah about what is written in this book that has been found. Great is the LORD's anger that is poured out on us because those who have gone before us have not kept the word of the LORD; they have not acted in accordance with all that is written in this book. (2 Chronicles 34:21)

He fell to his knees and repented for the wickedness of his nation, and God honored Josiah; however, it wasn't enough. God still had to judge the nation for its previous wickedness under the reign of Manasseh.

God spared Josiah during his reign, but after he died, judgment came upon the nation. No nation is immune from God's judgment.

Question

Are you concerned about the condition of our nation?

Father, help me to stand in the gap for my nation through prayer.

Grace

When He had said this, He breathed on them, and said to them,
"Receive the Holy Spirit."
JOHN 20:22 NKJV

How would you respond to a group of fellow workers if you were their leader and you poured your life into them, teaching them all you know for three years, only to have them disband and go their own way when troubles came? What would you say to them after you were reunited for the first time? Perhaps you might scold them. Perhaps you might cite each one's offense. At the least, you might shame them for their lack of faithfulness and courage.

After Jesus was crucified and raised from the dead, he appeared to the disciples. His first words to them were, "Peace be with you!" The word *grace* means "unmerited favor." When someone loves you unconditionally, without regard to your behavior in return, it becomes a powerful force in your life. Such was the case for the disciples when Jesus appeared to them after his resurrection. They could have expected reprimand. Instead, they received unconditional love and acceptance.

Jesus understood that the disciples needed to fail him as part of their training. It would be this failure that became their greatest motivation for service. Failure allowed them to experience incredible grace for the very first time. Grace would transform them as human beings. After he spoke those words of peace to them, he imparted the Holy Spirit upon their lives. He now wanted them to continue the mission to share his gospel.

Question

Have you experienced failing someone, and do you remember how it made you feel?

Father, I forgive myself when I feel I have failed you or others. Help me remain focused on my mission as your representative through the power of the Holy Spirit.

Motivations to Call

"Cheer up!
On your feet! He's calling you."
MARK 10:49 NIV

Do you recall the circumstances when God first called you into relationship with him? Were you in need of something? Were you in a crisis situation? Every day God calls someone into relationship with him through different circumstances. More often than not, the circumstances relate to a need in their life that only God can meet.

Bartimaeus had the need to see again. He was a poor, blind beggar who had heard about Jesus and the miracles he had done. The crowds rebuked him for seeking Jesus, yet he continued to cry out. "Many rebuked him and told him to be quiet, but he shouted all the more, 'Son of David, have mercy on me!'… Throwing his cloak aside, he jumped to his feet and came to Jesus" (vv. 48, 50). That day, Bartimaeus saw for the first time. But more than that, he saw with spiritual eyes for the first time.

Each workday, we rub shoulders with someone who has not met this Jesus we know personally. God uses our needs to draw us to himself. What need has he placed in a coworker that only Christ can meet? Perhaps you are the instrument he wants to use to introduce that person to himself. It requires availability and a willingness to look for people with needs; then we must point them to Christ to meet their needs.

Question

Can you think of someone you work with who needs Christ?

Father, I pray I can be used for any divine appointments you have for me today.

Going against the Flow

The whole assembly talked about stoning them.
NUMBERS 14:10 NIV

Have you ever had to stand up against the majority for a cause that wasn't popular? God brought the Israelites out of Egypt and promised he would lead them into a land of milk and honey. The process of moving out of Egypt was difficult. They could no longer do things the old way, for the old ways didn't work in the desert. God provided for them during this journey. But there came a point in which the people forgot what God had said. Their discomfort changed their belief about God.

Whenever God is slow to answer our prayers, what we believe about God is revealed. Do we change our plans and move in a different direction when pressure mounts? Or do we continue on the path God has directed for us? Four men believed what God said and were willing to stand; however, the crowd wanted to stone them.

Joshua and Caleb had spied the land. They believed God. They challenged the crowd. They seemed to know that if the Lord was not pleased with them, they would not enter into the promised land. Those who grumbled did not enter the promised land. Only Joshua and Caleb and a new generation saw the fulfillment of God's promise.

Question

Has God called you to stand for a cause bigger than yourself? You may have opposition to his call, and sometimes it even comes from those in your own camp.

Lord, today may I "be strong and courageous." May I not be terrified, nor be discouraged, for I know that the Lord my God will be with me wherever I go (Joshua 1:9).

Defining Moments

*Just outside the city, a brilliant light flashing from heaven
suddenly exploded all around him.*

ACTS 9:3 TPT

For Moses, it was the burning bush. For Peter, it was walking on water. For Shadrach, Meshach, and Abednego, it was walking through the burning furnace untouched. There have been many defining moments in the lives of human beings that changed their lives forever. These defining moments often set the course for the balance of their lives.

You may be in one of three stages of life: You may not have had your "defining moment," yet God may be preparing you with many important life experiences. You may have had your defining moment, and you are living out your call. Or you may be toward the end of your journey, and you have already experienced what I speak of.

We are all called to a relationship with God, and we are all called vocationally. Our vocations are often ushered in by a defining moment. And there can be more than one defining moment, each pointing you down a path that God foreordained from the foundation of the world. The secret of a great life is often a man's ability to discern the defining moments given to him, understanding them, and learning to walk in the path that leads him to his ultimate destination.

Once you have had a defining moment, you are never the same.

Question

What was your defining moment?

Father, give me eyes to see and ears to hear for any defining moment you have for me today.

True Repentance

God designed us to feel remorse over sin in order to produce repentance that leads to victory. This leaves us with no regrets. But the sorrow of the world works death.
2 CORINTHIANS 7:10 TPT

What does it mean to repent? A few years ago, a client severely wronged me and ultimately took our company for $160,000. In a court of law, I probably would have won the dispute. However, after I had already filed suit against the man, I realized that there was one aspect of the matter that I was wrong about. I could not effectively resolve the matter without taking the first step.

I made a decision to drop the lawsuit. However, I discovered the client had already filed a countersuit. I was completely exposed to liability if I dropped my suit.

I got his secretary on the line. "I want you to take this message down and give it to your boss. Please do not change the words at all. 'I have sinned against you. I know I do not deserve your forgiveness, but I ask your forgiveness for filing the lawsuit against you. You are no longer obligated to pay the balance you owe me if you feel you do not owe it.'" The secretary knew me and the gravity of what I was saying. She began to weep. She could not believe what she was hearing.

He dropped his countersuit. A few days later, I went to see the man and had dinner with him. He did not offer to pay any of the balance. It took three years for me to pay the vendors related to this situation. But I knew I had done the right thing in God's eyes.

Question

Is there anyone you need to seek forgiveness and restitution from?

Father, help me to acknowledge and repent of any wrong I have committed against anyone.

Faithfulness to Convict

"When he comes, he will expose sin and prove that the world is wrong about God's righteousness and his judgments."
JOHN 16:8 TPT

One day I realized I was experiencing a great cloud of oppression that had come over me. Each day I attempted to press through it but with no success. Fear, anxiety, doubt, and unbelief were setting in. I knew I was fretting over my future. I had been in a long period of transition in my work life. I was tired of waiting. It was definitely spiritual warfare. That night, I was reading a book regarding our calling from God. The author mentioned that we can become envious of others when we get into a place where we feel dissatisfied. I realized I was envying where other friends were in their lives. I was subconsciously angry at God. I had to repent.

That morning I turned on my computer to read my own devotional that was sent to my computer. The message was "Envying Others" and included the same Scripture reference as the authors in the book I had been reading. God used my own words to convict me of sin! To make the message even clearer, at lunchtime, I tuned into the local Christian radio station to hear an interview with the same author as he cited the very passage I had read the day before. I was shocked to realize how the Holy Spirit could be so precise in his ability to convict me of sin.

Question

Do you question if the Holy Spirit is active in your life? The Lord has promised that the Holy Spirit will convict us of sin when we move away from him.

Thank you, Holy Spirit, for convicting me of sin when I need it.

A Heavenly Strategic Planning Session

*"The Lord said, 'Who will entice Ahab into attacking Ramoth Gilead
and going to his death there?' One suggested this, and another that."*
1 KINGS 22:20 NIV

Rarely do we get a glimpse of what goes on in heaven. Here is one instance when the angels were conferring with the Lord about the judgment of King Ahab.

If God wanted to use you to impact your world for Jesus Christ, what would have to change for you to respond to his call? What would your response be should God and the angels conclude that the only way to move you into a position of fulfilling God's purposes was to remove some things that might be very dear to you? Would you agree with their plan if you knew this would be the only way you would achieve the purposes for which God made you?

This is the very thing God does in many who have been called for a special mission. Moses had to be stripped of his royal position in the family of Egypt and sit in the desert for forty years. The apostle Paul had to be knocked off his horse, blinded, and receive a personal visitation from Jesus.

The reason is that we do not seek God with a whole heart in times of prosperity and comfort. Prosperity and comfort tend to breed complacency and satisfaction. We often must have pain or crisis to motivate us. Eventually, that crisis bridges us to a new calling, and we embrace that calling if we are open to the Holy Spirit's work in us. We can actually thank God for the change that was required to get us to this place, but it is not without anguish of heart.

Question

Would you be willing to sit in the strategic planning session for your life and agree with the plans God has for your life?

Father God, give me the grace and trust in your love so that I can say yes.

Moving with the Cloud

Whether by day or by night,
whenever the cloud lifted, they set out.
NUMBERS 9:21 NIV

God brought the Israelites out of Egypt, and they had to pass through the desert on their way to the promised land. God was their guide by means of a cloud that appeared overhead. When it moved, they moved. When it stopped, they stopped—sometimes a day, a week, even a year.

Imagine living with the uncertainty of this situation. One day, you work at getting your "house" in order only to have to pull up the stakes and move. Your ability to plan is totally gone. But even greater is the temptation to move because you felt it was time to move even though the cloud did not move. For the Israelites, perhaps the grass was no longer green. Perhaps the water was not easily accessible. Perhaps the bugs were a problem. Whatever the case, they were strictly prohibited from moving if the cloud did not move.

It is still the same today. We are not to move unless the Holy Spirit instructs us to do so. We are not to make that business deal on the basis of whether or not it makes sense but on the leading of the Holy Spirit's "cloud" in our life. The Christian worker must learn to move when God says move; it is a sign of complete surrender and dependence on God's Spirit to direct our steps.

Question

Ask God today if you are sitting under his cloud. Or have you moved when he said stand still? He will show you.

Father, help me to be led by the Holy Spirit in my life.

Miracles at Work

The message I preached and how I preached it was not an attempt to sway you with persuasive arguments but to prove to you the almighty power of God's Holy Spirit. For God intended that your faith not be established on man's wisdom but by trusting in his almighty power.

1 CORINTHIANS 2:4–5 TPT

When is the last time you experienced a miracle in your work life?

In my book *31 Decrees of Blessing for Your Work Life*, I talk about the power of our words and the times God calls us to speak to problems using spiritual authority described in Matthew 16:19.

Recently my wife was preparing for a speaking engagement. She asked me to print some brochures using our copier. Our copier can print multipage documents and fold them and staple them. However, this time the copier was not cooperating. It would only print single pages and would not collate or staple. I wrestled with it for thirty minutes. I was very frustrated. I told my wife I did not think I was going to be able to get her what she wanted.

I decided to do something as a last resort. I laid my hands on the copier and said, "Copier, you were made to function the way you were designed. In the name of Jesus, I proclaim that you will function the way God intended you to function! Amen!"

I went back to my computer and clicked the print button again, not changing any settings. It printed all fifty brochures, collated, and stapled just the way it was supposed to.

Question

When is the last time you personally experienced a miracle in your work life?

Father, teach me to walk in the authority you have given me to manifest miracles in my work life.

Significance

May the favor of the LORD our God rest upon us;
establish the work of our hands for us—
yes, establish the work of our hands.

PSALM 90:17 NIV

Many of us begin our careers with the goal of achieving success. If we haven't entered our work as a result of God's calling, we will eventually face a chasm of deep frustration and emptiness. So often we enter careers with wrong motives—money, prestige, and even pressure from parents or peers. Some workers think that going into "full-time Christian work" will fill the emptiness they feel.

However, this only exacerbates the problem because they are again trying to put another square peg into a round hole. The problem is not whether we should be in "Christian work" or "secular work" but rather what work is inspired by our gifts and our calling. If there is one phrase I wish I could remove from the English language, it is "full-time Christian work." If you are a Christian, you are in full-time Christian work, whether you are driving nails or preaching the gospel. The question must be, are you achieving the God-given calling for your life? God has called people into their vocations to fulfill his purposes just as much as he has called people to be pastors or missionaries.

It is time for workplace believers to stop feeling like second-class citizens for being in their vocations. It is time workplace believers stop working toward financial independence so that they can concentrate on their "true spiritual calling." This is the great deception for those called to the workplace.

Question

Has God confirmed his calling on your life?

Father, thank you that every vocation is spiritual and is a high calling.

The Necessity of the Desert

"I have been a stranger in a foreign land."
EXODUS 2:22 NKJV

God's preparation of a leader involves training, extended times of waiting, pain, rejection, and isolation. Are you ready to sign up?

Moses was brought up in Pharaoh's court. He had the very best of everything—education, clothing, food, and personal care. But there came a time when the man God would use to free an entire people from slavery was going to have to learn to be the leader God wanted. At age forty, when most of us are at the height of our career, Moses was forced to flee to the desert.

Like Joseph and Abraham, Moses had to endure some difficult years of preparation that first involved removal from his current situation. He went from being a king's adopted son to living in obscurity, from limitless resources to no resources, from activity and action to inactivity and solitude. And, most importantly, he was left waiting. And waiting. He probably thought he would die in the land of Midian.

Then one day, a full forty years from the day Moses arrived, God appeared to him in a burning bush. Everything changed. God said, "It is time." The years had seasoned the vessel to prepare him to accomplish the work.

God is preparing many today. The circumstances may be different. The time frames may not be quite as long. But the characteristics of the training are still the same. Do not try to shortcut the desert time of God. It only leads to cul-de-sacs. Embrace them, so that he can use your life for something extraordinary.

Question

Have you been in a holding pattern with God?

Father, give me to grace to accept your timing in the fulfillment of my assignment.

Lack of Knowledge

It was because you, the Levites, did not bring it up the first time that the LORD our God broke out in anger against us. We did not inquire of him about how to do it in the prescribed way.

1 CHRONICLES 15:13 NIV

If you do not commit yourself to knowing what is in God's Word and following it, you will fail to know and experience God," I said to a friend. "God's Word is life to our souls. It provides knowledge that leads to life."

The prophet Hosea tells us, "My people are destroyed from lack of knowledge. Because you have rejected knowledge, I also reject you as my priests; because you have ignored the law of your God, I also will ignore your children" (Hosea 4:6).

God has given us his Word that has specific laws and principles that must be followed if we expect his blessing. King David forgot to follow one of those laws related to the ark. When they were transporting the ark, Uzzah reached to steady the ark but was immediately struck dead when his hands touched the ark of God. Did David know this law, or did he simply forget?

Many workplace believers I know take God's Word lightly. They believe they can violate his Word without consequence. This is not true; the Lord stands by to uphold his word. It can be life, or it can bring death. When God provides instructions, we need to follow them.

Question

Do you take God's Word seriously? Is it life or death for you? Do you feed upon his Word daily so that you might know him and know his precepts?

Father, thank you for the Word of God that gives life and instruction to me daily.

The Place of Tears

He said to them, "My heart is overwhelmed and crushed with grief.
It feels as though I'm dying. Stay here and keep watch with me."
MATTHEW 26:38 TPT

Often the place of our greatest pain becomes the place of our greatest triumph. Gethsemane was the place of Jesus' greatest trial. Three times he asked the Father to let this trial pass. It was not to be. The Father sent his Son to the cross to pay a debt owed by humanity.

Jesus was faced with his own temptation to quit, to not fulfill his destiny, to run from his assignment. It was a personal battle to persevere. Sometimes we face situations that cry out, "Quit! You cannot endure anymore!" We want to throw in our towel of what little faith we have left. We conclude that this faith thing simply does not work.

"Then an angel appeared to Him from heaven, strengthening Him" (Luke 22:43 NKJV). After Jesus asked the Father if this cup could pass, an angel was sent to him to comfort Jesus.

God will use your greatest failure or greatest sorrow to be a powerful force in your life and the lives of others. Your Valley of Baca ("weeping") becomes springs for you and others. You will go from strength to strength (Psalm 84:6–7). It is in the dying that the new springs are allowed to come forth and a new strength emerges.

Question

Do you find yourself in your own garden of Gethsemane? If so, lay yourself at the feet of the only one who can sustain you.

Father, I entrust myself to you.

The Way of God

O that my people would once and for all listen to me
and walk faithfully in my footsteps, following my ways.

PSALM 81:13 TPT

God has a specific training ground for leaders. There are three patterns of preparation that have been common among most of God's leaders. First, there is a time when the leader is separated from his old life. Consider Moses, Joseph, Abraham, and Paul. In order for God to mold and shape them into his nature, it appears that he had to remove them from the life of comfort. A teacher once said, "You cannot go with God and remain where you are."

Next, there is usually a time of solitude. God often brings leaders into a time of solitude in order to speak to them without other distractions. Hosea 2:14 says, "I will lead her into the desert and speak tenderly to her there" (NLT). Paul was sent to Arabia for two years for a time of solitude. Joseph spent years in the solitude of prison. Moses spent forty years in the wilderness herding sheep.

The third characteristic of God's preparation for leaders is discomfort. The setting in which the preparation takes place usually is not a place of comfort. Abraham traveled through the difficult deserts. David lived in caves fleeing Saul. Paul was frequently persecuted.

Like the people of Israel, I think we have something to do with the timetable of our education. "If my people would only listen to me, if Israel would only follow my ways, how quickly I would subdue their enemies and turn my hand against their foes!" (Psalm 81:13–14 NIV).

Question

Are you ready for the classroom of leadership preparation?

Father, thank you that you promise your grace is sufficient in all things.

The Butterfly Principle

The LORD hardened the heart of Pharaoh king of Egypt,
so that he pursued the Israelites, who were marching out boldly.
EXODUS 14:8 NIV

Overprotective parents do their children a great injustice. The caterpillar that lies inside the cocoon will never become the beautiful butterfly if someone cuts open the cocoon prematurely. It is the struggle itself that allows the butterfly to emerge as a strong, new creature of nature.

God understands how necessary this process is. That is why we are allowed to experience difficult, often life-changing events. He even orchestrates them—all for our benefit. What the Israelites thought was a cruel joke of God when Pharaoh sent troops to pursue them after they had been freed and penned against the shore of the Red Sea became the stage for the most publicized miracle of all time—the parting of the Red Sea. Generation after generation has heard this incredible story of deliverance. God puts us against the "Red Seas" in order to show his power in and through us. If we do not know God can deliver, then we can never learn to trust him. Circumstances that go beyond our capabilities of solving them place us at God's complete mercy. This is how he likes it.

Question

Do you overprotect your children from experiences they need for their growth?

Father, protect me from overprotecting those I love so that they can experience your power.

Unless the Lord Goes with Us

*Moses said to him, "If your Presence does not go with us,
do not send us up from here."*
EXODUS 33:15 NIV

Moses was in the middle of his journey through the wilderness, leading the people of Israel out of Egypt. The people had just sinned by worshiping the golden calf. Moses interceded for them, and God spared them their lives. Moses knew he could not lead this stubborn people without God's presence. He had come to realize that without God's presence, he could not do anything. "How will anyone know that you are pleased with me and with your people unless you go with us? What else will distinguish me and your people from all the other people on the face of the earth?" said Moses (v. 16).

Moses did not want to move farther without the assurance that God was moving with him. He knew it was a life-and-death situation. He sought the Lord with his whole heart on this one matter

The question is a good one. If we are to be effective in anything we do for the Lord, the Lord must be in the midst of it. Unless the Lord's power is seen among us, we will be just another person who has religion. Unless we manifest his life to others, they will see only good behavior that is easily counterfeited by nonbelievers. Moving out in presumption will end in failure and frustration.

Question

Are God's presence and power in your activities? If so, you will be assured that you will be distinguished among all the other people on the face of the earth.

Father, I invite your presence into every activity in my life.

Will You Enter?

*Then Moses raised his arm
and struck the rock twice with his staff.*

NUMBERS 20:11 NIV

Will you fulfill the destiny God has for your life? Perhaps you have never thought about it. God had a perfect plan for Moses to lead the people out of Egypt and into the promised land. It's been said the hardest place to score a touchdown is from the one-yard line. Perhaps you're almost there. But there is something about crossing over that makes those last few yards the most difficult. Moses failed from finishing well at the goal line of a glorious life of service for God.

The people of Israel were complaining that they did not have water to drink. It was another of many tests for Israel. Moses inquired of God and God said, "Speak to that rock before their eyes and it will pour out its water" (v. 8). Moses, in his frustration and anger with the people, began to act on his own and made a strategic mistake. Instead of speaking to the rock, he struck the rock twice in anger. In spite of his disobedience, the rock poured forth water.

God was calling Moses to a different dimension. Moses was to use his words to speak the miracle. However, he not only lost his temper, but he also took credit and dishonored God. He used his staff, the symbol of his work life as a shepherd, to force the provision.

Beware of solving problems in your own strength. God wants to bring you into the promised land of his blessing. But it will require walking in the spiritual dimension.

Question

Have you been obedient to the Lord's commands in your life?

Father, allow me to be obedient to every command you give me.

The Error of Positive Thinking

*"Not by might nor by power, but by my Spirit," says the L*ORD *Almighty.*
ZECHARIAH 4:6 NIV

God's people should be the most positive, joyful people on earth. This joy should be a by-product of a healthy, intimate relationship with Jesus. In today's workplace climate, we are barraged with every possible means of becoming more productive workplace believers. Positive thinking and self-help philosophy are promoted as tools for workplace believers to fulfill their potential and overcome the mountains in their lives. God calls each of us to be visionary leaders, but we must be careful that vision is born out of his Spirit, not the latest self-help program. These ideas lead us away from dependence on God to a self-based psychology designed to give us more power, prosperity, and significance.

The result is heresy. Our faith in God becomes faith in faith. It is born out of hard work and diligence rather than obedience to God's Spirit. The problem lies in that these philosophies sound good and can even be supported by Bible verses. Beware of anything that puts the burden of performance on you rather than God. There are times in our lives when God doesn't want us to climb every mountain. Sometimes he wants us to go around the mountain. Knowing the difference is the key to being a woman led by the Spirit. God has called us to affect the workplace through his Spirit, not by our might.

Question

Have you tapped into the real power source of the soul?

Father, I pray you reveal and empower me through your Spirit today.

Situational Ethics

Yahweh, who dares to dwell with you?
Who presumes the privilege of being close to you,
living next to you in your shining place of glory?
PSALM 15:1–2 TPT

I cannot believe they are not going to honor my bonus agreement," said the executive who was about to take another position in a new city. Her understanding of her present work agreement called for a bonus at the end of the year. Management saw the situation differently. "It's not right. I am entitled to that bonus!" she complained.

It was time to leave. The company had given her a laptop to use. However, when she left, she decided that because the company was not going to pay her the bonus she was entitled to, she would simply keep the laptop as compensation due her. "And they would never miss it," she reasoned. She was now in the employment of the new company. As each day passed, she grew uneasy about her decision. She could not get it off her mind.

Finally, she concluded that the Holy Spirit was telling her this decision was wrong and that she needed to call her former boss to confess her action. She called him and confessed what she had done and why she had done it. Her boss accepted her confession and forgave her. Strangely enough, he allowed her to keep the laptop computer.

Question

Have you had any experience in which you have used situational ethics? The Lord desires his people to have a higher standard, even at the cost of being wronged.

Father, reveal to me any business practices in which I may be guilty of situational ethics.

Speak to Your Mountain

"Whoever says to this mountain with great faith and does not doubt,
'Mountain, be lifted up and thrown into the midst of the sea,'
and believes that what he says will happen, it will be done."
MARK 11:23 TPT

Monika was in her religious instruction class held on Friday afternoons. The teacher told the students that they needed to pray boldly.

That day after class, she was walking with her friends through the church basement when they realized they were the last kids leaving and someone had turned out all the lights. They found themselves in total darkness in the room.

Monika recounted the story. "We slowly walked to the door, not able to see because it was so dark. The door was locked, so we pushed it and then banged on it. We yelled but couldn't get the door open. We thought to ourselves, 'It's Friday. We're going to be here all weekend in this dark basement until someone shows up for church on Sunday!'"

She admits, "I was so scared. My mind was racing. But the message that the nun had taught us that day was to speak boldly to God. So, I said a prayer. I put my hands on the door, and I spoke boldly, 'God, open this door!' and the lock released, and the door opened. I was so amazed and happy! I went running out of that basement!

"Sunday morning when I saw my teacher at church, I asked her if there was any way to open the door from the inside once it's been locked. She said, 'No. Once the doors are locked, they are locked and can't be opened without a key.' God had heard me, and he answered my prayer that I asked him boldly."

Question

Have you ever spoken for a mountain to be removed in your life?

Father, help me to make a decree over the problems I face where I see no way through.

Be as Little Children

Look with wonder at the depth of the Father's marvelous love that he has lavished on us! He has called us and made us his very own beloved children.

1 John 3:1 TPT

I have an important business meeting in the morning," I said to my wife. "Would you please set the alarm for 5:30 a.m.?"

"Oh, that won't be necessary," she replied. "Just tell the Lord what time you want to wake up. He does it for me all the time," my wife said.

I rolled my eyes. "Well, I'd feel more comfortable if we set the alarm."

"Okay, ye of little faith. But just to prove my point, I am going to ask the Lord to wake us up just before 5:30."

The next morning, I awoke before the alarm went off. I looked at the clock. It read 5:15. I looked at my wife, who had just awakened at the same time with an I-told-you-so smile.

Sometimes we wrongfully view God as someone we go to for only the "big things." The idea of "bothering God" for such a trivial matter seems foolish and presumptuous. However, when you were a child and had to get up in the morning for school, didn't your mom or dad come in your room to wake you up? They were your parents, and you could come to them with the most trivial concerns or requests.

Perhaps our problem is that we simply have not developed a level of intimacy with God so that we feel the freedom to approach him at these daily, routine levels.

Question

Do you allow the Lord to have this level of intimacy with you?

Father, increase my level of intimacy with you. I might just be able to get rid of my alarm clock.

A Fine-Tuned Instrument

"I will refine them like silver and test them like gold.
They will call on My name and I will answer them;
I will say, 'They are My people,' and they will say, 'The LORD is our God.'"

ZECHARIAH 13:9 NIV

My business career has been as an owner of an advertising agency. Over the years, I have had the privilege to work on many different and prestigious accounts. One of those accounts was Steinway Pianos, the maker of the world's finest pianos. Each piano is made from scratch; it takes over a year to make one Steinway. The soundboard is stretched to its maximum tolerance and allowed to sit for an extended period until it remains in the curved design.

After an extended time of stretching, the wood will never spring back to its original state. It is permanently changed. The piano is becoming a fine-tuned instrument. It takes eleven tons of pressure on a piano to tune it. Each step in the process moves the piano closer to a finished product that the world's finest musicians will ultimately play. These musicians desire a particular sound that only a Steinway piano can make.

God looks at each of us as a fine-tuned instrument. We begin as rough wood that he desires to transform into gold. Tuning us requires stretching our faith, our frame, and our very life. If we can stand the strain of this intense process, we will come forth as a fine-tuned instrument in his hand. It is painful to be stretched beyond our perceived limits, but the Lord knows this is necessary for us to become his instrument.

Question

Is the master craftsman stretching you and shaping you for his service?

Father, make me the instrument of your choosing.

Confrontation with God

They will be called oaks of righteousness,
a planting of the LORD for the display of his splendor.
ISAIAH 61:3 NIV

God, is this the way you treat someone who is faithful to you?" I yelled aloud on the top of the wooded hill. "I have waited and waited, and now this! I hate you, God! I have had enough!" Those were my words that day as I wrestled with news of an event that devastated me to the point where I broke down weeping.

I sat there among the trees, deciding what else I could say to God, but I was speechless. I was angry. I was confused. I wondered if he even existed. If he did, I felt like he really didn't honor my faith and obedience. I sat for hours wrestling internally with my feelings.

Finally, without answers and sensing that God wasn't answering me, I turned to leave. I had been sitting on an old oak tree that was broken at the base. The tree pointed toward the base of another huge oak tree. Finally, a still, quiet voice inside said, "Today, like this broken oak tree you are sitting on, you are a broken man. But this brokenness was needed in order for you to become this large oak tree you see."

Years later I would realize God's word to me was true. He began to replace the pain and disappointment with an inner joy that only his grace could provide. He birthed an international ministry from my pain.

Question

Have you ever wrestled with the events of life, feeling that God has deserted you? Have you been honest with God?

Father, I trust you to help me overcome the difficult situations I may face today.

Understanding What God Has Given

For we did not receive the spirit of this world system but the Spirit of God, so that we might come to understand and experience all that grace has lavished upon us.

1 CORINTHIANS 2:12 TPT

God desires for us to know what he has freely given to us. One of the responsibilities of the Holy Spirit is to reveal his plans and purposes to us. They may be hidden for a time, but if we seek him with our whole heart, we can know what he has given to us.

John the Baptist understood this principle. When asked if he was the Messiah, he replied, "A person can receive only what is given them from heaven" (John 3:27 NIV). John understood his role in the kingdom of God. He came to pave the way for the Messiah; he was not the Messiah himself. His ministry on earth was very brief, yet Jesus described his life in this way: "I tell you the truth, among those born of women, no one has arisen greater than John the Baptist. Yet the one who is least in the kingdom of heaven is greater than he is!" (Matthew 11:11 NET).

Once we understand what God has given to us, we can walk freely in our calling. However, if we strive to walk in a role that he never gave us, it will result in frustration and failure.

Question

Have you asked God to reveal what he has freely given to you? Pray that you receive and embrace only those things he has reserved for you to receive and to accomplish in your life.

Lord, help me to receive only what you have given me to receive.

A Faithful Woman

Her children arise and call her blessed;
her husband also, and he praises her.
PROVERBS 31:28 NIV

She was the vice president of household affairs for her entire adult life. She had a husband, four daughters, and one son, whose schedules she managed. Her workplace calling was the home. Her job description included sewing clothes for her twin girls, playing dolls, and even playing catch with her only son.

Then, midway in life, a telephone call came that changed everything. Her husband had tragically been killed in an airplane crash. She was in her early forties, still beautiful, with five kids to raise. The death of her husband removed their steady upper middle-class income. She hadn't worked outside the home for nearly twenty years. At her lowest moment, she cried out to God. God answered, "Trust me, Lillian." Those audible words became the strength to get her through the next forty years. That day she came to know her Savior personally and shared him with her family. Her children and grandchildren became the recipient of her prayers, and they came to know him too. She was building an inheritance in heaven, one soul at a time. She never remarried; Christ became her husband.

Whatever wisdom and encouragement have come to you through these devotionals, it is because of one who answered the call to the greatest and most important workplace there is: the home. You can thank my mom, Lillian Hillman, for whatever grace you have gained from these messages throughout the year, because she remained faithful to the call to invest in those she was called to love and serve.

Question

Has God called you to the home as your primary workplace?

Father, help me steward my home and my work for your glory.

Covenant Relationships

"I will establish My covenant with you, and you shall go into the ark—
you, your sons, your wife and your sons' wives with you."

GENESIS 6:18 NKJV

The Bible is filled with covenants God made with his people. Six of those covenants were made with Old Testament figures: Noah, Abraham, Isaac, Jacob, Moses, and David. The seventh was made with his own son, Jesus Christ. God is always the strongest partner in a covenant relationship.

God made a covenant with Noah in order to preserve the human race. This covenant involved Noah's participation by building an ark. He'd never built an ark before. He'd never had a boat. It was a totally new concept to Noah and the rest of the world. Why would he need a boat in a dry land?

Noah did not have to invent the ark; God gave him the plans—in specific dimensions and details. He did not have to gather the animals—God led them into the ark. God even closed the door when they all came on board. God made it rain to prove why the ark was needed.

The covenant provided all Noah needed to complete his mission in life. When God spoke to Noah, he needed only to respond to God's call to do it. Noah could rest in knowing the covenant made with God was going to be fulfilled if he fulfilled his part.

Each of us has a covenant with God. But we also enter covenants with others in our personal and work lives.

Question

How are you doing in fulfilling covenants to others?

Father, show me any unfulfilled covenants I need to honor.

An Audience of One

Stop imitating the ideals and opinions of the culture around you, but be inwardly transformed by the Holy Spirit through a total reformation of how you think.
ROMANS 12:2 TPT

What audience do you play to? Each day you are seen by many who will make a judgment about the way you handle yourself among different audiences. Politicians have learned to play to their audiences, customizing messages for the needs of their particular groups. Musicians have learned to play to their audiences. Pastors play to their congregations each Sunday morning. Workplace believers play to the audiences who will buy their product.

Christ has called us to play to one audience—the audience of himself. When you seek to please any other audience in your life, you become susceptible to situational ethics and motivations based on the need of the moment.

Pure obedience to pleasing God in our lives will often meet the needs of those around us. It is God's will that you and I love our spouses, provide good services to our customers, and look to the interests of others before ourselves. This will result in meeting many needs of the audiences in our lives.

However, there are other times when our audiences are asking for something contrary to God's will. When we are asked to go with the flow, we discover which audience is most important in our lives.

Question

Ask yourself why you are taking a particular action. Is it to please the audience of One? Or is it to please the audience of others who might negatively impact you should you not play to their tune?

Father, help me to play to the audience of One.

When Plans Are Thwarted

The prince of the Persian kingdom resisted me twenty-one days.
Then Michael, one of the chief princes, came to help me,
because I was detained there with the king of Persia.

DANIEL 10:13 NIV

I left at 5:00 a.m. to fly to another city to present to another organization some possible joint initiatives in ministry. I would have only an hour or so to meet with the board. I got into the city and taxied to the hotel. This is great, I thought. No glitches. I am even here an hour early. I asked where the meeting was. There was no record of such a meeting. I made several calls, to no avail. What had I missed? An hour and a half later I reached my wife by phone. She located a letter that seemed to indicate the meeting might be downtown. I took a cab and arrived at the location. "I am sorry, sir, there are no seventh-floor offices in use yet in this building."

Perplexed, I called my wife again. We made contact with yet another person who gave us another number to call. Finally, we located where the meeting was taking place. I got into the cab for another thirty-dollar cab ride. Forty-five minutes later the cab driver was lost. I was past the point of anger. I was laughing at this situation. We finally arrived at our destination, three and a half hours after our scheduled time. Sometimes plans are hindered for our purposes, sometimes we're in a spiritual battle, and sometimes we're being hindered to protect us.

Question

The next time your plans are thwarted, begin asking what is at the root of the calamities.

Father, thank you for discernment to know the causes of delays.

Tested for Abundance

We went through fire and water,
but you brought us to a place of abundance.
PSALM 66:12 NIV

It is nice to hear that God desires to bring us into abundance. In fact, many a preacher has promoted the goodness of the Lord and his ability to prosper his children. My experience is that this gospel of material abundance has little to do with the gospel of the kingdom as our Lord works in the realm of the sanctified soul. The passage above tells us that God does, in fact, bring us into better places than where we began. However, upon further study of the entire passage, we learn the route to this abundance.

God's economy of abundance often has little to do with material blessing. In God's economy, abundance is often measured in wisdom and knowledge of himself. It is then that we are truly blessed. Wisdom cannot be gained through intellectual pursuits. Wisdom comes only through experience. Real wisdom comes from the kinds of experiences that occur only through the deepest tests. Lessons of refinement lead us through the fire and water. This is the territory that we must travel to reach that place of abundance. It would seem strange that a loving God would use such means with his children. What we often fail to realize is that God's measuring stick is the character and likeness of Jesus Christ himself in each of us. This cannot be gained through a life of ease and pleasure. Ease and pleasure fail to refine.

Question

Is God using your workplace to refine you today? Has he placed you in a prison or laid burdens on your back?

Father, thank you for refining fires that bring me into a place of abundance.

The God of the Valley

"This is what the LORD says: 'Because the Arameans think the LORD is a god of the hills and not a god of the valleys, I will deliver this vast army into your hands, and you will know that I am the Lord.'"

1 KINGS 20:28 NIV

Whenever we stand on the mountain, we are able to see clearly. It is the best vantage point to see what lies ahead. Wouldn't it be great to live on the mountain all the time in order to anticipate what is ahead? God allows us to experience the mountaintop at times. Joseph's first mountaintop experience was as a young man. He had the favor of his father, Jacob. He was given a fine coat and even had a dream about his future. As a young man, Joseph had a sense of destiny about his life. God often gives us a picture of our future so that we will remember this picture when we are being tested to trust him in the valley. This picture usually does not reveal how God intends to bring about the visions for our life.

However, while we are on the mountain, none of us really derive the character qualities God desires for our lives. It is in the valley where the fruit is planted and harvested. It cannot grow on the mountain; it must grow in the valley. God is a God of the mountain, but he is even more a God of the valley.

Question

Has God brought you into the valley? Know that the valley is a place of fruitfulness; it is a place of testing.

Father, help me walk through the valley with grace and courage.

The Benefits of Obedience

*This is what the L*ORD *says—your Redeemer, the Holy One of Israel:*
*"I am the L*ORD *your God, who teaches you what is best for you,*
who directs you in the way you should go."

ISAIAH 48:17 NIV

My career has been in marketing and advertising. Early on, I learned to distinguish the difference between features and benefits. Features represent characteristics of a product or service. Benefits are those things that directly profit or benefit me by using the product or service. For instance, my new computer has incredible speed and lots of memory (feature). This allows me to do things more quickly and easily (benefit). People are more concerned about the benefits than the features.

God tells us in the above verse that there are some direct benefits to the features of his nature. He is a God who is committed to teaching his children in the way they should go. What is the real benefit of his teaching? He answers this in the next verse. "If only you had paid attention to my commands, your peace would have been like a river, your well-being like the waves of the sea" (v. 18). The Lord tells us that peace and righteousness are the benefits of allowing God to teach us and lead us in the way. Here is a guaranteed promise from God. I often use guarantees in my advertising claims. Here is God's immutable guarantee: You will have peace like a river and righteousness like the waves of the sea! What a great promise!

Question

Are you trusting God with the very details of your life so that he can lead you in the way you should go?

Father, teach me the way in which I should go.

The Root of Bitterness

*See to it that no one falls short of the grace of God
and that no bitter root grows up to cause trouble and defile many.*

HEBREWS 12:15 NIV

The enemy of our souls has a very specific strategy to destroy relationships. Whether these relationships are in business, marriage, or friendships, the strategy is the same. A conflict arises, judgments are made, and feelings are hurt. What happens next is the defining point of whether the enemy gains a foothold or the grace of God covers the wrong.

When a root of bitterness is allowed to be planted and grown, it not only affects that person, but it also affects all others who are involved. It is like a cancer. Breaking Satan's foothold requires at least one person to press into God's grace. It cannot happen when either party "feels" like it, for none of us will ever feel like forgiving. None of us feels like talking when we have been hurt. Our natural response is to withdraw or lash out at the offending party. It is only obedience that allows God's grace to cover the wrongs incurred. This grace prevents the parties from becoming victims who will seek compensation for their pain. Be a peacemaker and seek restoration.

Question

Is there anyone you carry bitterness against or anyone who carries bitterness against you?

Father, help me make restitution for any relationship that is broken and needs restitution.

The Power of Unity

*"I pray for them to become one with us
so that the world will recognize that you sent me."*
JOHN 17:21 TPT

What is the greatest power that allows the unsaved to make a decision for Jesus Christ? It isn't prayer, though this is important. It isn't good deeds, though deeds indicate a fruitful relationship with God. It isn't good behavior, though Christ commands us to be obedient as his children. The greatest power God's children have over darkness is unity. Jesus talked a great deal about his oneness with the Father and the importance of unity in the body of Christ. It is the most difficult command Jesus gave to the church because it wars against the evilest aspect of our sin nature—independence.

The walls of division and competition among his body are a stench in God's nostrils. He sees the competition and the pride of ownership and weeps for the lost who cannot come to him because they cannot see him in his body. When his body is one, the unbelieving see that Jesus was sent by God. It is like a supernatural key that unlocks heaven for the heathen soul. The key is in the hand of Christ's church. When there is unity, there is power. Scripture tells us five will chase one hundred, but one hundred will chase ten thousand (see Leviticus 26:8). We are a hundred times more effective when we are a unified group. Imagine what God could do with a unified church.

Question

Are you seeking to break down walls of competition among Christians, churches, denominations, and ethnic groups?

Father, I pray that you will unify the body of Christ to allow others to believe in you.

Are You Salty?

"Everyone will be salted with fire."
MARK 9:49 NIV

Jesus used parables to communicate principles of the kingdom of God. He said each believer's life should have the same impact on his or her world as salt has on food. Salt gives food flavor and brings out the best while at the same time it serves as a preservative.

What allows a Christian to become salty? Fire. God knows that each believer needs a degree of testing by fire in order for Christ's fragrance to be manifested. We cannot become salty without this deeper work of the Holy Spirit's fire in our lives. Fire purifies all that is not of Christ. It takes away all the impurities that prevent his nature from being revealed in us.

> In all this you greatly rejoice, though now for a little while you may have had to suffer grief in all kinds of trials. These have come so that the proven genuineness of your faith—of greater worth than gold, which perishes even though refined by fire—may result in praise, glory and honor when Jesus Christ is revealed. (1 Peter 1:6–7)

Let God allow your faith to be proven genuine.

Question

Are you a salty Christian?

Father, make me a salty Christian that I might impact others for your kingdom.

Great Is Your Faithfulness

Through the LORD's mercies we are not consumed,
because His compassions fail not.
They are new every morning;
great is Your faithfulness.
LAMENTATIONS 3:22–23 NKJV

Being a single mother with two children was a stressful time in Debbie's life. Although she had worked full time as a hairdresser, there never seemed to be enough money, but God always came through.

One time in particular, her pantry and refrigerator were bare, except for an onion, a bag of rice, and some flour. She cried out to the Lord, Father God, "You are a Father for the fatherless." She clutched her Bible and continued to pray aloud.

A neighbor came over to borrow an onion. Debbie thought, *You reap what you sow*, and she happily handed over the onion. Shortly after that, the landlord came for the rent, and he brought her a huge bag of freshly picked pears. Debbie prayed, *I stood on the Word, Father God, and I know you want better for my children. Just rice and pears won't cut it.*

Soon Debbie's other neighbor, who knew nothing about the situation, showed up with tears in his eyes. He was a pastor, and he told Debbie, "God laid you on my heart today when I was at Sam's."

Debbie recalls how that day, "the pastor filled my house with enough food to last my little family for two weeks. I baked him a chocolate cake, and we praised our Savior together. God is faithful!"

Someone once said regarding prayer, "God is never late, but he is rarely early" (see Habakkuk 2:3).

Question

Do you ever question the faithfulness of God?

Father, I believe and trust in your faithfulness for every need I have today.

A Remnant That Prays

One day, as Jesus was in prayer, one of his disciples came over to him as he finished and said, "Would you teach us a model prayer that we can pray, just as John did for his disciples?"

Luke 11:1 TPT

God is calling workplace women throughout the world who understand the role of prayer in their work. These women have learned that prayer is not a five-minute exercise in the morning devotion time, but it is a vital, strategic tool for discerning and knowing God's will and purposes in their work lives. You see, they have learned that their business lives are their ministries to God and others.

These women have entered into covenant relationships with intercessory prayer partners who help discern the activities they should be involved in. Some even have paid staff, who intercede for the decisions and activities in which they will be involved. They are a small remnant of workplace believers who know that skill and technique are not enough to fulfill God's purposes.

Someone once said, "Prayer is the rail for God's work. Indeed, prayer is to God's will as rails are to a train."[45] A train has great power but is useless without the rails to travel on. Without rails, the train will boggle down on the soft soil. And it would not stay on the intended course. Prayer is much like this. It is central to seeing God's activity move forward and for realizing breakthroughs.

Question

Is prayer a vital part of your strategic work-life practices? Put prayer on the front lines, instead of making it an afterthought.

Father, teach me to pray and see your hand at work.

The Isolation Chamber

Be still, and know that I am God.
PSALM 46:10 NKJV

There will be a time in our walk with God during which he sets us in a place of waiting. It is a place in which all past experiences are of no value. It is a time of such stillness that it can disturb the most faithful if we do not understand that he is the one who has brought us to this place for only a season. It is as if God has placed a wall around us. No new opportunities—simply inactivity.

During these times, God is calling us aside to fashion something new in us. It is an isolation chamber designed to call us to deeper roots of prayer and faith. It is not a comfortable place, especially for a task-driven workplace believer. Our nature cries out, "You must do something," while God is saying, "Be still, and know that I am God." You know the signs that you have been brought into this chamber when he has removed many things from your life, and you can't seem to change anything. Perhaps you are unemployed. Perhaps you are laid up with an illness.

God often allows us to hear best when there are no distractions.

Question

Has God brought you to a place of being still?

Father, help me remain still to see your hand move on my behalf.

Moving in Presumption

Nevertheless, in their presumption they went up toward the highest point in the hill country, though neither Moses nor the ark of the Lord's covenant moved from the camp.

NUMBERS 14:44 NIV

The people of Israel were brought out of Egypt to enter a new land—the promised land. This land was not handed over to them freely; it required the removing of God's enemies through battle. It required a partnership between God and the people. As long as the people remained true to God, they were victorious.

The people were camped at Kadesh Barnea, near the border entrance to the long-awaited promised land. All the hardships of their journey from Egypt were now culminating at this important crossing. However, Joshua and Caleb were the only scouts who proclaimed faith in God to take them into the land and conquer their enemies. The other spies saw all the dangers and refused to take the risk. The people of the camp shrank in fear because of their report. They decided not to enter.

God was angered at the people for their lack of faith. Moses had to intercede on their behalf. Once they realized what they had done, it was too late. But they thought their repentance was enough to right their wrong. They presumed this was all that was necessary.

Moses informed them they were deceived in their presumption of God's favor. They went to battle against the Amalekites only to be soundly defeated. Those who returned did not understand why they lost the battle.

Question

Do you know whether you have God's hand upon your endeavors? Presumption leads to failure. God's favor leads to success.

Father, I pray you confirm your hand in my endeavors.

Saved by a Prostitute

The same is true of the prostitute named Rahab who was found righteous in God's eyes by her works, for she received the spies into her home and helped them escape from the city by another route.

JAMES 2:25 TPT

God doesn't view current or past reputations as reasons for exclusion from usefulness in his kingdom. Such was the case for Rahab, a prostitute and innkeeper in Jericho, who would be a key player in allowing the Israelites to take the first city in the promised land. She, like Esther, became a critical player in the future of God's people when God placed her in a divine position to keep God's people from being destroyed.

It appears that she survived in life by operating a small inn and by a life of prostitution. She had heard about the exploits of Israel—parting of the Red Sea and winning many battles. It had caused fear in the townspeople. Some locals heard about the visitors and pressed her to expose them, but instead, she hid them on her roof. She made an agreement with them that she would hide them if they would protect her and her family when they attacked the city. A scarlet cloth hanging outside her inn was a sign during the battle that the Israelites were not to attack anyone who was in the inn. This is a prophetic sign of the blood of Jesus and the Passover.

Rahab would marry Salmon of the tribe of Judah and give birth to Boaz—the same Boaz who married Ruth, the great grandmother of King David, which puts Rahab directly in the lineage of Jesus himself.

Question

What does this story tell us about God's view of those willing to change and follow him?

Father, thank you that you redeem every life no matter how bad it is.

Led by the Spirit

The mature children of God are those who are moved
by the impulses of the Holy Spirit.
ROMANS 8:14 TPT

Penny was a nurse practitioner. She was often at a loss to know how to navigate the ever-changing face of health care in America. Her faith in God and his Word have been the best tool, followed closely by the *TGIF* daily devotions for workplace believers.

She wrote to me, "Almost every morning while reading *TGIF*, the Lord 'telegraphs' a name through my brain to share that day's devotion. Sometimes, it may be with another health-care provider, and other times it is a friend, neighbor, or family member."

On this particular day, the topic of the devotional was about listening to the voice of the Holy Spirit and being obedient at that moment. It prompted Penny to send a devotion to a friend who had surgery for breast cancer two days before and was battling nausea and severe pain.

Penny says, "I knew the Holy Spirit was telling me to call her, pray with her, and let her verbalize her feelings." The ailing friend sent Penny a text just before Penny received a request from *TGIF* for "God stories."

The woman thanked Penny for taking the time to check on her and pray for her. She said her "nausea had subsided, and the pain was minimal. Hallelujah!"

Without the *TGIF* devotion, Penny might have passed up the opportunity to allow the Holy Spirit to minister to her. She wrote, "The uncertainty of our world may be frightening, but the hope and courage to persevere that I receive from these devotions will keep me passing them along to others."

Question

Are you available to minister to others God brings to your mind?

Father, help me be sensitive to the leading of your Holy Spirit.

Discovering Root Causes

Now you must rid also yourselves of all such things as these:
anger, rage, malice, slander, and filthy language from your lips.
COLOSSIANS 3:8 NIV

The root issue you are dealing with is fear," I said to the woman who sat across the table from me. "The physical symptom is control, and when you cannot control, you get angry because of unmet expectations." These were the words I spoke during a conversation in a restaurant. My friend, who was separated from her husband, described her anger and how she never saw some of these characteristics in her life until her marriage.

A friend once said to me, "Anger is like the lights on a dashboard. They tell you something is going on under the hood. You must find out the source of the problem." Whenever we place expectations on another person and those expectations do not materialize, our tendency is to get angry. The source of the anger is often the fear that the unmet expectation will negatively impact us. We fear that our finances, our well-being, our image, or any number of things may be impacted by the unmet expectation. My friend's husband had not met her expectations in many areas of her life. This often led to harsh words between them and a diminishing level of respect and trust. Now, it was leading to a marriage crisis.

Question

Is there something that causes anger within you?

Father, I pray you reveal any source of anger in me.

Love the Lord Your God

Jesus answered him, "Love the Lord your God with every passion of your heart, with all the energy of your being, and with every thought that is within you."
MATTHEW 22:37 TPT

The doctors told Gisela that her husband of thirty-eight years had a rare disease and would only live a year. God gave her the wisdom to care for him, and he lived a much longer life. However, he died on a Sunday after being in church with me for the greater part of the day.

When he died, she was devasted and overwhelmed with grief. Even though he had been sick, his death was unexpected. That year they had planned a vacation, something they had not been able to do in over a decade. She remembered the week before his death that she thanked God because he was healing her husband. Now she questioned how God could do this to her. *How could he raise my hopes only to have them shattered?* She wanted to die. She did not want to live without her husband.

Suddenly, she felt the presence of the Holy Spirit, and a small, still voice asked her why she wanted to die. Was it because she wanted to be with her husband or because she wanted to be with the Lord? It was at that moment that she realized what she had done. She had put the love for her husband over her love for God. She felt she had hurt God's feelings. She immediately cried out, "I love you more! My love for my husband should have never come before my love for my God."

Question

Where is your love for a loved one today? Does it outweigh your love of God?

Father, forgive me for loving my spouse and children more than you.

Good Things versus God Things

When you yield to the life of the Spirit,
you will no longer be living under the law,
but soaring above it!
GALATIANS 5:18 TPT

The greatest sign that you and I are maturing in our walk with God is when we can discern the difference between "good things" and "God things."

Each of us must have the discernment to know when God is leading in a matter or if it is simply a good idea. There are so many things in which you and I can be involved, and the more successful we become, the greater the temptations to enter into areas where God has not called us. Entrepreneurs are especially prone to seeing all the opportunities.

I recall one time when I entered into a project that I thought was a great idea. It would help many people. After two years, the project had to be discontinued. It was a great lesson on understanding what projects have God's blessing on them. There are some projects you and I might get involved in that result in little fruit compared to the investment put into them. That is because they may never have been birthed by the Holy Spirit.

As a daughter of God, you are called to be led by the Spirit. This requires a level of dependence on God in which many do not want to invest. It requires listening, waiting, and moving only when God's Spirit tells you to move. Workplace believers are "action" people. We know how to get things done, but our greatest strength can be our greatest weakness.

Question

Are you submitting every project to the Lord to know if he is leading you to engage?

Father, make me a Galatians 5:18 woman who is led by the Spirit of God.

Freedom and Boundaries

Now the serpent was more crafty than any of the wild animals the LORD God had made. He said to the woman, "Did God really say, 'You must not eat from any tree in the garden'?"

GENESIS 3:1 NIV

God is big on giving us freedom and boundaries—freedom to manage what he has entrusted to us, boundaries to protect us from evil. The boundaries in the garden of Eden were not set for the purpose of limiting Adam and Eve. God had provided everything they would need for life. He also entrusted them with the responsibility to manage and work the garden. God gave them freedom in that responsibility. God knows we were made to express ourselves creatively through our work. Like Adam, we get into trouble when we question those boundaries.

Each of us must have freedom and boundaries in our work life. Whenever you are hired for a job, you must have the freedom to make certain decisions. You must have the authority to manage things within your area of expertise. You must also have limits within your area of responsibility. You need to know where those limits are and stay within them. Both freedom and boundaries are always under the umbrella of God's authority and our authority at work. We set boundaries with our children as well.

You and I are tempted every day to go beyond our God-ordained boundaries. Whether it is solving financial problems that have arisen through debt, making wrong decisions due to pressure, or manipulating someone in order to achieve our ends, it all represents rebellion toward God.

Question

Are you living within the boundaries God has set for you?

Father, thank you for giving me freedom and boundaries in my life. Help me live within those boundaries.

Staying Connected

Let the dawning day bring me revelation of your tender, unfailing love.
Give me light for my path and teach me, for I trust in you.
PSALM 143:8 TPT

Two of the greatest inventions of my time have been the laptop computer and email. The laptop means I no longer have to stay in one place to be productive in my business life. Email has allowed me to stay connected to people all around the world with the touch of a button.

The morning time with God is much like these situations. God pours his Word into my spirit, and I am recharged. This recharging has an important effect on my day. It allows me the greatest opportunity to hear the small voice that directs my steps. If I refuse to "get connected," I risk following my own ways of fulfilling the duties of my day. It sets forth the opportunity for God to speak into my spirit what he desires for me each day. It allows me to focus on God's purposes, not mine.

The only way to know someone is to spend time with them. The only way to discern the voice of another is to hear that person's voice. David, the author of this psalm, was a warrior, king, and businessman. He understood this principle of connecting with God in the morning. His morning allowed him to connect with God's love, renew his trust in him, and hear his directions for his life. Shouldn't you and I do the same?

Question

Are you staying connected to your Father every day?

Father, express your life through me in every activity today.

Avoiding Detours

Trust in the Lord completely, and do not rely on your own opinions. With all your heart rely on him to guide you, and he will lead you in every decision you make. Become intimate with him in whatever you do, and he will lead you wherever you go.

PROVERBS 3:5–6 TPT

I turned off the interstate to get gas for my car. I was returning from a speaking engagement, and it was very late. As I turned onto the road, I looked for the entrance ramp to get back on the interstate. It was dark, and I could not see any signs. I made a turn to the right that appeared to be the turn I needed to make. I could see the interstate was next to the road.

However, the road soon turned away from the interstate. It grew darker and darker. The road became a dirt road. I realized I was not going to get to the interstate on this road. Being a bit frustrated that I'd made the wrong turn, I turned around and went back, losing valuable time.

It's easy to make assumptions about the path we're on. If God's Spirit has not enlightened our reasoning, we are inclined to make the wrong choices. Our choices seem right at the time, but later we discover these choices have led us away from God because they were based on our own reasoning.

Question

Are you seeking God in all your ways today? Lean completely on him to reveal his direction for your life.

Father, thank you that you promise to direct my every step as I yield my life to you.

Signs and Wonders Today

Everyone became silent and listened carefully as Paul and Barnabas shared with the council at length about the signs and wonders and miracles God had worked through them.

ACTS 15:12 TPT

I was a pastor for nineteen years before I went into business," said the man sitting across the table from me as we were having lunch together. He shared this story with me.

I was a pastor of a particular denomination that did not embrace all of God's Word. At the time, I was also very ill and was about to be admitted to the hospital. I had been seeking God about whether he was truly a God of healing. Since the next day I was to go into the hospital, that night I cried out to the Lord. I confronted God about his Word. I asked him if he still did miracles today.

Just then, I turned on my TV and saw an evangelist preaching. At that very moment, he stopped preaching, looked into the TV camera, and said: "There is a man in the viewing audience who has been a pastor for many years and is struggling to know whether God heals today. God is healing you right now to demonstrate to you that his healing is for today, and you are to know that his Word is true for today just like it was for the early church."

God healed him that very night. He felt compelled to go before his church and witness to God's power in his life even though the congregation had different views. He was soon fired as pastor of his church, and this is what led him into business.

Question

Have you experienced the God of miracles in your life?

Father, I believe you can do miracles in my life. I am standing for one today.

Belief or Unbelief

"Abraham believed God,
and it was credited to him as righteousness."
ROMANS 4:3 NIV

Y ou can be a believer yet act as a Monday morning atheist. Whenever you fret over life circumstances, you immediately demonstrate unbelief. Whenever your motivation for action is fear or anxiety, you believe a lie about God's nature.

Each day your actions affirm or convict you of your belief system. It reveals who the central focus of your life really is—you or God. It reveals whom you place your ultimate trust in—you or God. It is one of the great paradoxes for believers. One day we can believe him to move mountains. The next day we can question his very existence.

- Peter believed God and walked on water.
- A sick woman touched the hem of his garment and was healed.
- A Canaanite woman believed and freed her daughter from demon possession.

Every day is a day to believe and experience the reality of a God who is involved in the daily affairs of his sons and daughters.

Question

In what circumstances do you act as an "unbeliever"?

Father, I pray I can be a faithful steward of all your gifts to me.

Angels at the Gate

*The angel of the Lord encamps all around those who fear Him,
and delivers them.*
PSALM 34:7 NKJV

Rebecca was a young, poor, single mom on her way home from a conference late in the evening when she arrived at the airport after the airplane door for her flight had already been closed and the gate agents were leaving. Most of the other late arrivers at the gate quickly left to get a hotel until the next flight, but Rebecca had no money for that. She did not know the city or what to do next. So she sat down in the empty concourse, feeling lost, and prayed, *What now, Lord?*

Suddenly a far door opened, and out came a handsome young man dressed in an airline uniform. Rebecca relates, "He came straight to me and asked me if he could help. I explained my situation and my need to get home to my kids. He said, 'Just a minute.' He proceeded to open the jetway door and disappeared. Not even a minute later he returned with a smile. 'Go on,' he said, 'your seat is waiting for you.'"

When Rebecca got to her window seat, the man sitting next to her asked, "Who are *you?*" She was baffled, and then he continued. "I have never seen them open the door once it is shut. You must be someone important."

Rebecca said, "I shook my head, thinking, *Lord, what did you do?*"

So, Rebecca got home to her children on time. She wrote to me to tell me, "I think God sent an angel disguised as an airline employee to take care of me. Many, many times I have thought back to what God did for me that day and have been encouraged in the Lord."

Question

Are you bold enough to ask God to do the extraordinary?

Thank you, Father, that you still do miracles today!

Living Forward, Understanding Backward

*The one who calls you is faithful
and he will do it.*

1 THESSALONIANS 5:24 NIV

When I was in my twenties, I participated in a wilderness-training course in a desert and mountain area. For our "final exam," we were blindfolded, placed in the back of a pickup truck, and taken to a remote area. We were dropped off and told to meet back at the camp in three days. We did not know where we were. We had to determine our location with our compasses. It was a frightening experience for four young people who had just learned to navigate through the use of a compass.

With our food and water on our backs, we began our trek. It had just snowed that morning, so the way was difficult. We walked through valleys, canyons, snow-covered hills, and forests. In all, we walked more than sixty miles in three days. There were times when we did not think we could go another foot. Exhaustion and nearly frostbitten feet were taking their toll. However, we finally made it to our base camp successfully. Surprisingly, we were the first ones among the groups of patrols to make it back.

At the conclusion of our journey, we were able to stand on top of a ridge, look behind us, and see the beautiful terrain that we had just scaled. The pain of what we had just endured seemed to subside. We could not believe we had actually walked through those valleys and snowcapped hills. There was a sense of accomplishment.

Question

Are you in the midst of a difficult journey that seems almost impossible to continue?

Father, thank you for the grace to continue on the journey.

Disappointments

Hope deferred makes the heart sick,
but a longing fulfilled is a tree of life.
PROVERBS 13:12 NIV

Life is filled with disappointments. Many of God's greatest servants experienced deep disappointment in their journeys of faithfulness to God. After spending years as a slave and in jail for crimes that he did not commit, Joseph revealed deep disappointment when he was forgotten for another two years in prison. John the Baptist, when awaiting execution, questioned whether Jesus was, in fact, the Christ because John was sitting there awaiting his death. Elijah, losing all hope and despondent to the point of death, asked God to take his life in the desert. Peter, who left his fishing business and invested three years of his life only to watch his Savior crucified, wondered whether the purpose of those three years could be justified.

When life doesn't add up, it leaves the heart sick. When we have done all we know to do and the formula has not worked, we may find ourselves questioning. These are times that try the very souls of men and women. There is no human sense to be made of it. We are left with a choice: to cling or not to cling. There are times when holding on to our Master's robe is all that we can do. It is all that he wants us to do.

There is only one answer to life's disappointments. Like the psalmist, we must find rest: "My soul, wait silently for God alone, for my expectation is from Him. He only is my rock and my salvation; He is my defense; I shall not be moved" (Psalm 62:5–6 NKJV).

Question

Is your heart sick with disappointment?

Father, give me grace to walk with you through every trial I may face.

One Flock, One Shepherd

*"I have other sheep that are not of this sheep pen. I must bring them also.
They too will listen to my voice, and there shall be one flock and one shepherd."*
JOHN 10:16 NIV

A friend of mine told me a story about an experience he had in Israel. They were in the country visiting some of the famous biblical sites when they saw a group of sheepherders. A shepherd brought his flock of sheep into a round pen for the night. Then, a few minutes later, another shepherd brought his flock into the pen. Then, a few minutes later, yet another shepherd brought his sheep into the pen. There were three groups of sheep in the pen with no identifying marks among any of them. My friend wondered how in the world they would separate their sheep the next day.

The next morning, a shepherd came over to the pen and said something in his own language to his sheep. One by one, the sheep filed out to follow him. The other two shepherds did the same. Only their own sheep followed their voice. My friend said it was an amazing scene to see only that shepherd's sheep follow him and the others remain in the pen. What a picture of Jesus' words spoken centuries earlier!

Hearing and responding to Jesus' voice is the key to having a two-way relationship with God. It is the difference between having religion and a relationship.

Question

Can you recognize God's voice in your life? Are you listening to the shepherd's voice? Do you respond when he calls?

Father, help me increase my ability to hear your voice.

I Give Myself Away

When they came up out of the water, Philip was suddenly snatched up by the Spirit of the Lord and instantly carried away to the city of Ashdod, where he reappeared, preaching the gospel in that city.

ACTS 8:39–40 TPT

Joann and her ministry team were invited to travel to South Africa to train teams in inner healing ministry. She was also scheduled to speak at a women's conference, at two Bible studies, and at a Sunday church service.

However, twelve hours into the flight, she started feeling very ill. Being diabetic, she closely monitored her blood glucose levels and was alarmed to see them becoming increasingly high. She tried increasing insulin intake, but levels continued to rise because her insulin pump was malfunctioning. When she arrived at Cape Town, she was in an acute state of ketoacidosis. She was taken to the hospital ICU.

Around one in the morning, her heart stopped beating, and she had to be resuscitated. During this brief time of unresponsiveness, she says, "God sent my spirit to Uganda while I was unconscious."

After three days in intensive care, Joann was released from the hospital. That same evening, she returned to her mission and ministered nonstop for the next five days. "I was weak," she reports, "but God held me up."

After returning home, Joann spoke with a friend who happened to be in Uganda during Joann's trip. While there, the friend also became ill and was bedridden. During the night, while in bed, the friend remembers turning and seeing Joann standing there by her bed. Joann spoke a word from God to her. It was the same night and time when Joann was in ICU being resuscitated.

Question

Is God able to take you outside the box for his purposes?

Father, help me not to limit you in your ways.

Encounter at the Movie Theatre

Through our union with Christ we too have been claimed by God as his own inheritance. Before we were even born, he gave us our destiny; that we would fulfill the plan of God who always accomplishes every purpose and plan in his heart.

EPHESIANS 1:11 TPT

Pamela's good friend Polly invited her to a movie premiere called *Captive*. As they entered the theater, Polly spotted an old friend sitting next to the producer, and they immediately recognized each other. Polly introduced the man to Pamela, "This is my friend, Pamela Winderweedle. A producer wants to do a movie on her life, and she just received a contract. Maybe you could help her with it since you know something about the movie industry."

He responded with a smile, "What would make your life so interesting that someone would want to do a movie about you?"

Pamela just said, "It's really complicated…and a very long story!"

So, he handed her his card and smiled, "I would like to hear more." She gave the man her card in return, and the two women took their seats. Pamela had been single fifteen years at the time.

She looked over at him, thinking, "I wonder what it would be like to be married to a man like that?" She knew nothing about him, but she says, "Just a moment with him revealed a wise, fine-looking man filled with kindness. His eyes showed he had a heart for Jesus." She was so intrigued and hoped he wasn't married. Would he actually call her?

Two days later the man called Pamela. It turned out they lived only two exits from each other. They dated for eight months, and God confirmed their relationship.

Note: Os and Pamela were married May 17, 2016.

Question

Have you ever had a divine appointment?

Father, thank you that you orchestrate every detail of our lives.

Paul's Personal Mission Statement

I want to know Christ and the power of his resurrection and the sharing of his sufferings by becoming like him in his death, if somehow I may attain the resurrection from the dead.

PHILIPPIANS 3:10–11 NRSVUE

Paul understood his personal mission, which should be the personal mission of every believer in Jesus Christ. It is the one summary statement that best describes the purpose of our existence on earth and the goal of our Christian experience. It can be reduced to three important characteristics.

1. To know Christ
2. To know and experience his power
3. To identify with his sufferings

All that flows from these three objectives becomes a by-product. Salvation is a by-product. Miracles are a by-product. Christlikeness is a by-product. Paul's focus was on relationship. He understood that the deeper the relationship, the more power he would experience. He also understood that as he grew in this relationship, there would be suffering. Whenever the kingdom of light confronts the kingdom of darkness, there is a battle, and this often results in casualties. Christ confronted these earthly kingdoms and suffered for it. If we are living at this level of obedience, we, too, will face similar battles; it simply comes with the territory.

Question

Does this sound like your personal mission statement? Is your focus in life centered on knowing Christ and the power of his resurrection?

Father, may I experience your power daily in my walk with you.

Recognizing Our Source

Remember the LORD your God,
for it is he who gives you power to get wealth.

DEUTERONOMY 8:18 NRSVUE

Pride is the greatest temptation to a successful workplace minister. When we begin accumulating wealth, managing people, and becoming known for our workplace expertise, we are most susceptible to falling to the most devious sin in God's eyes—pride. The Bible tells us that God is the reason we are able to produce wealth. It is not of our own making. As soon as we move into the place where we begin to think more highly of ourselves than we ought, God says he will take action.

> You may say to yourself, "My power and the strength of my hands have produced this wealth for me." But remember the LORD your God, for it is he who gives you the ability to produce wealth…
>
> If you ever forget the LORD your God and follow other gods and worship and bow down to them, I testify against you today that you will surely be destroyed. Like the nations the LORD destroyed before you, so you will be destroyed for not obeying the LORD your God. (Deuteronomy 8:17–20 NIV)

Question

Are there any areas of pride that you need to remove and repent of today?

Father, reveal any pride in my life so that I might attract your presence in all I do.

Hearing God's Voice

Now Samuel did not yet know the Lord:
The word of the Lord had not yet been revealed to him.

1 SAMUEL 3:7 NIV

Samuel was born to Hannah, a woman who had a deep commitment to God. She was barren, but she cried out to God for a son. The Lord gave her Samuel, whom she completely gave to the Lord for his service. After weaning Samuel, she took him to the house of the Lord to be reared by the priests. Eli was the priest of Israel, but he was not a godly leader. He had allowed much corruption, including the sins of his own sons, in God's house. God was not pleased with Eli and later judged him and his household.

Samuel grew up in the temple serving God. He also grew up seeing the hypocrisy of Eli's household, yet this did not change the young man. God was with him. We learn that even though young Samuel had a belief in God, he had not yet experienced a personal relationship with him. God called to Samuel three times, but Samuel thought it was Eli, the priest, calling him. Finally, Eli told him to say, "Speak, Lord, for your servant is listening" (v. 9). This is what Samuel did, and God began telling Samuel important things to come.

Question

Do you know God's voice? Can you recognize it when he speaks?

Father, help me discern your voice when you speak to me.

No Rooms Available

She gave birth to her firstborn, a son. S
he wrapped him in cloths and placed him in a manger,
because there was no guest room available for them.

Luke 2:7 NIV

Imagine if the God of the universe decided to visit earth as a new baby, and you were given the opportunity to host his first night in your hotel. Think of the future promotional possibilities: "God stayed here his first night!" You could sell tickets to see the room where he was born. What an opportunity to make history as a small-business owner!

God had need of a business owner's establishment one night over two thousand years ago. But there was no room for God in this business that night. There was no room for the unexpected miracle, no awareness of what was taking place in the heavenlies, no sign that God might be reaching out to this workplace believer so God could use him or her like no other in all of history.

Every day, God has need of some man or woman's workplace. He wants to demonstrate miracles in their work. But there is no room in their work for Jesus. They do not ask him to participate.

That night God slept in a stable. That night a business opportunity from heaven was missed. It was business as usual.

Question

Are you living with spiritual eyes and ears to know when our Master desires what he has entrusted to us for his purposes?

Father, help me recognize when you want to use my workplace for your purposes.

The Power of Serving Others

*Every believer has received grace gifts, so use them to serve one another
as faithful stewards of the many-colored tapestry of God's grace.*
1 PETER 4:10 TPT

There is a kingdom principle I find few really understand. The principle is this: when you focus on serving others, your need is often met through God's supernatural law of serving.

I've seen this happen so many times. The law of sowing and reaping comes into play in this kingdom principle. "Sow righteousness for yourselves, reap the fruit of unfailing love" (Hosea 10:12 NIV). God is able to abundantly bless those who generously reap.

Remember this: Whoever sows sparingly will also reap sparingly, and whoever sows generously will also reap generously. Each of you should give what you have decided in your heart to give, not reluctantly or under compulsion, for God loves a cheerful giver. And God is able to bless you abundantly, so that in all things at all times, having all that you need, you will abound in every good work. (2 Corinthians 9:6–8 NIV)

Whenever God calls me to serve another person with my time and resources, I notice how God measures resources back to me from unrelated sources. Sometimes it comes through an unexpected donation to our ministry or a speaking engagement or a new opportunity. It is uncanny how this happens consistently when I serve others. We are never to view people or organizations as competition. The Bible says that God has already assigned our portion. We do not have to manipulate outcomes.

Question

Are you a person who consistently serves others?

Father, make me a servant just as you are a servant.

The Finger of God

*When the L*ORD *finished speaking to Moses on Mount Sinai, he gave him the two tablets of the covenant law, the tablets of stone inscribed by the finger of God.*

EXODUS 31:18 NIV

Throughout the Bible, the word *testimony* is used in many ways. *Testimony* comes from the Hebrew word *eduwth*, which means "witness." The ark of the covenant contained the Ten Commandments, written and inscribed personally by God and given to Moses on Mount Sinai. These became known as the testimony. The ark was a divinely inspired structure that was to be used as a witness to the people of Israel and the whole world of God's power and majesty. These divinely created tablets were a witness of God's activity on earth with man.

Throughout the Bible, God looked to create testimonies with his people. At the Red Sea, he created a testimony through Moses. God created a testimony through Joshua when he parted the Jordan River and allowed the people with the ark to cross on dry land. When Lazarus lay dead for days, Jesus came and created a testimony of his ability to raise the dead.

God wants to create a testimony in every aspect of your life—your family, your work, your church, and your community. He is waiting to put his finger on your next endeavor to reveal his power through your life. Look carefully at the events where God might want to create a testimony out of an impossible situation. He delights in using his children for this purpose because it brings him glory.

Question

Are you a testimony of his activity in your life?

Father, make my life a living testimony.

Brigid's Legacy

Every time you give to the poor you make a loan to the Lord.
Don't worry—you'll be repaid in full for all the good you've done.
PROVERBS 19:17 TPT

Brigid was born from a sexual encounter between an Irish king and one of his slaves. She was raised enslaved within the king's household and was required to perform hard work on the king's farm. From the beginning, Brigid took notice of the plight of the less fortunate. She would give the butter from the king's kitchen to working boys. She once gave the king's sword to a passing leper. The king was enraged! One day, Brigid fled the king's house and committed herself to belonging only to Christ. But the king also concluded that Brigid was so generous and caring of others that her Christian commitment should allow her freedom to live fully for Christ.

Brigid found seven women who organized as a community of nuns that became known as the Abbey of Kildare, a place where many thatch-roofed dwellings were built and where artist studios, workshops, guest chambers, a library, and a church evolved. These and other settlements became little industries all to themselves, producing some of the greatest craftsmanship in all of Europe. Many of the poor had their lives bettered because of Brigid's ministry to them.

When she died in 453, it is estimated thirteen thousand people had escaped from slavery and poverty to Christian service and industry. She was a woman who turned a life of slavery and defeat into a life lived for a cause greater than herself. She became a nationally known figure, and the Irish people still celebrate her each February 1.[46]

Question

Are you serving your community like Brigid did?

Father, help me use my gifts and talents to improve the plight of the poor.

Betrayals

It wasn't an enemy who taunted me. If it was my enemy, filled with pride and hatred, then I could have endured it. I would have just run away. But it was you, my intimate friend—one like a brother to me. It was you, my adviser, the companion I walked with and worked with!

PSALM 55:12–13 TPT

Y ou will always be attacked in the place of your inheritance," said the man sitting across the breakfast table from me. "God has called you to bring people together and to impact other people's lives as a result of this anointing in your life. You must make sure that you seek to maintain righteousness in all of your relationships." Those words came from someone who had the wisdom and authority to speak them to me.

Loving those who betray you is "graduate-level Christianity." The religious community and one of his closest friends betrayed Jesus. Those who were closest to David betrayed him. Joseph's own family betrayed him. Loving our enemies cannot be accomplished by mustering it up. It can only happen when we have come to a death in ourselves so that Christ can love through us.

If you are a leader, you can be sure God will allow you to experience betrayal. It is one of those courses in the kingdom that may not be required until God has seen that you have successfully passed other tests. It is the most difficult and most gut-wrenching of all tests. A godly response goes against all that is in us.

Question

Will you ask God to build his nature in you now so that when such attacks come, you will be aware that it is a test and will respond in righteousness?

Father, help me to forgiven and bless those who betray me.

The Gospel of the Kingdom

*"Manifest your kingdom realm, and cause your every purpose
to be fulfilled on earth, just as it is in heaven."*
MATTHEW 6:10 TPT

Imagine that you have never driven a car. All you are told about this car is that you are about to receive something that will get you anywhere you need to go. The day arrives, and you are given a brand-new car. You get in and drive the car. However, the emergency brake is on, preventing you from going faster than twenty miles per hour. No one tells you that you need to unlock the brake. You are not told that the car has lights, which would allow you to drive at night. Neither are you told about the many other wonderful features of the car. Still, you are excited because you no longer have to walk to your destination. For the rest of your life, you drive this incredible car only during the daytime and only at twenty miles per hour.

When Jesus came to earth, he came in order to penetrate the very kingdom of darkness with light. He came to bring healing to sickness, replace sadness with joy, and fill meaninglessness with purpose. He came to change things for the better for a world that had no hope outside of God.

Jesus did not come to merely give us a ticket to heaven (a car that you drive only in the daytime at twenty miles per hour). He came to bring us much more—the kingdom of God on earth. Nowhere in the Bible will you find the term *gospel of salvation*. The church does not exist for heaven but for earth. If it existed only for heaven, then each of us would immediately be taken to heaven when we accept Jesus into our lives.

Question

Will you ask God to show you how he wants to penetrate the darkness of your domain with his light?

Father, I pray you bring heaven on earth through me.

Effective Leadership

When the Israelites saw the great power the LORD had used against the Egyptians, they feared the LORD and believed in him and in his servant Moses.

ExODUS 14:31 GW

W hat makes an effective Christian woman leader today? Is it charisma? Is it ability? Is it communication and oratory skills? God's view of an effective leader has nothing to do with these qualities. They may be a part of an effective leader. However, the core attribute of a Christian leader is her integrity with God and her obedience to follow him.

When this happens, God manifests his power in and through that leader. Moses was effective because he was willing to obey the commands God gave him. When Moses did this, God manifested his presence in him. The result was that people followed. They followed because they saw God working in and through the leader. They saw that this leader was worthy of following because God's anointing was on him.

When people see the Lord's power manifested in your life, they will have a healthy fear of the Lord. They will look at you and say, "This person has something I don't have that is worthy of more investigation." Your challenge is to seek the Lord with your whole heart, resulting in God's power being manifested in the daily activities of your life.

Question

What makes you different from your neighbor? Is your experience with God noticeably different from that of the woman next door?

Father, make me a leader others will want to follow.

Endnotes

1   Sara Blakely, "Spanx Founder: My Dad Encouraged Me to Fail," interview by CNN Business, March 30, 2018, YouTube video, 3:59, https://www.youtube.com/watch?v=_TeV9op6Mp8.

2   Corrie ten Boom and Jamie Buckingham, *Tramp for the Lord* (Fort Washington, PA: CLC Publications, 2011), 153–55.

3   Junious Epps Jr., *There's Enough Woman Left to Be Your Lady* (Maitland, FL: Xulon Press, 2003), 99–100.

4   Mother Teresa, "Address to the National Prayer Breakfast," delivered February 3, 1994, at the Washington Hilton Hotel, Washington, DC, in *National Prayer Breakfast* video, 57:11, https://www.c-span.org/video/?54274-1/national-prayer-breakfast.

5   Robert J. Morgan, *On This Day: 365 Amazing and Inspiring Stories about Saints, Martyrs and Heroes* (Nashville, TN: Thomas Nelson Publishers, 1997), January 8.

6   Billy Graham, *How to Be Born Again* (Nashville, TN: Thomas Nelson, 1989), 38–39.

7   Marvin Wilson, *Our Father Abraham* (Grand Rapids, MI: Wm. B. Eerdmans, 1989), 284–86.

8   Robert J. Morgan, *On This Day: 365 Amazing and Inspiring Stories about Saints, Martyrs and Heroes* (Nashville, TN: Thomas Nelson Publishers, 1997), January 23.

9   Billy Graham, *The Holy Spirit: Activating God's Power in Your Life* (Grand Rapids, MI: Zondervan, 2002), 103–4.

10   Charles Hembree, *Fruits of the Spirit* (Grand Rapids, MI: Baker Book House, 1969), 7.

11 See https://www.lifechangerslegacy.org/ to learn about Pamela's ministry and how you can get involved.

12 *Braveheart*, directed by Mel Gibson (1995; Sherman Oaks, CA: Paramount Pictures, 2000), DVD, 178 min.

13 Charlie Renfroe, "What Our Readers Are Saying: Remembering Dr. Sam Peeples, Jr.," AL.com, last modified January 13, 2019, https://www.al.com/opinion/2014/07/what_our_readers_are_saying_re_9.html.

14 Allan Luks, "Helper's High: Volunteering Makes People Feel Good, Physically and Emotionally," *Psychology Today*, October 1988, 39–42.

15 Wikipedia, s.v. "Betty James," last modified on December 6, 2021, https://en.wikipedia.org/wiki/Betty_James.

16 Zachary Crockett, "The Invention of the Slinky," Priceonomics, December 3, 2014, https://priceonomics.com/the-invention-of-the-slinky/.

17 Rachael Lallensack, "The Accidental Invention of the Slinky," *Smithsonian Magazine*, August 29, 2019, https://www.smithsonianmag.com/innovation/accidental-invention-slinky-180973016/.

18 Wikipedia, "Betty James."

19 Robert J. Morgan, *On This Day: 365 Amazing and Inspiring Stories about Saints, Martyrs and Heroes* (Nashville, TN: Thomas Nelson Publishers, 1997), January 26.

20 John Woodbridge, ed., *More Than Conquerors* (Chicago: Moody Press, 1992), 100–102.

21 John Woodbridge, ed., *More Than Conquerors* (Chicago: Moody Press, 1992), 131–33.

22 Mary Bellis, "Biography of Ruth Handler, Inventor of Barbie Dolls," ThoughtCo., last modified January 28, 2020, https://www.thoughtco.com/history-of-barbie-dolls-1991344.

23 Robert J. Morgan, *On This Day: 365 Amazing and Inspiring Stories about Saints, Martyrs and Heroes* (Nashville, TN: Thomas Nelson Publishers, 1997), February 5.

24 The author heard this on a radio show from Key Life Ministries with Steve Brown, based in Orlando, Florida.

25 Warren W. Wiersbe and Lloyd M. Perry, *The Wycliffe Handbook of Preaching and Preachers* (Chicago: Moody Press, 1984), 193.

26 Wikipedia, s.v. "Charles Studd," last modified on October 24, 2021, https://en.wikipedia.org/wiki/Charles_Studd.

27 Corrie ten Boom and Jamie Buckingham, *Tramp for the Lord* (Fort Washington, PA: CLC Publications, 2001), 56–57.

28 Jim Gilbert, "Symmetry of Birds in Group Flight Is All about Efficiency," *Star Tribune*, November 5, 2020, https://www.startribune.com/symmetry-of-birds-in-group-flight-is-all-about-efficiency/572985262/.

29 Len Wilson, "5 Things Geese Can Teach Us about Teamwork," last modified January 4, 2012, https://lenwilson.us/5-thing-geese-can-teach-us-about-teamwork/.

30 "What Is the 10/40 Window?" The Joshua Project, Frontier Ventures Ministries, accessed November 6. 2021, https://joshuaproject.net/resources/articles/10_40_window.

31 Janelle Powers, "Six Women from the Persecuted Church to Be Inspired by on International Women's Day," Open Doors, March 8, 2017, https://www.opendoorsusa.org/christian-persecution/stories/six-women-persecuted-church-inspired-international-womens-day.

32 Larry Crabb, *Inside Out* (Colorado Springs: Navpress, 2013), 98–99.

33 Henry Blackaby, Richard Blackaby, and Claude King, *Experiencing God: Knowing and Doing the Will of God*, rev. ed. (Nashville, TN: Lifeway Press, 2007), 21.

34 Dave Willis, "7 Marriage Lessons from the Reagans," *Time*, March 9, 2016, https://time.com/4253249/marriage-lessons-reagans/.

35 Alvin L. Reid, *Join the Movement: God Is Calling You to Change the World* (Grand Rapids, MI: Kregel, 2007), 94–98.

36 John Woodbridge, ed., *More Than Conquerors* (Chicago: Moody, 1992), 308–12.

37 Wikipedia, s.v. "Post-it Note," last modified on December 6, 2021, https://en.wikipedia.org/wiki/Post-it_Note.

38 Wikipedia, s.v. "Alan Amron," last modified on October 12, 2021, https://en.wikipedia.org/wiki/Alan_Amron.

39 Eileen Reynolds, "On 9/11, Women Were Heroes Too," New York University (website), last modified on September 9, 2016, https://www.nyu.edu/about/news-publications/news/2016/september/fdny-captain-brenda-berkman-on-9-11.html.

40 Jewell Johnson, *The Top 100 Women of the Christian Faith* (Uhrichsville, OH: Barbour Publishing, 2013), 50–51.

41 F. B. Meyer, "The Great Benefit of Suffering for Christ," SafeGuardYourSoul, accessed on November 8, 2021, https://safeguardyoursoul.com/the-great-benefit-of-suffering-for-christ-by-f-b-meyer/.

42 S. S. Times, "August 16," in *Streams in the Desert*, ed. Mrs. Charles E. Cowman (Los Angeles: The Oriental Missionary Society, 1925), 240.

43 Bob Buford, *Halftime: Moving from Success to Significance* (Grand Rapids, MI: Zondervan, 2011).

44 Visit https://www.iwork4him.com/ for more information.

45 Watchman Nee, *Let Us Pray* (New York: Christian Fellowship Publishers, 1977), 11.

46 Cynthia Long, "The Generosity of Saint Brigid," Orthodox Christian Network, February 1, 2015, https://myocn.net/generosity-saint-brigid/.

About the Author

Os Hillman is an internationally recognized speaker, author, and consultant on the subject of faith at work.

He is the founder and president of Marketplace Leaders Ministries, an organization whose purpose is to train men and women to fulfill their calling in and through their work life and to view their work as ministry.

Os formerly owned and operated an ad agency in Atlanta for twelve years. He has written over two dozen books on faith and work-related subjects and a daily workplace email devotional entitled *TGIF: Today God Is First* that is read by hundreds of thousands of people daily in 105 countries. He has been featured on TBN, CNBC, NBC, *The Los Angeles Times*, *The New York Times*, *The Associated Press, Newsmax*, and many other national media as a spokesperson on faith at work. Os has spoken in twenty-six countries.

Os attended the University of South Carolina and Calvary Chapel Bible School, a ministry of Calvary Chapel of Costa Mesa, California. Os is married to his incredible wife, Pamela, and they live in north Atlanta with their four dogs. Os has one daughter, Charis, and son-in-law, Justin.

Additional Resources
from Os Hillman

Other Books by Os Hillman

31 Decrees of Blessing for Your Work Life

Overcoming Hindrances to Fulfill Your Destiny

Listening to the Father's Heart

Experiencing the Father's Love

The Upside of Adversity: From the Pit to Greatness

Change Agent: Engaging Your Passion to Be the One Who Makes a Difference

The 9 to 5 Window: How Faith Can Transform the Workplace

The Purposes of Money

Faith & Work: Do They Mix?

Faith@Work Movement: What Every Pastor and Church Leader Should Know

How to Discover Why God Made Me (Booklet)

TGIF: 270 Four-Minute Meditations Arranged by Topic (Paperback)

TGIF (Pocket Version)

TGIF: Volume 2 (Hardcover)

TGIF: Small Group Bible Study

TGIF for Men

The Joseph Calling: 6 Stages to Discover, Navigate, and Fulfill Your Purpose

The Joseph Calling: 12-Week Bible Study

Proven Strategies for Business Success

So You Want to Write a Book?

Are You a Biblical Worker? Self-Assessment

To order: TGIFBookstore.com

678.455.6262 x103

info@marketplaceleaders.org

Websites and Electronic Resources

TodayGodIsFirst.com
CAMasterMentor.com
MarketplaceLeaders.org
TGIFBookstore.com

Subscribe free to *TGIF: Today God Is First* at TodayGodIsFirst.com.
Download our free app TGIF Os Hillman via Google Play or iTunes app store.

To Contact Os Hillman

os@marketplaceleaders.org
678-455-6262 x103
Marketplace Leaders, P.O. Box 69, Cumming, GA 30028

Want to be mentored by Os Hillman? Check out the Change Agent
MasterMentor program at CAMasterMentor.com.